P9-ARD-355

Daughters of Valor

Daughters of Valor

Contemporary Jewish American Women Writers

Edited by

Jay L. Halio and Ben Siegel

Newark: University of Delaware Press
London: Associated University Presses

Associated University Presses
440 Forsgate Drive
Cranbury, NJ 08512

Associated University Presses
16 Barter Street
London WC1A 2AH, England

Associated University Presses
P.O. Box 338, Port Credit
Mississauga, Ontario
Canada L5G 4L8

The paper used in this publication meets the requirements of the American National Standard for Permanence of Paper for Printed Library Materials Z39.48–1984.

Library of Congress Cataloging-in-Publication Data

Daughters of valor : contemporary Jewish American women writers / edited by Jay L. Halio and Ben Siegel.
p. cm.
Includes bibliographical references and index.
ISBN 0-87413-611-3 (alk. paper)
1. American literature—Jewish authors—History and criticism. 2. American literature—Women authors—History and criticism. 3. Jews in literature. 4. Holocaust, Jewish (1939–1945), in literature. 5. Jewish women—United States—Intellectual life. 6. American literature—20th century—History and criticism. I. Halio, Jay L. II. Siegel, Ben, 1925– .
PS153.J4D38 1997
810.9′9287′089924—dc20 96-26164
CIP

PRINTED IN THE UNITED STATES OF AMERICA

For

Amy and Sharon,

our own valiant daughters

Contents

Preface

THE growing numbers of Jewish American women writers, as well as their increasing literary, intellectual, and social significance, have led to the publication of this book. Earlier discussions of Jewish American literature have been dominated by the works of male authors like Saul Bellow, Philip Roth, Bernard Malamud, Herbert Gold, Chaim Potok, Bruce Jay Friedman, Stanley Elkin, Karl Shapiro, and Delmore Schwartz, among others. But experienced teachers of contemporary American literature, especially those with a special interest in Jewish American writing, have realized that for several decades now the most significant literary achievements in this area have been by women. A number of impressive anthologies have offered tangible evidence of this salient fact. But there have been relatively few collections of critical essays evaluating and placing these Jewish women writers and their work into proper literary and cultural perspective. Hence we decided to undertake a volume of original essays by outstanding scholar-critics dealing with some of the major women writers in this country whose novels and short stories, poems, plays, and essays have been shaped and colored by their own Jewishness and by the special cultural or religious strains and pressures, joys and pains of that rich heritage. The result is this gathering of essays—centered fully or in part—on the writings of Cynthia Ozick, Anne Roiphe, Susan Fromberg Schaeffer, Lesléa Newman, Francine Prose, Erica Jong, Ilona Karmel, Henryka Karmel-Wolfe, Marcie Hershman, Marge Piercy, Norma Rosen, Lynn Sharon Schwartz, Adrienne Rich, Pauline Kael, Wendy Wasserstein, and Allegra Goodman. Some of these writers have, of course, been less influenced by their Jewishness than have others. Still, all can be said to perceive the world as they do, and write as they do, to some degree at least, because of being Jewish.

So far as we are aware, ours is the first volume devoted entirely to Jewish women writers edited by men. This fact may strike some readers as odd or, perhaps, unfortunate. If so, then that reaction may be yet another reason for this book's appearance.

For we feel strongly that however vital gender may be in current criticism, it is not of the utmost importance. Certainly questions of gender do not in themselves supersede intellectual acuity, literary style, emotional sensitivity, or the ability to transmute those qualities into literature. A more logical basis for debate, perhaps, was our decision to focus on those writers who have achieved recognition since World War II. In doing so, we have no wish to ignore earlier writers such as Tillie Olsen, Hortense Calisher, or Gracy Paley, nor the talented young writers only now starting their careers. In short, we wished to be as inclusive as possible, but inevitably our contributors, by their selections, determined which writers they would discuss. These very busy scholar-critics put other pressing matters aside to provide us with essays on writers of special interest to them. We asked these critics to consider the various ways each subject-author's "Jewishness" shapes the central elements in her work. In short, we asked that each essay illuminate those ways in which the author—through her subjects, characters, and themes—reveals herself to be a "Jewish writer" rather than a writer who is "simply Jewish." We did so despite our awareness that some critics consider this a distinction without a difference.

We wished this collection to be a significant addition to that growing but still modest body of monographs, anthologies, and essay-collections that now deal with Jewish American women writers. For these writers are among those who for too long were given short shrift in the conventional literary histories. If not conspicuous by their absence, Jewish women writers were, at best, grouped with other "ethnic" or "minority" writers and given little space or emphasis. We hope to help rectify that shortcoming.

In his Introduction, therefore, Ben Siegel attempts to place the writings of contemporary Jewish American women within the larger historical and literary context of the Jewish experience in America. Starting with the earliest immigrants to these shores, Siegel traces the acculturative process through its literary manifestations to the Holocaust in Europe and the creation of the State of Israel. For these two momentous events dominate, nor surprisingly, much of the thinking and writing about being Jewish in twentieth-century America and suggest how a definition of Jewish literature—specifically Jewish American literature—can be formulated.

Susanne Klingenstein then focuses on both of these salient issues in her essay on novelist Cynthia Ozick. Discussing in detail Ozick's conception of Jewish literature as the "intellectual grammar of rabbinic thought," she explains Ozick's take on the rabbinic tradition's "unsettling nature." Klingenstein also turns her attention to a hitherto neglected aspect of Ozick's achievement—her translations of Yiddish poetry—and in the process also treats important aspects of her fiction. Both Miriyam Glazer and Jay Halio deal with the novels of Anne Roiphe. Glazer places Roiphe in the broad perspective of men and women writers who are grappling with the often combative tensions of "Jewishness" versus "Judaism." Halio scrutinizes Roiphe's novels in terms of her own sharply defined context: her personal quest for a satisfactory identity as a secular Jew in contemporary America.

Victoria Aarons also considers some of the attempts by Jewish women writers to formulate new means of expression to meet the demands of American life today. Melding the Jewish literary past and present, Aarons discerns in the fiction of Susan Fromberg Schaeffer, Lesléa Newman, and Francine Prose connections to older literary masters and forms. She traces specific links, for example, to those tales of Sholom Aleichem that transform ordinary life into "extraordinary moment[s] of vision." Then, in an essay likely to surprise some readers, Charlotte Templin delineates Erica Jong's wholehearted embrace of her long-neglected Jewishness. She illustrates—as few other critics have—how even Jong's early novels are informed by her Jewish origins.

Sara Horowitz refocuses our attention on the Holocaust and on some of the ways Jewish women writers have treated that cataclysmic event. She explains how Norma Rosen, Ilona Karmel, Henryka Karmel-Wolfe, Cynthia Ozick, Marcie Hershman, Marge Piercy, among others, have used the Holocaust and its lingering traumas as a literary means of probing human character and exploring modern cultural and political issues. Among the first to do so was Norma Rosen, whom Lillian Kremer discusses at length with insight and empathy. Returning to the pre-Holocaust years, James Mellard centers on what he terms the "back-story"—that is, Jewish experience of the Other—in the fiction of Lynn Sharon Schwartz. Mellard shows, in several highly significant stories, how Schwartz explores the attempts of two different generations to deal with their Jewish heritage. Whereas the older generation is less than enthusiastic to acknowledge that heritage, the younger one is eager to discover, understand, and embrace it.

Equally varied responses to Judaism's rich tradition provide issues central to understanding writers as different as Adrienne Rich and Pauline Kael. For example, Karen Klein probes Rich's responses to her divided heritage (Jewish father, Christian mother) in terms of her "inherited ambivalence" as a Jew. Steven Kellman explains how Kael's Jewish background influenced, both directly and indirectly, her film criticism. This influence is especially discernible, Kellman notes, in Kael's critical candor and frequently unpopular positions. Wendy Wasserstein exemplifies a different dichotomy. Steven Whitfield points out that both Jewishness and feminism are key elements in her writing, for they link Wasserstein in varied ways to other Jewish women writers who have also found feminism as important as their Jewish heritage—and as problematical within that heritage.

Our collection ends on a "youthful" note. Gloria Cronin offers one of the earliest critical pieces on the fiction of Allegra Goodman, a promising member of the latest generation of Jewish American women writers and the youngest writer represented here. Allegra Goodman herself then contributes the volume's final essay. Disdaining restrictive labels, Goodman insists on a rather broad literary stance. She views her work as determined by her separate—albeit interlocking—roles (as Cronin also demonstrates) of writer and woman, of American and academic, and of Jew. Like other contemporary writers (older and younger), she sees present Jewish American literature as needful of new inspiration and strength from traditional Jewish religious thought and culture.

We wish by this volume to thank the Jewish women writers who are here being discussed. But we are equally grateful to the many who are not, and we hope to pay them homage on another occasion. We also want to express our gratitude and appreciation to each of our distinguished contributors. As is evident, both men and women, Jews and non-Jews, have contributed to this modest collection. Such diversity seems appropriate in a multicultural America nearing century's end. Yet, in truth, we gave little thought initially to gender or ethnicity in inviting contributors. Our selection criteria were directed primarily at those individuals whose interests and critical skills would enable them, in our opinion, to develop our book's main focus: to bring fresh and useful perspectives to a body of writings whose literary, intellectual, and cultural importance had already been established by critical consensus.

We wish to express a final and special thanks to Elizabeth Reynolds, a textual editor without peer. After more than twenty years of dedicated and superior service, Elizabeth is retiring as editor of the University of Delaware Press to accept a new post in the university. The members of the editorial board, as well as the many authors whose works she has so skillfully guided to publication, wish her godspeed and good fortune.

Daughters of Valor

Introduction: Erasing and Embracing the Past: America and Its Jewish Writers—Men and Women

Ben Siegel

THE world's very first writer is said to have been Enheduanna. The daughter of the Sumerian warrior-king Sargon, she was a high priestess in the service of the moon-god (Nanna) and his daughter (Inanna). Enheduanna is credited with inscribing on cuneiform tablets, about 2300 B.C., her hymns to Inanna, in praise of the moon-goddess's "fierceness that accompanies her power and beauty." But Enheduanna's own verses, translator Jane Hirshfield observes, prove a significant "representation . . . of the fierce female energy found in spiritual traditions throughout the world." Whether this formidable lady was truly the first individual to record for posterity her impressions and beliefs is now, perhaps, of small consequence. But if true, her efforts do signify how long women have struggled to express in story and song their "fierce female energy"[1] through their deepest internal convictions and external thoughts, often against harsh odds and obstacles.

JEWISH WRITER/JEWISH BOOK: SOME ATTEMPTS AT DEFINITION

In America today, such odds and obstacles have grown less stringent for those women who strive for literary expression. But other significant factors of belief and ethnic background merit consideration. Indeed, any discussion of American Jewish writing, whether by men or women, raises a number of questions. For many writers and critics not only challenge the accuracy of terms like "American-Jewish fiction" or "the American-Jewish novel" or "American-Jewish poetry," but they also deny that such entities even exist. Other observers seem concerned primarily with semantics—that is, whether such terms might not be rendered more accurately as "Jewish-American" when applied to certain novels, poems, or plays. Whatever its validity, this questioning attitude does have its ironies: Many protesters or deniers have built their own professional reputations either writing Jewish fiction or writing about it. Cynthia Ozick is at present one such writer. Allegra Goodman here recalls that Ozick, in conversation, dismissed the label of "Jewish-American writer" as derogatory, simplistic, and reductive. "It reduces art and ideas to ethnic commodities. The very word ethnic, she said, is a hateful term; it is really a slur, a term of alienation, with its root word *ethnos* connoting foreign and heathen. To label fiction Jewish-American fiction, to think of it as ethnic, is not merely to categorize it but to attack it."

Ozick is entitled to her views, even if they contradict opinions she has expressed in the past. Certainly it is understandable that writers like Ozick and Bellow, Malamud and Roth, among others, should reject, at least on occasion, the "Jewish writer" label. Considering themselves unique, independent artists, they resent being grouped or stereotyped. One can sympathize with the intent and logic of their disclaimers. However, a large body of empirical evidence suggests that there does exist—and indeed has existed for a very long time in American literature—a significant and definable segment that can be labeled Jewish fiction. Such an assertion, however, does raise several basic queries. The first would appear to be: Who is a Jew? Jewish ecclesiastical law decrees that a Jew is anyone born of a Jewish mother. But in recent years the state of Israel has struggled to develop a broader definition of Jewishness acceptable to most of its citizens. Logic dictates that anyone who practices Judaism is clearly a Jew. But many individuals who consider themselves Jewish, as critics are fond of pointing out, know little of Judaic and Hebraic culture, have had little Jewish education, and do not adhere to Jewish religious practices. One self-mocking definition has it that "A Jew is anyone another Jew says is a Jew." But the most generally accepted definition is that a Jew is any person who identifies him or herself as such, anyone, in short, who affirms a Jewish heritage.[2]

Our concerns here are more narrowly focused. Our key preliminary questions are *Who* is a Jewish writer? and *What* is a Jewish book? In this area, too, replies and definitions have been numerous. How could they have been otherwise? They have had to encompass figures as different, for example, as Saul Bellow and Herman Wouk, Philip Roth and Chaim Potok, Cynthia Ozick and Erica Jong, Elie Wiesel and Leon Uris—all of whom have been classified as "Jewish writers." Indeed, these definitions generally raise more questions than they answer. At one time the standard rejoinder was embodied in Ludwig Lewisohn's dictum that a Jewish book is one written by a man who is aware he is a Jew. But even when its obvious gender bias is set aside, Lewisohn's definition proves fuzzy and inadequate. Joseph Lowin, who has thought hard about the subject, offers his own perspective. "What is it that makes a story Jewish?" he asks. "Is it, for example, the subject? Can one not write a non-Jewish story on a Jewish subject, the way it is possible to paint a Christian painting on an Old Testament theme? Is it the language—Yiddish or Hebrew or Ladino—in which the author writes?" Or perhaps, he says, "it is the author's intention that his or her story be Jewish that makes it so." This suggests it may be "Jewish readers who make a story Jewish." But even that possibility lacks total validity. No, Jewish stories are, at least for him, those depicting "Jews as they really are."[3]

This means that a truly Jewish story, Lowin explains, must have "meaning" but must not "make a totem, an idol, out of the imagination." It should also "distinguish between what is Jewish and what is not." Generally, Jewish narrative "swims against the tide of Western culture and with the tide of Jewish history." This is due primarily to the fact that "Jews are text-centered, if not to say text-obsessed." Hence Jews are distinguished from other storytellers by their habit of spending "their most precious time commenting on text, judging text and, in the process, judging the world. For the Jews, a story may be funny, but it must have moral seriousness." Indeed, a truly Jewish story, Lowin reasons, is likely to have—like the Talmud, that most Jewish of all Jewish texts—both *halaka* (law) and *haggada* (lore). For together, "law and lore promise that tomorrow there will be more law and lore." In other words, "the Jewish idea involves an ongoing process." For in Jewish writing, says Lowin, "Story begets commentary, which in its turn begets judgment, which in its turn begets further story and so on." The result is that "Jewish history is only partly the narrative of events, the story of national calamity and of national triumph." More precisely, Jews focus on commentary rather than event. "They comment on their history and, more importantly, they comment on their texts." In the process, they "judge their history and the world, giving meaning to both."[4]

Lowin is correct. Both history and the world have given Jews ample opportunity to exercise their storytelling gifts. Nowhere was this more tragically apparent than in the besieged Warsaw Ghetto. There its doomed inhabitants, painfully aware of their imminent destruction, placed in the crevices of their stone walls "little rolled pieces of paper with notes, diary entries, anecdotes, letters." In the face of death, they felt the need to roll up and leave these notes, not knowing whether anyone would later find and read them. Why then did they bother to write? "Because," explains Roger Rosenblatt, "telling the stories keeps us from drowning, so we can stay afloat and go on. That is the story of us. And we will continue to tell that story until we get it right. And then we may get each other right. When we do, the killing will stop and the drowning will stop. And we will all be part of one story that finally makes sense. And we will come together as around a fire in a single story."[5] One storyteller who has not stopped relating the tragic circumstances of his personal history is Elie Wiesel. He is also one who offers his own definition of the Jewish writer. "A Jewish writer is, in the final analysis," states Wiesel, "a Jew who has chosen the art of writing to extol or to condemn a certain way of living, believing, fighting, or in one word: being. He remains a Jew even if he writes against Jews. Except that in this case, he will be an apologetic Jew and an inauthentic writer."[6]

These varied attempts at definition are obviously thoughtful and well-intentioned. Still, even simpler, more logical and specific definitions of the terms "Jewish book" and "Jewish writer" may be extracted from these and other efforts. A Jewish book, it can be argued, is one that deals with characters *motivated to action by their sense of Jewishness.* Yet even this touchstone speaks only for the *book* and not the writer. A non-Jewish writer may write such a book, as John Hersey did in *The Wall* or James Michener in *The Source* or, in the last century, George Eliot in *Daniel Deronda.* Citing these titles, Sol Liptzin once argued that "It is, therefore, obvious that a book written by a non-Jew may be a Jewish book, while many a book whose author is of Jewish origin cannot lay claim to this designation." To support his view, Liptzin insisted that *The Source* was decidely a Jewish book because "It did more to further an understanding of Israel's right to its homeland than all the propaganda releases of the past decade." However, author-translator Hillel Halkin, speaking on the same Jerusalem International Book Fair panel, disagreed. He thought it "silly to speak of Jewish books written by Non-

Jews." The relevant question, he argued, was which novels written by Jews reflected "an authentic Jewish concern." Franz Kafka wrote Jewish books, declared Halkin, despite their lack of the word "Jew." Yet they were Jewish books because Kafka's "fears, neurosis and inner struggles were very Jewish." Conversely, Marcel Proust referred to Jews "frequently, almost compulsively," but was "not a particularly Jewish author." The same was true, if for different reasons, of American novelists like Saul Bellow, Bernard Malamud, and Philip Roth. Their works would not gain entrance to the "corpus of Jewish literature," said Halkin, because they were in a language "not exclusively Jewish." This means, he reasoned, the readership will inevitably be "mainly non-Jewish," a situation causing "basic ambiguities."[7]

Language aside for the moment, most critics would appear to agree that a Jewish writer is one who embodies in words aspects of his or her human experience as a Jew. Clearly, Jews need not and do not write only about Jews. After all, Jews who are writers have the same freedom as non-Jewish writers to select the characters, subjects, and themes that appeal to them. Some critics have argued that many writers who happen to be Jews have so weak a grasp of Judaism—that is, of the Judaic religious, cultural, literary, or linguistic traditions—that they should avoid Jewish subject matter. Other commentators merely observe how easy it has been to pose as a Jewish writer. "Even out of great ignorance," Norma Rosen states, referring to an earlier generation, "it was still possible for a 'Jewish writer' to write a 'Jewish book' merely because of living in New York, or Cleveland, or similar places. One had inherited, literarily speaking, a trust fund. Without even trying, one had certain speech rhythms in one's head—colloquialisms that were inherently funny, relationships always good for a cutting down by wit, and a large, energy-radiating store of culture-abrasions." But that time has passed, argues Rosen. "To write as a Jew in America," she insists, "it is no longer enough to draw on the interest of what was put in the bank long ago by others."[8]

So widespread is this view at present that many writers readily acknowledge—at times with an exaggerated pride—their own cultural shortcomings. In an introspective mood, they might well describe their plight in terms somewhat similar to those Philip Roth attributes to his protagonist at the conclusion of his novel *The Counterlife.* Eight weeks of ethnic isolation in a decidedly non-Jewish London have moved the writer Nathan Zuckerman to reassert his Jewishness. But this proves no easy task for one who characterizes himself pathetically as "a Jew among Gentiles and a Gentile among Jews." More specifically, he is, Zuckerman shamefacedly concedes, "a Jew without Jews, without Judaism, without Zionism, without Jewishness, without a temple or an army or even a pistol, a Jew clearly without a home, just the object itself, like a glass or an apple."[9]

Such ethnic uncertainties are today widespread among Jews. But the fact remains that when writers of Jewish origin deal in their fiction, poems, or plays with characters and ideas, interests and actions that can be identified historically or culturally as Jewish, they are themselves then working "Jewish writers." So when Saul Bellow writes *The Victim, Herzog,* or *Mr. Sammler's Planet* and Bernard Malamud writes *The Assistant* or *The Fixer,* and Philip Roth writes *Goodbye, Columbus* or *Portnoy's Complaint* or even his Zuckerman narratives, each is functioning as a *Jewish* writer. When these novelists write *Henderson the Rain King* or *The Natural* or *When She Was Good,* novels in which there are no Jewish characters, they are functioning as writers who happen to be Jewish. Some critics may argue that even in these "non-Jewish" works each writer's Jewish sensibilities inevitably come into play, albeit in less obvious or more subtle ways. This is very likely true, but it is equally true that the writer's Jewishness has in such instances been rendered irrelevant. The question of Jewish writer becomes more complex, however, with a book like Bellow's *Seize the Day* or Malamud's *A New Life* or Roth's *Letting Go,* in which Jewish protagonists are less motivated by their Jewishness than by their humanness.

Shaped by Their Jewishness

These are not merely academic questions for an essay collection such as this one. We have asked our contributors to focus on the various ways their author's "Jewishness" shapes the central elements in her work. In other words, we wanted every essay to illuminate those ways in which that author—through her subjects, characters, and themes—reveals herself to be a "Jewish writer" rather than a writer who is "simply Jewish." This distinction, as Ted Solotaroff points out, is now more difficult than in the past. Twenty-five years ago, he states "there was a clear distinction between the writer who was a Jew and the Jew who was a writer." Then the former insisted "on the right to explore the Jewish subject, as one did any other, by one's experience and imagination." The latter held "that her or his experience and imagination were largely formed by and served the history and mission of the Jewish people. It was fairly easy to tell the 'marginal' writers from the 'authentic' ones since the protagonists of each were, broadly speaking, the antagonists of the other. Things are no longer so clear-cut."[10]

But Cynthia Ozick, a writer given to subtle distinctions, has decided there is even a difference between being a Jew and being a writer. "To be a Jew," she states, "is an act of the strenuous mind as it stands before the fakeries and lying seductions of the world, saying no and no again as they parade by in all their allure. And to be a writer is to plunge into the parade and become one of the delirious marchers."[11] In keeping with Ozick's logic then, a Jewish writer is a strenuous nay-sayer who ultimately plunges into the "delirious march" that is life. But the very label has at times been distasteful to her. She recalls once saying that "The phrase 'Jewish writer' . . . may be what rhetoricians call an 'oxymoron'—a pointed contradiction in which one arm of the phrase clashes profoundly with the other as to annihilate it."[12] Admittedly, Ozick's efforts at definition, as well as the others cited, prove rather rhetorically ambiguous. Collectively, they remind us how challenging it still is to define Jewish writing or the Jewish writer.

There are other difficulties as well. When panels or symposia on American Jewish writing are held, the argument is inevitably made that novelists, poets, dramatists, and even essayists have used up the mother lode that was the "American Jewish immigrant experience." The panelists (many of them writers themselves) concede the settlement process had provided writers with rich, if parochial, subject matter for more than a half-century. But the immigrant vein, they argue, ran dry in the 1950s and 1960s. Jewish American writers today then should realize there is nothing of significance left to be said not only about their parents' immigrant lives but also about their own "postimmigrant" doings. So if they want to write "as Jews," literary aspirants are advised, they should deal either with the Holocaust or Israel and their related metaphysical or theological issues.

Hence the Holocaust and Israel are now viewed by many writers and commentators (American and foreign) as the touchstones for *Jewish* writing in America. Israeli novelist Amos Oz, appearing on a panel at UC Berkeley titled "The Writer in the Jewish Community," has summarized succinctly the case for his homeland as theme. "Now suppose a new Kafka is growing up right now, here in San Francisco, California," he argued. "Suppose he is fourteen years old right now. Let's call him Chuck Bernstein. Let's assume that he is every bit of a genius as Kafka was in his time. His future must, as I see it, depend on an uncle in Jerusalem or an experience by the Dead Sea, or a cousin in a kibbutz or something inspired by the Israeli live drama. Otherwise, with the exception of the possibility that he is growing among the ultra-Orthodox, he will be an American writer of Jewish origin—not a Jewish American writer." Oz concedes such a writer "may become a new Faulkner, but not a new Kafka." In short, he is "suggesting that even individual creation in the future, to the extent that it is going to be Jewish, will depend on Israel to some extent." What he is saying, Oz further explains, is "that in the long run individual creation springs from the fertile ground of collective creation, and as I maintain that perhaps there is no collective creation in the present Diaspora, the only choice for Jews is either to turn to Israel or maybe despair."[13]

Appearing on the same panel, and responding to Oz, was Cynthia Ozick. She quickly rejected geographical and cultural boundaries in favor of a universal "substratum" of the Jewish creative imagination. "Cultural imagination, it seems to me," declared Ozick, "is a diminishing thing, an impoverishing, above all a transient and gossamer thing: an ad hoc thing, a temporary and contemporary contrivance, readily obsolescent." But culture is less of a problem than is, surprisingly, language itself. "We call ourselves Jews, we think of ourselves as one people," she argued, "but not because of culture. After a while—and not a very long while, either—culture divides. Language especially divides, because language is the preeminent vessel and vehicle of culture."[14]

Some Jewish writers share Ozick's disdain of culture because of its transitory and shifting nature. But not many are likely to agree with her rejection of language as a primary bonding force for Jews. For most writers, words generate the power that defines their Jewishness. Saul Bellow, for example, insists that Jews express not only their Jewishness but also their humanity in their native idioms. "Your language is the principal instrument of your humanity," he states. "When the doors of the gas chambers were shut, the German Jews—and, for that matter, the Polish Jews—called upon God in the language of their murderers, for they had no other. Your language is your spiritual base. Yes, I know the word 'spiritual' is in disrepute, but what I am saying can, if you like, be framed more acceptably if you put it that existence is, finally, a mystery, a radical mystery graspable, if at all, by language."[15]

Years earlier, Irving Howe had expressed a similar view. "Finally, it has been upon language that the American Jewish writers have most sharply left their mark," Howe stated in his introduction to a collection of Jewish stories. "To the language of fiction they have brought turnings of voice, feats of irony, and tempos of delivery that helped create a new American style." Howe conceded "it was likely a shortlived style and one that reached its fulfillment in a mere handful of writers," but he insisted it was "a new style nonetheless." He explained that "style speaks of sensibility, slant, vision." Here, he added, it "speaks . . . of a certain high excitability, a rich pumping of blood, a grating mixture of the sardonic and the sentimental, which the Jews brought across the Atlantic together with their baggage." Howe thought it no exaggeration to claim "that since Faulkner and Hemingway the one major innovation in American prose style has been the yoking of street raciness and high-culture mandarin that we associate with the American Jewish writers." He did not mean "all of them," he conceded, for there obviously is no one "style shared by all these writers." Still he did want to emphasize "that the dominant American Jewish style is the one brought to a pitch by Saul Bellow and imitated and modified by a good many others."[16]

Like Bellow and Howe, many non-American Jewish writers have insisted on the importance to them of their language. Israeli novelist David Schuetz, for example, also argues the singularity of his native tongue in articulating his Jewishness. "I tell stories," he explains. "To unlock some of these doors that still need magic to open, I read books in Hebrew and I write my stories in Hebrew. English, for example, refuses to let me into its secrets. And so my world remains the world of the Hebrew language." Schuetz reasons that "this obsessions with *words* is *Jewish*." Indeed, this verbal obsession is literally the very "hallmark of the Jewish heritage to the world: words upon words to describe it, to tame it, to make the hidden visible." He has experienced for himself language's true power. "I became a real Jew," he declares, "when I started to see my world through words and verbal images, when I realized that we have no paintings, no sculptures, no buildings, no music, and no machines. We have words. We have the STORY."[17]

Forgetting Things Past

Ultimately, few writers and critics can disallow the importance to them of language. Yet history teaches that spiritual or communal or linguistic unity, although devoutly to be desired, has hardly been the shaping force either within Jewish life and thought or between Jews and their neighbors. Even traditional Jewish writings underscore the divisiveness between God and man, between the higher reality of God's world as opposed to the unreality of this world. In Old Testament and Talmud this world also belongs to God, and His Jews are expected to be grateful and obedient for being permitted to share it. But for the descendants of Adam and Eve obedience comes hard and backsliding easy. In modern Jewish fiction, too, this world always belongs to somebody else, so that the Jew has to struggle in a world not of his own making or control. Many non-Jews have been acutely aware of the inherent irony. John Jay Chapman, for instance, observed that the heart of the world is Jewish. But Chapman's view has hardly proved the historically dominant one. Even Jewish fiction writers have viewed the cosmos differently. They, too, see an uncertain, hostile world dominated by strangers, with the Jews as marginal beings—that is, as displaced newcomers or parvenus in an uneasy relation to the society or culture in which they find themselves. There is special irony here: The Jew-as-writer accepts and employs the non-Jewish view of Jews as latecomers and fringe creatures even when history indicates otherwise. After nearly a thousand years of living in Poland, for example, Jews accepted their marginal status there as inevitable.

Jewish American fiction generally has echoed the same marginal note. But the plain historical truth is that Jews were not latecomers to America. Elias Legardo, the first known Jew to reach these shores, landed in Virginia in 1621. With his arrival, Jewish "immigration" to this continent was launched. Indeed, no migratory people is more tightly linked by history to America than are its Jews. Historical forces were already at work in the fabled year of 1492, when Columbus was discovering America and Ferdinand and Isabella were driving the Jews from Spain. The two monarchs were motivated by their religious zeal for the Spanish Inquisition—a movement which soon drove the Jews from Portugal as well, and then a handful from the Portuguese colony of Brazil to New Amsterdam in 1654. This latter group of 23 Jews established the first Jewish community in the North American colonies. New Amsterdam (later to become New York) was administered by the Dutch West India Company. It had as its governor Peter Stuyvesant, who was not happy to have Jews in his community. Similar Sephardic or Spanish and Portuguese Jews kept arriving throughout the colonial period. Soon Jews other than the Sephardim came in numbers. Some of them, like Hayim Solomon (1740–85) and the "Sons of Liberty," participated in the American Revolution. In 1776, the American colonies had about 2,000 Jews.

Any serious attempt to put Jewish immigration to the New World into historical perspective reveals its one central theme to be that of conflict. Admittedly, the conflicts between Europe and America's cultures, societies, religions, lifestyles, and values are integral to all American immigrant groups and their literatures, but they are particularly crucial in Jewish literature. Throughout history, it would appear, civilizations, empires, dynasties, city states have taken turns disgorging their Jews. Usually they have done so willingly, even eagerly, but occasionally with considerable reluctance, as with Egypt's pharoah or Russia's communist regime. The Book of Exodus could be described as the first "immigration" narrative, one clearly embodying the qualities of a prose epic.

The journey to America was not always a direct one. Many Jews first fled to Holland then crossed the Atlantic from there. (Something of the impact these Jews made on the American literary mind is suggested by Henry Wadsworth Longfellow's poem "The Jewish Cemetery at Newport," which describes a Sephardic cemetery.) The first literary efforts by this early group of Jewish Americans were religious writings in Hebrew. But the first Jewish American poet to achieve recognition for verse written in English was Emma Lazarus, who wrote the well known lines on the base of the Statue of Liberty: "Give me your tired, your poor . . . Your huddled masses, yearning to breathe free." Yet even liberal-minded Americans found Jews exotic, mysterious figures. Lazarus had sent Ralph Waldo Emerson her poems over a period of years. But when she visited Concord in 1876, Alfred Kazin has noted, "she was the first Jew Emerson had ever met." Emerson's daughter Ellen, a seasoned Sunday School teacher, was astonished "to get at a real unconverted Jew (who had no objection to calling herself one, and talked freely about 'our Church' and 'we Jews'), and to hear how Old Testament sounds to her, and find she has been brought up to keep the

Law, and the Feast of the Passover, and the day of Atonement. The interior view was more interesting than I could have imagined."[18]

As noted, some critics lament the "ignorance" of American writers of their Jewish heritage. These critics apparently can neither forgive nor understand how so sad a state of affairs has come to be. Such commentators (often themselves writers, but writers who perhaps had stayed longer in *cheder*) often hint darkly of intellectual laziness or myopia or assimilationism on the part of their less knowledgable literary colleagues. But the true causes are both more complex and yet painfully obvious. They are to be discerned primarily in American immigrant fiction, both Jewish and non-Jewish. Some causes or answers may even be found in a brief comparative glance at what was once termed the "Catholic novel"—that is, the parochial novels of a James T. Farrell, J. F. Powers, or Edwin O'Connor. These dealt generally with Irish Catholics, but Italians and Poles could also be included. For these three groups shared with the Jews the urban tenement neighborhoods of cities like New York, Boston, and Chicago. Like the Jews, these Catholic groups also were told that their old ways and beliefs were outmoded, parochial, narrow. But they all had a major psychological and sociological advantage over the Jews: They had come from their *own* countries where, if they had been poor and hungry, they were at least not marginal beings, outsiders, intruders, transients. They had the status bequeathed by a homeland: a nationality. If told to "go back to where you come from," they had a clear idea where that was. The Jews did not. In addition, these peoples could become fully Americanized or assimilated and still remain devout Catholics. They did not have to feel guilty for having deserted their faith or religion. Instead, they could look to a future in which they could cling to their Church and its dogmas and still be considered Americans. In other words, believing Catholics could live and function as untarnished Christians in a modern industrial society.

Orthodox Jews were less fortunate. For them, becoming fully acculturated, much less assimilated, meant the men had to shave their beards and sideburns. Women were expected to remove their *sheitels,* or marriage wigs. Both were pressured to wear westernized clothing and generally grow more flexible—if not lax—in *kashrut,* the dietary laws. Often they had to desecrate the sabbath to hold a desperately needed job. Such choices contributed to the Jewish trauma of transition—that is, of accepting the prevailing "Melting Pot" concept. One major result of this acculturative process was that contemporary Jewish writers (an occasional Chaim Potok or Herman Wouk notwithstanding) felt absurd advocating past Jewish beliefs, much less lifestyles. At best, they could hope to retain only an ethnic or cultural identity, or some moral and ethical values embodied in Judaism's historical tradition. The problem was that many of those values were now embodied in a Western humanistic tradition that had long absorbed the Judeo-Christian ethic. Not surprisingly, therefore, the Jewish novel in twentieth-century America has lacked theological context, tone, or dimension. If it sounded a recurrent lament for things past, that lament was marked by nostalgia, by a wistfulness for a time when the individual Jew knew his or her place and identity.

Shaping most Jewish immigrant fiction then was a tearing question: How much loyalty was owed to God in a society where both Deity and belief appeared increasingly irrelevant? How much Old Country orthodoxy then should the individual Jew attempt to retain in a new country where acceptance and success depended to a great extent on looking, sounding, and acting like everyone else? Resembling your acculturated neighbors was what being an American meant in this century's early years. The vaunted "Melting Pot" was visualized as a crucible wherein all foreign differences would be boiled away, leaving a slightly dehydrated but cleansed new being. The nation's public schools were the primary crucible: they were expected to turn immigrant children (whether Jewish, Italian, Polish, or German) into this idealized conception of an American citizen.

In his highly praised study of immigration, *The Uprooted,* Oscar Handlin observed that "the history of immigration is a history of alienation and its consequences."[19] In other words, immigration—whatever its blessings, and they were and are many—left emotional scars. These scars often resulted from the newcomers being told their old ways, beliefs, values were simply not good enough. Readers today, therefore, should not be surprised that immigrant fiction and later Jewish American writings nurtured a sense of apartness or alienation. This feeling was especially strong in immigrant novels, plays, and stories. So if America's Jews, as many commentators have pointed out, did not see themselves as a separate nationality in the East European sense, they did for decades feel themselves a people set apart in their new country. Their folk memory of a common history and religion formed them into a virtually self-contained community within the larger American society. Still, if they viewed themselves as an integrated minority within a Christian culture, America's Jews harbored at least a sense of *shared* alienation.

For all their gratitude and love for their new home, immigrant Jews, therefore, quickly began expressing disappointment that the Golden Land's streets were not paved with gold. Of course, many were pleased with what they found, but few exhibited the exuberant optimism of novelist Herbert Gold's father. Arriving on these shores at age thirteen, the senior Gold adopted his surname, his son reports, "in honor of the freedom given to men by the gold in the streets of New York."[20] The newcomers, writes Gold, came jammed into the hold of the ships, bringing with them "feathers to make pillows, cloth to make hats, charms to melt into junk. Some rode happy and seasick through the storm, planning heaven in the promised land. A few had schemes and thought they knew what Columbus had found. Some merely sang, living through another day. And some feared they were noplace, nowhere, and dreamed of sinking in the sullen ocean."[21] Another survivor later recalled the Atlantic crossing as "a kind of hell that cleanses a man of his sins before coming to the land of Columbus."[22]

Settled in their new homeland, Jewish immigrants soon realized that, despite their high expectations, life would remain difficult and their labors arduous. In 1882, for example, Abraham Cahan, in a letter written for a Russian newspaper, gave voice to the disillusionment of a "greenhorn" generation: "Curse you, emigration. Accursed are the conditions that have brought you forth! How many lives have you broken, how many brave and mighty have you rubbed out like dust!" After citing these words, Irving Howe observes that "Such sentiments were not at all unusual in the eighties and nineties." Arriving in this country "with inflamed hopes, some of the immigrants became demoralized and others permanently undone. Not only was their physical situation wretched—that, after all, they had long been accustomed to. Far worse was the spiritual confusion that enclosed their lives."[23] In the face of such bitter disillusionment, not surprisingly, the "Old Country" took on a certain nostalgic charm. For if life under the czars in shtetl, ghetto, or city street generally had been grim and hard, it had also proved, at least on occasion, warm and pleasant. The new Americans expressed their disappointment in terms such as *Amerika gonef* ("America the thief") or *a klug tsu Columbus* ("a curse or plague on Columbus"). In effect, the immigrants and their children soon found themselves struggling between the cultural fragments of two countries, and the resulting mixture confused and frightened them.

Many critics have underscored the multicultural aspects of the Jewish experience. "The Jew," Leslie Fiedler notes, has served as "the gateway into Europe for America; for he has carried with him, almost against his will, his own history, two thousand years of which is European."[24] This heritage helps explain why Jewish immigrant fiction has been credited with serving as a barometer for the entire American immigrant experience. This is not surprising, as it was a heritage that contained always a literary component. Through many centuries and locales, Mark Shechner points out, the Jewish devotion to words, "to the reading and writing of books," had proved unwavering.[25] So revered was the Word among Jews that when sacred books grew old and tattered, they were not thrown away. Instead, they were treated like human remains and buried in sacred ground. In Orthodox homes even Yiddish newspapers—because they were written in Hebrew letters—were not to be spread on the floor or stepped on. Even today, in synagogue or temple, the Torah is generally read not from printed volumes but from parchment scrolls inscribed by a scribe or *sofer* (the Hebrew word for writer). "The sofer," Judd Teller explains, "made his first appearance in Jewish history in the Fifth Century B.C.E., and was apparently also an interpreter of the law and successor to the prophets." For over two millennia then, the Jews "have been conditioned . . . to defer to the writer, and, for longer than that, to the castigator. They have also handed down the tradition that wisdom is not their monopoly. Their respect for other cultures is expressed in an age-old Hebrew phrase, *chachmat yavan,* 'the wisdom of Greece.' The Jewish writer who remains outside his tradition is still revered as a carrier of *chachmat yavan.*"[26]

Seemingly, most Jewish writers in America would be considered carriers of *chachmat yavan.* In any event, the country offered fresh literary opportunities. Despite their new surroundings, and "often crushing poverty," notes Mark Shechner, Jews "brought with them a rich tradition of literacy and scholarship and the beginnings of a secular fiction that needed only translation into modern terms to gain entry into American writing."[27] No sooner settled, the newcomers began to write. Like the Jewish tradition itself, Jewish fiction in America (immigrant and postimmigrant) quickly emphasized moral and social responsibility, or the individual's need to accommodate his or her needs to those of the community. But this process has never been an easy one. Hence Jewish writers concentrated for several decades on themes of social acceptance and rejection, assimilation and intermarriage. These feelings were most evident in fiction of the first native-born generation, the one that came to maturity in the 1920s and 1930s. The novels, stories, and plays of Ludwig Lewisohn, Ben Hecht, Meyer Levin, Sidney Meller, Daniel Fuchs, Albert Halper, Michael Gold, and Clifford Odets, among others, are pervaded by a sense of ever-pending crisis and a wry, self-deprecating humor.

These qualities are also to be found in the immigrant and Depression-decade literary efforts of Jewish women writers of those trying years. Mary Antin, Anzia Yezierska, Edna Ferber, Fannie Hurst, Tess Slesinger, Jo Sinclair, and Tillie Olson, among others, filled their writings, as did the men, with the exotic speech patterns, street experiences, kitchen smells, and synagogue sounds of Jewish city life. In her introduction to *Her Face in the Mirror,* a volume of stories and poems by Jewish women, editor Fay Moskowitz suggests the special problems confronting these writers. She complains of the paucity of past literary opportunities available to Jewish women. For "in the past," she states, "expectations of Jewish women in the Jewish community have been essentially conservative." Until recent years there existed "few avenues for self-expression within the tradition. A Jewish woman's canvas, if she had one at all, would depict the details of domesticity, the food and furnishings and the ritual celebrations both religious and secular that have traditionally been both a woman's purview and her purdah, the means by which she was at once empowered and, some would say, kept powerless."[28] But the aforementioned women writers, most of whom Moskowitz cites, proved that strong-willed, talented Jewish women could find their literary voices and garner considerable public recognition and acclaim, both within and beyond the Jewish community. If they often focused on the home and ritual (as did the men), most of these women were not reluctant to deal with social acceptance and rejection or the other moral and political issues that confronted America's Jews in the immigrant and postimmigrant years.

Still, despite women writers' valiant efforts to deal with the same pressures confronting Jews in America as did men, there is no denying the cultural and literary differences posed by gender. "If we look back at the literary histories that mainly describe male experience," says Ann Shapiro, "we need to rethink every chapter to include the experience of the Jewish woman. For example, the immigrant experience recorded by Abraham Cahan is not the same experience as that of Anzia Yezierska." This is because "assimilation poses different problems for Henry Roth and Edna Ferber." In other words, "the alienation of which Delmore Schwartz writes is distinct from the alienation conceptualized by Adrienne Rich." Certainly in the big cities "the problems of urbanization were different for Tess Slesinger and Albert Halper." Nor has the situation, Shapiro insists, been much different in Israel itself. "Israel may be the promised land for some," she declares, "but at least one American feminist, Marcia Freedman, describes herself as an 'exile in the promised land' in her book by that title." Indeed, the problems confronting the woman writer extend beyond geography to the roots of Judaism itself. For "whatever *halakhah* might mean for a male writer," says Shapiro, "it has been infinitely more complicated for the Jewish woman, who often saw herself as excluded from the Covenant entirely." Even writing of the Holocaust raises questions of gender. "Holocaust literature is especially problematic," she states, "because, as Marlene Heinemann has observed, 'Even the most impartial and sensitive male survivor will be unable to provide an insider's picture of women's experiences in the Nazi camps, since male and female prisoners were segregated in separate camps.'"[29] Elaine Showalter voices a similar caveat. "We must invent new paradigms and myths to describe the writing of Jewish American women," she declares. "Too many literary abstractions which claim to be universal have in fact described only male perceptions, experience, and options." The ideas they embody "have falsified the social and personal contexts in which literature is produced and consumed."[30]

Earlier literary commentators, however, did not concern themselves with such gender differences. The familiar elements offered by most Jewish writers convinced some critics that Jewish American writing was clearly defined by specific communal characteristics. Conceding the "many differences among American Jewish writers," Irving Howe, for example, was still convinced that there were also "shared memories, shared experiences, shared sensibilities. How could there not be?" Howe contended that "novelists like Henry Roth and Saul Bellow, storytellers like Delmore Schwartz and Bernard Malamud have been blessed, sometimes cursed, with a collective memory that arches over their work, at once liberating and confining the imagination." This collective Jewish memory has, he insisted, at least one positive result: Jewish writers in America need not engage in "that frantic casting about for material, that desperate search for action and setting through which a writer can give fiction body to a glimpsed idea." Howe referred to that specific "plight of deracination" he felt was then (1977) "characterizing so much of American writing." He thought that problem had been absent "from their earlier work, when they are still in the fierce grip of childhood and adolescent memories." But time, he cautioned, could deprive them of that advantage. For "later, as they drain their memories, they may come to share the plight of other American writers."[31]

Hence many Jewish writers began "with the assumption that there remains—perhaps in secure possession, perhaps no longer in their grasp—a body of inherited traditions, values, and attitudes that we call 'Jewishness.'" That these inherent elements are important to both the lives and work of this country's Jewish writers appears to Howe to be "beyond dispute." At times these ideas are significant "as positive beliefs, sometimes as negations hard to shake off." The problem is that "the very term 'Jewishness' suggests a certain vagueness, pointing to the diffusion of a cultural heritage." Howe then distinguished between "Jewishness" and "Judaism." He explained that when a person alludes to "Judaism or the Jewish religion," he does so "to invoke a coherent tradition of belief and custom." When he refers to "Jewishness," however, he "invokes a spectrum of styles and symbols, a range of cultural memories, no longer as ordered or weighty as once they were yet still able to affect experience." But just what is that "distinctiveness that Jews experience?" Howe asked. "No two writers may quite agree. Yet there are felt connections, overlappings of sensibility, kinships of belief."[32]

A prime element of this distinctive Jewish destiny, Howe suggested, was "the centrality of the family in Jewish life, and thereby in the fiction written about that life." The good news was the family served the immigrants as "an agency of discipline and coherence" while providing their children with "enormous emotional resources." The bad news was the same family structure bequeathed them "also a mess of psychic troubles." For the individual who has grown up "in an immigrant Jewish milieu," Howe explained, will inevitably "be persuaded that the family is an institution unbreakable and inviolable, the one bulwark against the chaos of the world." Ironically, the family also proves "the one barrier to tasting its delights." In Jewish American fiction, therefore, the family is generally "an overwhelming, indeed, obsessive presence: it is container of narrative, theater of character, agent of significance." Saul Bellow's "The Old System" proves prototypical. This story reads for Howe "like a compressed version of those leisurely family chronicles which European novelists wrote at the turn of the century." In other words, Bellow's characters matter primarily "as representative figures in the saga of a family."[33]

Howe's point merits both consideration and elaboration. For example, Bellow, who has edited a collection of Jewish stories by other writers, adds to the family theme several other elements he finds central to Jewish fiction: laughter and trembling. "[I]n the stories of the Jewish tradition," Bellow observes, "the world, and even the universe, have a human meaning. Indeed the Jewish imagination has sometimes been found guilty of overhumanizing everything, of making too much of a case for us, for mankind, and of investing externals with too many meanings." A careful reading of Jewish stories also reveals that in them "laughter and trembling are so curiously mingled that it is not easy to determine the relations of the two." On some occasions the laughter appears "simply to restore the equilibrium of sanity." But, on other occasions, the characters in "the story, or parable, appear to invite or encourage trembling with the secret aim of overcoming it by means of laughter."[34]

A Shift of Gender

Many of the themes and elements discussed to this point have persisted through the years. Other have virtually disappeared. But the search for a valid Jewish self-identity continues, most directly and centrally at present in the fiction and nonfiction of Jewish American women writers. This gender shift can be viewed as part of a significant cultural change that started asserting itself in the 1960s. During that decade—the "golden age" of Jewish American writing—writers and critics began proclaiming the demise of the immigrant tradition as a central theme in Jewish writing. Several decades later, Pearl K. Bell offered a retroactive overview of the immigrant period and its aftermath. "In the shifting tides of Jewish writing in America," she noted, "the first generation consisted of those who grew up in Europe and whose literary language was Yiddish. In the early novels of Sholem Asch, such as *Salvation* and *Mottke the Thief,* in family sagas like I. J. Singer's *The Brothers Ashkenazi,* the writer sought to preserve the *shtetl* memory which he felt had been threatened by transplantation to an alien land." During the same years, said Bell, "there emerged another generation, the first Jewish novelists born in America to immigrant parents." Among these the most prominent proved to be Michael Gold, Meyer Levin, Daniel Fuchs, and Henry Roth. These writers were not equal in talent, she conceded, but all revealed "a fierce need to capture not only the stifling life of the ghetto but [also] their own struggle to escape it, often into the world of radicalism."[35]

But it soon became clear, Bell explained, that "the ground of experience—namely, the Yiddish-speaking immigrant life"—had almost vanished. Gone with that life were the familiar Jewish themes so easily available in earlier decades, themes that had enabled these novelists to bridge "the chasm" dividing their generation's "American aspirations" from their parents' European culture and values. Still, neither the earlier "Yiddish novelists nor the first-generation Americans who began publishing in the 1920's and 1930's," Bell argued, had "left any substantial trace as memory or influence on the young writers who followed. Except for the work of [Henry] Roth and [Daniel] Fuchs, who have remained cult figures despite periodic revivals, most of the Jewish fiction published in the first third of the century rapidly came to seem ideological or lachrymose, and . . . badly dated."[36]

It seems hardly surprising, therefore, that following World War II, young Jews began recording in fiction and essay their efforts to escape not only the Jewish life of their parents but also Judaism itself. Religious leaders and other communal spokesmen began expressing their concern, persisting to the present, that assimilation, primarily intermarriage, was endangering the existence of the Jewish community as a discrete, identifiable cultural entity. Jews were entering the American mainstream in increasing numbers—at least in economic, professional, and cultural terms. Norman Podhoretz even provided his contemporaries with a handbook to success in literary journalism. In *Making It,* he glorified in personal terms the country's four-decade-old "dirty little secret": the driving hunger of immigrants and their children for acceptance and success. He did so by emphasizing his own cultural journey from Brownsville to Manhattan. "One of the longest journeys in the world," Podhoretz boasted, "is the journey from Brooklyn to Manhattan—or at least from certain neighborhoods in Brooklyn to certain parts of Manhattan."[37]

Norman Podhoretz was hardly alone. Many Jews had *made it* in America. Some were now not only experiencing a change in mood and attitude but were also reassessing their ethnic and religious identities. Causes for this change were numerous, among them the Holocaust and the founding of the State of Israel. In addition, they and other Americans were also now living amid the harsh realities—whether central or peripheral to their individual lives—of the civil rights movement, the assassinations of John and Robert Kennedy and Martin Luther King, the Viet Nam war and its protestors, the sexual revolution, the feminist movement, and the Cold War. These events would soon be followed by the demise of Soviet communism, the AIDS epidemic, terrorism abroad and at home, and one military expedition after another.

Ironically, the feminist movement came slowly to the Jewish community, despite the fact that some of its leaders—like Betty Friedan and Gloria Steinem—were Jewish or partly Jewish. Indeed, the 1950s were especially unrewarding years for all American women, Jewish and non-Jewish, who wished to assert their creativity. That decade, according to Elaine Showalter, was literally the low point for American women writers in this century. For these were the years when medical and media Freudians emphasized "the tragedy of American women" and domestic "experts" urged their "return to their kitchens and nurseries." In college texts and anthologies of American literature, adds Showalter, "women averaged only about 3 percent of the writers represented." Talented young women like Sylvia Plath and Ann Sexton, who grew up in the 1940s and 1950s, were deeply discouraged by the lack of women role models. These ambitious literary aspirants wished "to distinguish themselves from other women writers who had failed. In 1958, Anne Sexton wrote to her mentor, the poet W. D. Snodgrass, 'I wish I were a man—I would rather write the way a man writes.'" To these sad words Showalter adds: "This was the generation that all too often seemed to pay for its literary achievements in depression, alcoholism, and suicide."[38]

The sixties, however, were to be a very different decade, bringing numerous changes for women and a range of ethnic minorities. It proved to be a truly pivotal period for America and, toward the end, especially for its Jews. Ted Solotaroff, a veteran observer of the Jewish scene, cites 1967 as the year that marked "a turning point in American Jewish consciousness." He points out that "1967 was the year of the Six-Day War." That war started "as the darkest moment in the history of the new state of Israel, [but it] ended as the brightest, and lives on in its consequences as the most problematic." The war's "very brevity," as well as "the dramatic transformation of horrified concern to intense relief and vaulting pride," Solotaroff reasons, "changed the way that American Jews thought not only about Israel but [also] about themselves." Commentators, he states, have noted that "Israel henceforth became the religion of American Jews, the transcendent object of their politics and philanthropy and pilgrimages and as such a new source of loyalty and solidarity, and in time of dogma and controversy."[39]

Yet other events also affected the Jewish psyche at that time. The most significant, Solotaroff explains, was the recognition of the Holocaust. That cataclysmic horror emerged "from the darkness and silence of relative repression in the previous decade into the public light and clamor of the Eichmann trial and of its aftermath." For in this trial "the issue of the cooperation of European Jewry in its own destruction was raised by Hannah Arendt's *Eichmann in Jerusalem* and debated and soul-searched by everyone."[40] One result of this painful soul-searching was that the Holocaust became a literary *subject,* both for some who survived and for others who were able to filter its horrific events through their imaginations. Norma Rosen and Cynthia Ozick, Ilona Karmel and her sister, Henryka Karmel-Wolfe, Marge Piercy, Irena Klepfisz, and Marcie Hershman are among those who have transmuted catacysm into literary art. For most of these women at least, the reasons are personal as well as professional.[41]

But there were also basic, primary questions confronting all the fiction writers—whether European or American, male or female—who gave thought to dealing with the Holocaust. Norma Rosen stated matters bluntly. "But how was the Holocaust to be written about?" she asked. "How could the virtues of fiction—indirection, irony, ambivalence—be used to make art out of this unspeakable occurrence?" In short, was it even "possible to make art of it"? Her next query was even closer to the point: "Should art be made of it at all?" Dealing with those horrendous years, she emphasized, offered difficulties both numerous and horrifying. Above all, there was still "too much pain, too recently felt, still felt." So perhaps the most logical response to the Holocaust, Rosen suggested, "might be silence, or an endless scream."

But while those options were tempting, the sad truth was, she admitted, that neither silence nor endless screaming "makes art." But if art were to be made of this horror, then perhaps women were better prepared than men to do so. Hard experience has always conditioned women to sustain life amid the world's most dire horrors.[42]

Indeed, one of the most compelling notes struck in literature by Jewish American women, according to Miriyam Glazer, "is precisely this visceral identification of women with the forces of life." Whether confronting Holocaust horrors, "Depression-era poverty, or bleak urban chaos, the women depicted by such writers as Ilona Karmel, Tillie Olsen, Cynthia Ozick, Grace Paley, Marge Piercy, and Susan Fromberg Schaeffer defy despair." It is as if there is embedded "in the very marrow of their consciousness," Glazer suggests, "a refusal to succumb to the devastation of death. That is one of our moorings. That is what binds us."[43] Women's accounts of their death-camp experiences bear out this claim. "Unlike male writers' texts," Lillian Kremer observes, "women's narratives frequently acknowledge female prisoners' vulnerability as sexual beings in the male-dominated Nazi universe." Yet despite their biological vulnerability, women's "gender-based domestic training and resourcefulness—in food management, clothing repair, housekeeping, nurturing, and nursing—enhanced their chances for survival."[44]

Several other cultural shocks of the 1950s and 1960s strongly affected Jewish women and men, and soon were reflected in both journalism and fiction. One was the new antagonism between Jews and African-Americans. This conflict had its special ironies in that Jews had been the strongest allies of black activists in the civil rights movement. Joshua Muravchik has recently recalled the strong Jewish emotional, political, and financial support of black Americans in those years. Throughout this country, he states, Jewish organizations assigned staff members to work for civil rights. For to be Jewish and liberal then meant, almost by definition, to be a champion of black rights and aspirations. So it was in the Muravchik family. Sadly enough, the "cardinal victories" of the Civil Rights Act (1964) and the Voting Rights Act (1965) moved many black activists to become advocates of "black power" and to vent their "rage over racial humiliation."[45] Jews quickly become the symbols of white oppression, with ethnic tensions exacerbated and focused by the New York City school strike of 1967–68. The central issue was local school control, Ted Solotaroff claims. It pitted "black militants against the American Federation of Teachers, the most powerful remnant of the waning Jewish labor movement." The ensuing "vehement rhetoric generated on both sides brought into the open the class feelings and prejudices that had long smoldered in the Northern ghettos." This was the lone area "where the Jew wasn't the underdog and remained as the most visible white presence." Jews filled the ranks of "teachers and school officials as well as merchants, landlords, and employers."[46] Clear indications of the strike's vitriolic debate, says Muravchik, were the leaflets that attacked "Jewish teachers as 'Middle-East murderers of colored people,' and a viciously anti-Semitic poem [that] was read over the radio by the black activist Leslie Campbell."[47] Many of the Jewish administrators and teachers drawn into the conflict were women, who have since retained their leadership roles in New York City's educational system.

As the 1960s drew to a close, Jewish women also participated in an internal religious movement centered in the Boston area as well as around Brandeis University. A group of educated young Jews who had grown dissatisfied "with suburban Judaism," reports Solataroff, initiated their own services and began to study traditional texts. They also wanted to lessen the patriarchal restrictions that reduced women to second-class status in orthodox congregations. They were determined not to distinguish "between the sexes in leading the prayer service, reading from the Torah, and interpreting the text." Soon known as the Boston Havurah, they witnessed "their intense and yet informal mode of Jewish practice" spread to other Eastern seaboard cities and then across the nation. These young people had created "a movement of spiritual activism" that was welcomed by many rabbis as a means of energizing their congregations.[48]

Freedom and Diversity

By the late 1960s and early 1970s, forces external to Judaism coalesced to affect all American women, but especially writers and artists. An activist surge, termed by Elaine Showalter "a second wave of American feminism," generated a fresh interest in women's writing. Feminist critics and activists—non-Jewish as well as Jewish—now emphasized the importance of women's personal experiences in shaping their artistic opportunities, choices, and careers. They explored women's youthful relationships with their parents, their sexuality, their decisions about marriage and motherhood, their friendships with other women, and the ways they dealt with the aging process. These elements were all viewed as feeding into women's creative lives. With surprising suddeness, or so it seemed, women's writings attained a new importance. Forgotten women writers were remembered and their works reprinted for the classroom, there "to be read, taught, and discussed." Invigorated by this fresh "attention and devotion of feminist criticism, and by the burgeoning market for their work, American women writers entered a renaissance."[49]

A central and ongoing aspect of this renaissance was the reaching out to wider audiences by black and Asian and Jewish American women writers, as well as those from other ethnic and racial backgrounds. These literary women found doors open as never before, and they have remained open. "For a serious American writer, especially a woman writer," Joyce Carol Oates has declared, "this has been by far the best era in which to live."[50] Inspired by this new literary feminism, Solotaroff says, Jewish women have in their writings blended a growing "spiritual activism" with a strong need to assert "their identity, kinship, and creativity." In doing so, they have pushed these issues "to the forefront of contemporary Jewish thought and art."[51]

Other forces, too, have affected Jewish women writers. Some influences extend beyond gender or territorial borders. A key presence has been the state of Israel and its related effects on language and culture, religion and identity. Together these factors have contributed to a "Jewish revival, both religious and cultural." The existence of Israel has enabled many more Jews to be conversant with Hebrew as a living language and culture than their forebears were." Solotaroff then puts matters another way: "Yiddishkeit has not dried up and blown away." Instead, it "is being both supplanted and to some extent resuscitated by a nascent contemporary Jewish culture that lives on easier and perhaps more fertile terms with religious Judaism than does the Israeli one." As a result, many reawakened Jews now attempt to draw upon Judaism's rich literary tradition.[52]

Tradition may take many forms, but generally these forms tend to be less biological than cultural and literary. What too often is viewed as the "female tradition" in American literature, Showalter explains, is basically "the product of literary exchanges." She suggests that "There is nothing essentially feminine in women's imagination determined by their biology, bodies, or psyches that leads them to write about particular subjects in particular ways." Instead, women have learned from one another. Obviously, American women writers have "read and revised each other's work across generations, regions, and even races."[53] Still, postwar practices took time to shift and reformulate into coherent new patterns. In 1981, Pearl K. Bell could argue that "we cannot yet speak confidently about a 'new generation' of Jewish novelists, though clearly a conscious effort is being made—or at least felt—by some writers to have done with a secular older generation trapped in the modernist worship of experience." These younger writers," she reasoned, "in their sense of themselves as Jews, feel that they are no longer beholden to the literary postures of alienation and victimization." Instead, these young writers have turned for literary inspiration to "Jewish tradition and belief."[54]

Bell was right, for clearly tradition can involve searching history for intellectual sustenance. In recent years, Jewish literary women have done just that. They have gleaned Judaism's sacred texts for new insights and plots, with their stories often emerging as commentary or *midrash* on various means of female survival. "This exploration of women as guardians of survival, through their determination, through the sheer force of personality, and through their readiness to bond," notes Miriyam Glazer, "is just one of the powerful and recurrent themes that winds its way through recent Jewish-American women's literature." Another idea of equal force, she adds, "expresses less our social, cultural, and historical experience as Jewish women than it does our spiritual thirst." Still vivid and painful for them is the "memory of their long exclusion from participation in the central religious rites of the faith." Now Jewish American women are literally "grappling with Judaism." Releasing by their struggles an "immense creativity," they have produced a steady stream of "songs . . . innovative *midrash* . . . narrative fiction . . . [and] new ceremonies." They also have revealed their longings "for significant spiritual expression."[55] Some of them, like Elizabeth Swados and Shirley Kaufman, have turned to the Old Testament for subject matter and utilized talmudic-like commentary to establish the style and structure of their fiction. But younger writers like Rebecca Goldstein and Allegra Goodman have drawn upon tradition by blending past and present. Their fictional characters are often contemporary intellectuals imbued with Jewish traditional ideas and values that prove difficult to reconcile with life in America today.[56]

American life, of course, has always presented its Jews with special complications and choices. At no time has this been more true then at present with this society's ongoing cultural and technological shifts. Men and women alike are confronted almost daily by life-changing decisions. Such challenges are usually compounded for women. Jewish women have generally written, at least in part, out of a cumulative experience shared with other women and men—Jewish and non-Jewish. In doing so they have found themselves creating freshly particularized themes, concepts, and myths. One such particularized theme today centers on shifting relationships between Jewish mothers and daughters. Rapid changes in women's societal roles have left both older and younger women without functional role models. Not surprisingly, women writers have been more inclined to deal with gender-driven dilemmas than male writers. Hence feminist critics evince little surprise that the mother-daughter relationship "is more significant to women than to men." After all, the males have been "reared in a Jewish American milieu," notes Ann Shapiro, "that Irving Howe identified as 'the world of our fathers.'"[57]

Yet Howe's description represents for Shapiro a "falsification of Jewish literary history and criticism." Still it remains the one sustained by critics who have developed their "paradigms" by reading Saul Bellow and Philip Roth, among other male writers. This renders "the world of our mothers," Shapiro feels, "still largely uncharted territory." She believes most men enter women's texts with difficulty, but that for many Jewish men the problem is intensified. Shapiro refers to those males who tend to "challenge the very authenticity of the writing of Jewish American women." For them the Jewish woman-as-author represents a deviation not only from long literary practice, but also from that rich patriarchal tradition that has shaped so much of their masculine lives.[58]

A Quick Look Back

Shapiro speaks here for a number of Jewish women writers. Certainly her claims have a certain resonance. But women writers past and present have hardly gone unappreciated by male critics, scholars, and lay readers. More to the point, given the creative vigor of today's Jewish American writers of both sexes, it seems unlikely they will in their future writings divide so neatly along gender lines. But then literary prophecy is a topic for another occasion. For with the century drawing to a close, it is more tempting to look back and attempt to graph, albeit sketchily, the literary trends and currents already discussed. What should now be obvious is that for nearly four decades critics and historians, as well an expanding general readership, have grown acutely aware of America's women writers. "Women have revised the fundamental themes and conventions of American literature," declares Elaine Showalter. They have reshaped our literature's "myths of individuality, community, language, and the frontier." It is now evident, she adds, that "feminine imagination and feminine energy" have proved important forces in this nation's cultural heritage. No history of American literature that excludes the contribution of women, therefore, can be considered valid, much less "complete."[59] Norma Rosen, as a Jewish writer discussing Jewish women writers, clearly agrees. Rosen points out that in recent years "there has been an outpouring of writing by women about women. It is as if the woman's movement gave a kind of support that led to an exuberant letting go, out of imagination or memory." Some of the resultant writing is "very good writing, some of it art, some of it confessional and documentary." What makes much of it interesting, however, is that "the confessed and documented matters haven't been written about before."[60] In fact, a good deal of what women writers—Jewish and non-Jewish—have been revealing in recent years has not before been exposed.

Indeed, the essays here collected make clear that Jewish American women writers have proved increasingly outspoken and candid in revealing the forms and substance of their experiences not only as women and Jews, but also as Americans and human beings. Still, as a group, they have faced special challenges and complexities. For even as they search for new truths in old myths, Jewish women writers continue to recall old pains. Like their male colleagues, they have also known what it is to be marginal beings or outsiders in a world where anti-Semitism refuses to die and takes "new forms in every generation." But for women "the problem is compounded," according to Ann Shapiro. For Jewish women "are not only outsiders in a Gentile world," but they are also "outsiders in the double patriarchy of secular society and Judaism," yet even more irritating than their "exclusion from the full legal protection" of Judaic law has been their exclusion from sacred study." A prime example, says Shapiro, "is the Woman of Valor described in Proverbs 31." This valiant woman is a dutiful "housekeeper and breadwinner, but reading and study are reserved for her husband" and other males. Still, for her modern sisters societal conditions and lifestyles have been changing, albeit slowly and painfully. Most Jewish women now are steadily overcoming the barriers excluding them from any textuality, Jewish or not. Those among them who choose to do so, therefore, are participating more fully in the new liturgies and literature, poetics and culture being articulated by Jewish feminist writers and critics.[61]

A cautionary note, however, does appear in order: Readers should not expect these valiant women to articulate, in whatever their chosen genres, a monolithic body of writings. Any discussion of their "commonalities," Shapiro warns, should also acknowledge "their wide diversity." Introducing her own collection of bio-critical essays on Jewish American women writers, she observes that the writers represented in it "include communists and proponents of the American dream; assimilated Jews and those who celebrate their faith and ethnicity." Some of the women are "radical feminists and traditional wives and mothers." Others are "lesbians who have come out and lesbians who have not." There are also, of course, "straight women; orthodox believers and atheists. Some are well known and others barely recognized." But the significant factor is that all have contributed "to the braid of many strands that represents Jewish American women's writing."[62] Her caveat is an apt one for this collection as well. With this warning in mind, the reader is well prepared to move on to the essays that follow.

Notes

1. Jane Hirshfield, "Enheduanna," in *Women in Praise of the Sacred: 43 Centuries of Spiritual Poetry by Women,* ed. Jane Hirshfield (New York: HarperCollins Publishers, 1994), 3.

2. See Sam Welles, "The Jewish Elan," *Fortune* 61, no. 2 (February 1960): 137.

3. Joseph Lowin, "A Novel Tradition," *Hadassah Magazine* (March 1987): 19–20.

4. Lowin, 19–21.

5. Roger Rosenblatt, "Remarks," *People for the American Way News* 1, no. 3 (Spring 1995): 4.

6. Elie Wiesel, foreword to *The Literature of American Jews,* ed. Theodore L. Gross (New York: The Free Press, 1973), xiii.

7. William J. Drummond, "Publishers Ask: What Is Jewish Book?" *Los Angeles Times,* 11 May 1975, pt. 8, sec. 4. All quotations in the paragraph are from this article.

8. Norma Rosen, "The Holocaust and the American-Jewish Novelist," in

Accidents of Influence: Writing as a Woman and a Jew in America (Albany: State University of New York Press, 1992), 17, 9.

9. Philip Roth, *The Counterlife* (1986; reprint, New York: Penguin Books, 1988), 370.

10. Ted Solotaroff, "The Open Community," in *Writing Our Way Home: Contemporary Stories by American Jewish Writers,* ed. Ted Solotaroff and Nessa Rapoport (New York: Schocken Books 1992), xx.

11. See Elaine M. Kauvar, "An Interview with Cynthia Ozick," *Contemporary Literature* 34, no. 3 (Fall 1993): 3.

12. Cynthia Ozick, "Of Polished Mirrors," in *The Writer in the Jewish Community: An Israeli-North American Dialogue,* ed. Richard Siegel and Tamar Sofer (Rutherford, N.J.: Fairleigh Dickinson University Press, 1993), 50.

13. Amos Oz, "Imagining the Other: 1," in *The Writer in the Jewish Community,* 122.

14. Ozick, "Imagining the Other: 2," in *The Writer in the Jewish Community,* 126–27.

15. Saul Bellow, "A Jewish Writer: Is There a Cure for Anti-Semitism?: A Symposium," *Partisan Review* 61, no. 3 (Summer 1994): 373.

16. Irving Howe, introduction to *Jewish-American Stories,* ed. Irving Howe (New York: New American Library, 1977), 13–14.

17. David Schuetz, "The Storyteller as a Jew," in *The Writer in the Jewish Community,* 27.

18. See Alfred Kazin, "The Jew as Modern Writer," *Commentary* (April 1966): 37.

19. Oscar Handlin, *The Uprooted: The Epic Story of the Great Migrations That Made the American People* (New York: Grosset & Dunlap, 1951), 4.

20. Herbert Gold, *Fathers: A Novel in the Form of a Memoir* (New York: Random House, 1966), 16.

21. Gold, 22.

22. George Price, *Yidn in amerika* (1891), quoted in Irving Howe, *World of Our Fathers* (New York: Harcourt Brace Jovanovich, 1976), 36.

23. Howe, *World of Our Fathers,* 70.

24. Leslie A. Fiedler, "Negro and Jew: Encounter in America," in *No! In Thunder: Essays in Myth and Literature* (Boston: Beacon Press, 1960), 234.

25. Mark Shechner, "Jewish Writers," in *Harvard Guide to Contemporary American Writing,* ed Daniel Hoffman (Cambridge: Harvard University Press, 1979), 193.

26. Judd L. Teller, "From Yiddish to Neo-Brahmin," in *Strangers and Natives: The Evolution of the American Jew from 1921 to the Present* (New York: Delacorte Press, 1968), 272.

27. Shechner, 193.

28. Faye Moskowitz, introduction to *Her Face in the Mirror: Jewish Women on Mothers and Daughters,* ed. Faye Moskowitz (Boston: Beacon Press, 1994), xvi–xvii.

29. Anne R. Shapiro, "Introduction: The Braided Tradition: Ethnicity, History, and Ethics," in *Jewish American Women Writers: A Bio-Bibliographical and Critical Sourcebook,* ed. Ann R. Shapiro, Sara R. Horowitz, Ellen Schiff, and Miriyam Glazer (Westport, Conn.: Greenwood Press, 1994), 6–7.

30. Elaine Showalter, "Toward a Feminist Poetics," in *Feminist Criticism: Essays on Women, Literature, and Theory,* ed. Elaine Showalter (New York: Pantheon, 1985), 127.

31. Howe, *Jewish-American Stories,* 4.
32. Howe, *Jewish-American Stories,* 9–11.
33. Howe, *Jewish-American Stories,* 8–9.
34. Saul Bellow, introduction to *Great Jewish Short Stories,* ed. Saul Bellow (New York: Dell, 1963), 10, 12.
35. Pearl K. Bell, "New Jewish Voices," *Commentary* (June 1981): 62.
36. Bell, 62.
37. Norman Podhoretz, *Making It* (New York: Random House, 1967), 3.
38. Elaine Showalter, introduction to *Modern American Women Writers,* ed. Elaine Showalter, Lea Baechler, and A. Walton Litz (New York: Macmillan, 1991; reprint, New York: Collier Books, 1993), xiv.
39. Solotaroff, xv.
40. Solotaroff, xv–xvi.
41. See, for example, Norma Rosen, "The Holocaust and the American-Jewish Novelist," in *Accidents of Influence: Writing as a Woman and a Jew in America* (Albany: State University of New York Press, 1992), 3–17.
42. Rosen, 9–10.
43. Miriyam Glazer, "The Will to Be Known: An Introduction to Contemporary Jewish-American Women Writers," in *Studies in American Jewish Literature,* ed. Daniel Walden and Miriyam Glazer 2 no. 2 (Fall 1992): 125–26.
44. S. Lillian Kremer, "Holocaust-Wrought Women: Portraits by Four American Writers," in *Studies in American Jewish Literature,* ed. Daniel Walden and Miriyam Glazer 2 no. 2 (Fall 1992): 150.
45. Joshua Muravchik, "Facing Up to Black Anti-Semitism," *Commentary* (December 1995): 26–27.
46. Solotaroff, xvii.
47. Muravchik, 27.
48. Solotaroff, xviii.
49. Showalter, *Modern American Women Writers,* xiv, ix.
50. Showalter, *Modern American Women Writers,* xiv.
51. Solotaroff, xviii.
52. Solotaroff, xviii–xix.
53. Showalter, *Modern American Women Writers,* xi.
54. Bell, 66.
55. Glazer, 126–27.
56. See Shapiro, 1–2.
57. Shapiro, 5–6.
58. Shapiro, 5–9.
59. Showalter, *Modern American Women Writers,* xiv–xv.
60. Rosen, "Women? Writers?", *Accidents of Influence,* 146.
61. Shapiro, 7–9.
62. Shapiro, 3.

"In Life I Am Not Free": The Writer Cynthia Ozick and Her Jewish Obligations

Susanne Klingenstein

Writer without Program

It is a truth universally acknowledged that biographies are a species of fiction. The hard reality of this truth dawned on me when I was invited to contribute a portrait of Cynthia Ozick to this collection of essays. My friend for many years, she is also a literary intellectual whose mind has profoundly shaped the direction of my work. I realized quickly that despite my familiarity with many facets of her life and work, I would not be able to grasp her inner gestalt. Ozick's fundamental sense of self, the core of her being, would still elude my pen.

Writers cannot be adequately described with the help of social categories. Writers *are* the passionate moments of literary creation. They are coextensive with the span of time when something comes into being on the page. The writer's social circumstances are secondary to the acts of literary creation. His or her situation in life—gender, class, religion—may inspire elements of plot, for instance, but it does not determine the writer's artistry. In short, it is quite meaningless to speak of an author as a woman, Jew, or middle-class American. One does not thereby say anything that goes to the core of the writing process, because the writer is just that, a writer. "Art comes first," Ozick declared. "The writer who is the real thing begins with the lure, mandate, and bliss of the alphabet, and then falls, who knows how, into content. Writers who begin with subject and content are bound to be programmatic, and a programmatic writer is by definition second-rate."[1] Virginia Woolf, speaking about women and fiction writing, said very much the same thing. "The desire to plead some personal cause or to make a character the mouthpiece of some personal discontent or grievance always has a distressing effect," she wrote. "It introduces a distortion and is frequently the cause of weakness."[2]

Cynthia Ozick therefore may be somewhat less than happy to find her portrait included in a collection whose explicit purpose is to assemble essays on Jewish American women writers. While it is true that she is a Jewish woman living in America and a writer by profession, she has always insisted that the social and biological coordinates of her life do not define her as a writer:

> When I write, I am free. I am, as a writer, whatever I wish to become. I can think myself into a male, or a female, or a stone, or a raindrop, or a block of wood, or a Tibetan, or the spine of a cactus.
>
> In life, I am not free. In life, female or male, no one is free. In life, female or male, I have tasks; I have obligations and responsibilities . . . I am devoured by drudgery and fragmentation. My freedom is contingent on need. I am, in short, claimed. . . .
>
> But when I write . . . I am in command of a grand *As If.* I write *As If* I were truly free. And this *As If* is not a myth. As soon as I proclaim it, as soon as my conduct as a writer expresses it, it comes into being.[3]

Ozick has emphatically protested both against being called a woman writer, because she disagrees with the political program of segregation that this appellation currently entails, and against being called a Jewish American writer, because, as she said, she was becoming "more and more skeptical—doubtful—of the meaning of 'American Jewish writing' anyhow. . . . I am getting deeply bored by unliterary approaches, as exemplified by a woman's question at the [New York Public] Library: How does the growing rate of intermarriage affect your writing?"[4] The woman's question was addressed to a panel that included, along with Ozick, Max Apple, Michael Chabon, and Ted Solotaroff (as moderator), and it was asked in response to the panelists' discussion of American Jewish writing. In her brief opening remarks Ozick had argued that the epithet *Jewish writer,* connoting either subject matter or descent, was inappropriate as a definition for the kind of writer she wanted to be. Ozick concluded that

> Jewish writers, whatever language they write in, and whether they are in Israel or the various Diasporas, must be writers first, and then Jews; otherwise it may turn out that there is prose on Jewish themes, but no Jewish *literature*—which is something different from prose on Jewish themes. . . .
>
> But by and large, if you lead with Jewish themes, your fiction will falter and stutter into polemic, politics, tendentiousness. Maurice Samuel is resplendent as essayist, but his theme-novel on the ancient Ebionites, is secondary work. A fictionized essay is not litera-

ture. The work of the intellect is not the work of fiction-making, which is dream-and-word work. . . . No one can *will* to make a novel: novels and stories are not willed but surprised into being.

In the same way, Jewish writers are surprised into being. Real writers know about themselves only that they must write, not to write is a dying. Then the world comes, looks at content and subject, and says, "Eureka! You are a Jewish writer," as if the writer had all along intended to press a cause. Writers as citizens may have causes; writers as Jews do indeed have causes; but writers as writers have only the alphabet, a certain chaotic dreaminess, and the wish to leave something standing that was not there before the wish began.[5]

Taking my cue from these remarks, I examine in this essay some of the Jewish causes that have left their imprint on Ozick's writing. I shall try to spell out what it means to her, in terms of "obligations and responsibilities," to be Jewish. My intention, however, is not primarily to comment on Ozick as a fiction writer. The recent slew of monographs and critical articles on Ozick's fiction allows me to bypass many of her novels and stories and to focus on some less accessible sources.[6] In particular, I want to examine Ozick's preoccupation with Yiddish poetry.[7] I will illuminate some Jewish facets of the citizen Cynthia Ozick and illustrate how those aspects of her being in which she is not free but "claimed" do impose themselves on her freedom as a writer. There is little doubt that in the areas of Jewish life and thought she "falls, who knows how, into content."

The Chimera of the Third Thing—the Jewish Writer

"To be Jewish," Ozick once declared, "is to be a member of a civilization—a civilization with a long, long history, a history that is, in one way of viewing it, a procession of ideas. Jewish history is intellectual history. And all this can become the content of a writer's mind; but it isn't equal to a writer's mind. To be a writer is one thing; to be a Jew is another thing. To combine them is third thing."[8]

Few would doubt that Ozick has successfully combined being a writer and a Jew, and produced not "prose on Jewish themes, but . . . Jewish *literature*." Her fiction, which may or may not be written in an overtly Jewish lexicon, using Jewish protagonists, settings, or subject matters, is inescapably shaped by the structure of Jewish thought, which evolved from the intellectual axioms of Torah and Talmud. Ozick's fictions are written, then, in the intellectual grammar of rabbinic thought, and it matters very little whether the lexicon her fictions use (the naming of protagonists, settings, and subject matters) is Italian, Swedish, American, or Jewish.

The intellectual grammar that shapes Ozick's fictional work is in fact very simple. The starting point of all Jewish thought, that of the Talmudic rabbis as well as Ozick's, is the basic tenet of Judaism posited in the first verses of Genesis, which declare the radical separation of the material and the divine, of immanence and transcendence. The axiom of separation, which may be summarized quite simply as God is not in nature although nature is God's creation, is so scary—leaving humanity to fend for itself—that there have been many attempts to reverse or undo it and to put God back into nature. The most successful attempt was Christianity.

If one accepts the axiom of separation, as the Torah does, however, the problem arises of how one establishes a relation between the two incommensurate realms. The Torah presents an ingenious metaphor to allow humanity a relationship with the divine without being too presumptuous about the realm of transcendence, which is, by definition, beyond humanity's ken. The Torah's metaphor is that of the covenant *(brith)*; it defines the relation between God and his chosen people as contractual—that is, regulated by the voluntary agreement of both parties to abide by the terms spelled out in a contract. As the Torah tells the story, God had a hard time gaining recognition as Master of the Universe until He found the ear of a certain Avram. In exchange for the promise of land and descendants—that is, physical continuity through space and time—Avram promised to translate the will of God into deeds (causing God to change his name to Abraham, "father of a multitude of nations," as a sign that He intended to fulfill His part of the contract). Hence, the only way transcendence manifests itself in immanence is through the deeds of those bound by the covenant to execute the divine will. The Jews define themselves as heirs to Abraham's *brith*; "to be a Jew is to be covenanted," Ozick wrote.[9]

The two constituent works of the Jewish tradition, Torah and Talmud, document how the Jews came to inherit and pass on the legacy of the covenant and explain precisely what obligations adherence to the contract entails. The rabbinic discussions, compiled and edited in the second century of the Common Era, amount to more or less informed guesses as to how the will of God is best translated into deed. Halakhah—Jewish law, or, better yet, precepts of Jewish conduct—spells out Abraham's part of the contract. There is little speculation about God's obligations beyond the hope that He may preserve the executors of His will (a hope that was disappointed often enough). But this is where Jews draw the line: it would be presumptuous of those confined to immanence to assess and describe what is, by definition, beyond their reach. All speculation about the divine is unequivocally cut off in Deuteronomy 29:29, where Moses announces to the people of Israel: "The secret [unsayable] things belong to the Lord our God; but the things that are revealed [in God's speech to Moses] belong to us and to our children for ever that we may do all the words of his law." The emphasis is on *doing* the word, on translating will into deed.

In Ozick's early fiction the basic source of tension lies in the incompatibility of the realms of moral conduct and "volcanic high imagination."[10] The obligation to a life of moral conduct stands over and against the temptation to approach the realm of high imagination and to disappear in its hallucinogenic vortex. Isaac Kornfeld in "The Pagan Rabbi," Ruth Puttermesser in "Puttermesser and Xanthippe," and Lars Andemening in *The Messiah of Stockholm* spin in ecstatic bliss until the creative drive they released spins out of control and turns destructive. While Ruth and Lars escape their brush with high imagination by regaining their rational faculty and hence self-control, Isaac Kornfeld is consumed in a passionate *Liebestod* (death in the act of love).

It is evident that even in her fiction, Ozick not only accepts but agrees with the admonition of Deuteronomy 29:29. This has tempted critics to conclude that she condemns the writing of fiction. The fact is, however, that Ozick sees no fundamental contradiction between the moral life and the production of literature. "The novel at its nineteenth-century pinnacle," she once declared, "was a Judaized novel: George Eliot and Dickens and Tolstoy were all touched by the Jewish covenant: they wrote of conduct and of the consequences of conduct: they were concerned with a society of will and commandment."[11] Yet as a writer, she is propelled, as if by a perverse impulse, to explore precisely the force that separates her from ordinary life and chains her to the desk.

The nature of the creative drive, condemned in Genesis as *yetzer ha-ra* (Gen. 6:5, 8:21), is the fundamental issue broached in all of Ozick's early fiction. The way it is broached, namely as an illicit subject—as pagan-poetic impulse, cannibalistic drive, or imagemaking shop set up in competition with the Creator[12]—evokes as its cultural frame of reference not only the rabbinic suspicion of the imaginative faculty but also the Jewish tradition of fictional and historical narratives about runaway imaginations in the shape of idols, golems, dybbuks, false messiahs, and the like. But what Ozick pursues, despite the rabbinic censure of indulgence in the ecstasy of the creative impulse, is a vision of pure writing in which the impediments of subject matter, the bits and pieces of ordinary life that cling to the writer as she walks into her study, are consumed in the fiery passion of the creative act.

Ozick's image of the writer, contrived when she had just finished the manuscript of her third novel, *The Messiah of Stockholm* (1987), was that of a "beast howling inside a coal-furnace, heaping the coals on itself to increase the fire. The only thing more tormenting than writing is not writing. . . . What *I* did, a child crazed by literature, was to go like an eremite into a cavern and spin; I imagined that I would emerge with a masterpiece. Instead I emerged as an unnatural writing-beast, sooty with coal dust, my fingers burned and my heart burning up."[13]

It is perhaps no coincidence that in *The Messiah of Stockholm,* Ozick's most ambitious fiction to date about literary passion and the vortex of the imagination, fire is the decisive leitmotiv, beginning with the "smell of something roasting," that seems to hang in Stockholm's night air. The odor evokes in the literature-crazed protagonist Lars Andemening the recollection of the verse "O the chimneys" by Nellie Sachs, who in 1940 had found refuge from the Nazis in Sweden. Lars, a book reviewer for the unread Monday pages of the newspaper *Morgontörn,* has a singular way of producing his highbrow literary reviews. He reads from morning till afternoon, and then falls into bed, exhausted from the effort.

> When he awoke at seven into full blackness of night, he felt oddly fat—he was sated with his idea, he understood what he thought. He sat down immediately to his review. He wrote it straight off, a furnace burning fat. It was as if his pen, sputtering along the line of rapid letters it ignited, flung out haloes of hot grease. The air brightened, then charred.[14]

Lars imagines himself the son of the Jewish writer and artist Bruno Schulz, who was shot dead by SS in Drohobycz, a small town in Nazi-occupied Poland, in 1942. When Lars finally holds in his hands what he believes to be the lost manuscript of his father's only novel, *The Messiah,* he discovers that it is about the occupation of Drohobycz by idols, who eventually burn each other up in ever-increasing bonfires "in a frenzy of mutual adoration" (*Messiah* 109). Recovering from his gluttonous reading of the manuscript, Lars is shaken in his belief that he has seen the authentic *Messiah.*

Yet he is pushed by the proprietors of the manuscript into accepting its authenticity and to become *The Messiah*'s prophet in the pages of the *Morgontörn.* He is asked to announce there the resurrection of *The Messiah* from the ashes of Jewish culture. But Lars is suddenly shocked into recognition of the truth:

> "Fakery. I've lived for fakery." . . .
> His transient little fear. His hands were hot. His fingers were heating up like the staves of a fence on fire.
> "*The Messiah* went into the camps with its keeper." Lars shook: the ape had him by the throat. "That's all that could have happened, nothing else. *The Messiah* was burned up in those places. Behind those fences, in those ovens. It was burned, Mrs. Eklund, burned!" (*Messiah* 121)

At this point the fires of Andemening's literary imagination are reigned in by their real-life counterparts—the fires of the Shoah. In much of Ozick's fiction, the destruction of the European Jews functions as the reality that renders morally dubious, if not even illicit, any indulgence in the pleasures of art. In *The Messiah of Stockholm* Ozick, self-critically, equates the passion for the hermetic life of literary idol-worship with a ferocious, pagan passion for aesthetic perfection, which, in her view, found its culmination in the Nazis' obsession with racial hygiene, their compulsion to cleanse the master race of its imperfect elements. In 1970 Ozick declared,

> The German Final Solution was an aesthetic solution: it was a job of editing, it was the artist's finger removing a smudge, it simply annihilated what was considered not harmonious. In daily life the morality of Germans continued as before, neighbors were kindly, who can deny it? From the German point of view, getting rid of the Jew had nothing to do with conduct and everything to do with art. The religion of Art isolates the Jew—only the Jew is indifferent to aesthetics, only the Jew wants to "passionately wallow in the human reality." . . . Even now, in the whole planet of diverse cultures, the Jew is the only one who stands there naked without art. The Jewish

writer, if he intends himself really to be a *Jewish* writer, is all alone, judging culture like mad, while the rest of culture just goes on *being* culture.[15]

In many of Ozick's fictions the representatives of history, Jews touched by the Shoah, judge those who indulge in the freedom of art. In the short story "The Pagan Rabbi" (1966), Sheindl, whose life began in a concentration camp, condemns her husband's love affair with nature and poetry. In "The Suitcase" (1971), the artist's Jewish lover, Genevieve, declares that the scene at a gallery opening resembles a concentration camp. "'Everybody staring through the barbed wire hoping for rescue and knowing it's no use.'"[16] She compares the paintings of her love, who is of German descent, to "'shredded swastikas, that's what,' Genevieve announced. 'Every single damn thing he does. All that terrible pre*cis*ion. Every last one a pot of shredded swastikas, you see that'" (109). In "Bloodshed" (1970) the protagonist's guns, the real one and the toy gun—the latter a symbol of deadly make-believe that is compared to the "toy showerheads, out of which no drop fell"—are confiscated by a Hasidic rebbe, who is a survivor of Buchenwald.[17]

At all points Ozick's artists are either mocked or stopped from going further in their imaginations by representatives of history, by those for whom death was not make-believe but real. It is precisely here that Ozick's obligations as a Jew intrude on her freedom as a writer and judge her literary pursuits. Although she claims, "I am trying to give myself the freedom to be free—to do whatever I damn please, however I damn please,"[18] being a Jew curtails her sense of being entitled to such freedom. As she once said in a debate about the Holocaust, during which she argued that the destruction of the European Jews ought to be perceived not as a past but as a contemporary event, "To be a Jew means to be a carrier of that kind of history."[19] It is Ozick's intense awareness of the deadly facts of Jewish history that makes her suspect the moral legitimacy of the flights of fancy to which she wants to yield as a writer.

The distinctions Ozick draws between being a writer, a Jew, and a combination of the two are less clear than she would have us believe. In much of her fiction she has achieved the "third thing" by writing within the moral and intellectual framework of rabbinic Judaism about the subject that compels her, the unsettling nature of the creative imagination. At the same time she insists that she is keeping separate her obligations as a Jew and her desires as a writer. In 1989 she explained that, "To be a Jew is an act of the strenuous mind as it stands before the fakeries and lying seductions of the world, saying no and no again as they parade by in all their allure. And to be a writer is to plunge into the parade and become one of the delirious marchers."[20] Yet more often than not in Ozick's fiction the Jew grabs the Writer by the collar just as she is ready to plunge and restrains her by pointing out that "the fakeries and lying seductions of this world" spell the death of the Jews.

In all other respects, however, it is true that Ozick separates her passions as a writer and her causes as a Jew. In a short essay, responding to the question "Does the Jewish writer have a particular responsibility to the Jewish community?," Ozick declared that she could not put her writing into the service of political causes, even when she recognized their importance. She maintained that stories are "the central human purpose around which all politics flows." She continued,

> But how to prove it? How to prove, for instance, that one sentence in a single story of Agnon's is worth an armada of op-ed pieces?. . . . How can one argue that a story about polished mirrors is as much a service as, say, being a nurse or a neurologist in Hadassah Hospital? It is a difficult, perhaps an impossible, argument, and I don't know how to make it. But I bring my devotion to such a proposition, if only out of a tremulous hope of exculpation; the hope that a polished mirror, itself no more than a bauble, will somehow catch a reflection of Sinai.[21]

Writers as Jews Do Indeed Have Causes

As a writer Ozick does not hope to do more for the Jews than provide them with fiction written within the moral framework to which Jews committed themselves at Mount Sinai; as a Jew, however, she has devoted time, energy, and her skills to causes essential to the preservation of the Jews and their culture. Foremost among these causes is the safety of the state of Israel and, concommitantly, the adequate representation of its policies in the American press. Since 1973 Ozick has written numerous op-ed pieces for and letters to the *New York Times,* as well as a few articles for other publications on Israel and the Palestinian problem.

Needless to say, Ozick accords language great political force.

She thinks of Hebrew not only as the vessel and vehicle of Israeli culture but also of Jewish moral ideals and principles of civilization. Because ancient and modern Hebrew are recognizably continuous, Ozick can indeed assign Hebrew the function of a "unifying substratum," linking temporally and spatially widely dispersed Jewish cultures in a tight fabric of one Jewish people. The language of the diaspora Ozick considers "perishable" tongues, whereas Hebrew was the "language of perpetuation."[22]

The diaspora language that perished most dramatically and painfully was, of course, Yiddish. Between the two world wars there were an estimated 11 million Yiddish speakers, among them also Ozick's parents and grandparents. It was one thing to declare dispassionately that Yiddish shared the ontological status of all diaspora tongues, and quite another to witness its death through atrophy in America and murder in Europe. Yiddish was too intimately connected with Ozick's personal and cultural identity to allow her to sit still. And while she could not revive the language, she might at least rescue what it once conveyed. She began to translate Yiddish poetry into English, first on her own, then for Irving Howe's famous anthologies. This translation project, a constant in Ozick's life for some twenty-five years, has been overlooked by most critics. And yet her translation of Yiddish literature "with the fury of lost love" illuminates, like few other examples, the confluence of Jewish subject matter and literary craftsmanship, or the emergence of Ozick as a Jewish writer.[23]

Translating Yiddish with the Fury of Lost Love

Ozick's involvement in what was really Howe's rescue effort for Yiddish literature dates back to the early 1960s when she became, almost by accident, one of the translators in Howe's illustrious stable of American poets, essayists, and educators literate in Yiddish. In 1963, when Ozick had just finished but not yet published her long first novel, *Trust,* she read somewhere that Irving Howe and Eliezer Greenberg were planning to edit an anthology of Yiddish poetry in translation. She wrote to them and sent along a story by David Bergelson she had translated on her own, "just for the fun of it."[24] Some two years later a batch of Yiddish poems arrived. The timing was perfect. In September 1965 Ozick's daughter Rachel was born. She seriously disrupted her mother's nocturnal "visionary toil."[25] For despite the fact that Virginia Woolf had famously claimed that the novel, as "the least concentrated form of art,"[26] could be interrupted without detriment by domestic chores, Ozick did not find this to be the case. Yet a translation was "perfect to do with a baby because you could pick it up and you could put it down. I would make endless versions, endless drafts. I would have pages and pages for two lines" *(TI)*.

Ozick's toil on the poetry of David Einhorn, H. Leivick, and Chaim Grade was fired by her passion for language as artistic material—that is, by the mental gymnastics cum aesthetic judgment required by the task of coming up with *le mot juste*. This sums up Ozick's early view of writing, which Elaine Kauvar has aptly called "the struggle for exactitude."[27] Although Kauvar's phrase refers to the writing of Ozick's first novel, *Trust* (1966), which consumed the author's late twenties and early thirties (1956 to 1963), it could just as well refer to the poetry Ozick composed at the time.[28] In fact, she has often emphasized the linguistic range and lyrical qualities of *Trust*. To her critic Victor Strandberg Ozick wrote in 1991, "The energy and meticulous language-love that went into that book drew on sources that were never again so abundant. In certain ways it is simply an immensely long poem."[29] Whether these sources were indeed "never again so abundant" will be questioned by any reader familiar with Ozick's later work. What is important, however, is that her language-love and sense of linguistic wealth propelled her to try her hand at the tricky task of literary translation.

In the early 1960s, Ozick recalled recently, "I was really interested in poetry and in translating and in Yiddish. Also I was in an insatiable belles lettres place where I wanted to try my hand at everything, which explains my current theatrical folly." For Howe's project it was almost more important to be a superb poet than to be a competent Yiddish speaker, because he wanted, as Ozick recalls, "not a translation but another poem in English." The finished text "had to stand as a poem in English while at the same time being as faithful as possible a translation. His criterion and Ruth's [Wisse, who replaced Eliezer Greenberg as collaborator after his death] was a poem that could last forever in English" *(TI)*. When *A Treasury of Yiddish Poetry* appeared in 1969, the anthology looked very much like a collection of English poems, not least of all because a good quarter of the translators were themselves distinguished poets. They included Irving Feldman, Edward Field, John Hollander, Carolyn Kizer, Stanley Kunitz, William Merwin, Adrienne Rich, Jerome Rothenberg, Harvey Shapiro, Karl Shapiro, and James Wright. How successful some of their translations were was indicated by Harold Bloom's wicked praise, meaning "not to dispraise Hollander in judging his version of [Moshe Leib] Halpern's 'The Bird' to be his best poem so far."[30]

While finding herself in such company strengthened Ozick's somewhat shaky self-confidence, the actual labor on the translations and the "astonishing education" she acquired as she moved into the language and explored the cultural contexts of the Yiddish poems, had, of course, a much more lasting effect on her as a writer. When she started her work, she recalls, "I didn't know these poets by name; I knew nothing about the history of Yiddish poetry; I was a total tabula rasa" *(TI)*. As a child she had had some exposure to Yiddish poetry because her parents, immigrants from a small town near Minsk in White Russia, subscribed to the *Tog*, the most literary of the American Yiddish dailies. It featured a daily poem, which Ozick used to read. "I was not aware of it then, but those poems were by the great Yiddish writers of the time" *(TI)*.

For Ozick, who was born in the Bronx, New York, in 1928, and grew up with English as her mother tongue, Yiddish was a household language until the death of her grandmother in 1939, when it declined into the "speech of reminiscence" for her parents.[31] Her entire education in written Yiddish was acquired "in four hours in four days, one hour a day, over a week in *heder*, when the rabbi announced that this week we were going to learn Yiddish. Since we already knew the Hebrew alphabet, it was a simple thing to learn. My so-called Yiddish literacy, which is at a very low level, came from that week in *heder*" *(TI)*. Like other New York Jewish children with immigrant parents and grandparents, she did not cherish the language that was to her such a simple and natural part of family life. Instead she was fascinated by the initially unfamiliar. "I went the way of my not very distinguished generation, and forgot, if I had ever really known it, that there was a world of Yiddish letters; or, rather, I forgot, like almost everyone of my shamed generation, that the world of Yiddish letters mattered. I entered the life of the universities and became obsessed by English and American literature."[32] It was not until she had embarked seriously on the translations for Howe's anthology that she began to recover bits of an extraordinary Jewish world that had been slipping away from her. But she could not have caught it by the coattails without her father.

Unlike Ozick's mother, who was brought to America at the age of nine, Ozick's father arrived at twenty-one as a "finished adult" *(TI)*. He had graduated from a Russian Gymnasium, where he had studied Latin and German, yet he had retained his ability to write "beautiful Hebrew paragraphs" and to read "in Yiddish all of Sholom Aleichem and Peretz." He also read Bernard Malamud's novel *The Assistant* when his daughter asked him to.[33] In America Velvl became William, who made a living as the *apteker* of the Park View Pharmacy in Pelham Bay, New York. "My father grinds and mixes powders, weighs them out in tiny snowy heaps on an apothecary scale, folds them into delicate translucent papers or meticulously drops them into gelatin capsules."[34]

But when the Yiddish poems arrived, Velvl stepped out from behind William. He sat down with his daughter and explained the poems to her. "He would not only help me with the deep inner meanings of words and phrases but with all kinds of cultural contexts that I didn't understand, whether they were religious, linguistic, historical, or sociological references" *(TI)*. Velvl, who was Mr. O. to his wife, unfolded his past before the eyes of his daughter. It is easy to imagine that with the exuberance of discovery came also excruciating pain at the extent of what was lost in the murder of the Eastern European Jews. "For the whole of the project," Ozick wrote, "I came as a suppliant to Yiddish, imploring it to let me reenter the language. I drank the dictionary, supped on idiom, and explored my father's brains and life—and with the pursuit of each poem, I more and more recovered, and also discovered, not only what had been, but what would be, and not only the future but the present."[35] That discovery would be turned into story, but not until a few years later.

When after endless drafts Ozick arrived at a "final polished version, that which I regarded as completely finished," she would send it to Irving Howe. "Generally, he accepted them as is, but once in a while he quarreled with a word. In [Chaim Grade's] 'Elegy for the Soviet Yiddish Writers' he tampered with phrases, making them much too prosaic. Always, I thought, his touch was on the side of prose" *(TI)*. Ozick was not merely unhappy with Howe's interference but genuinely upset about it because Howe's changes destroyed what, as a poet, she believed to be the Yiddish poem's English equivalent. "The poem's translation," she held, "is not the poem's shadow or reflection. The poem and its translation are two separate artifacts, each equal to the other; and not only 'equal' in the sense of being 'alike,' but each having become the other." She maintained, moreover, that the original poem's equivalent could be "found" in an arduous process of linguistic work, during which the translator *became* the poet.[36]

When Ozick sent off a "final polished version," she was sending Howe the poem he had asked for. But while Howe was indeed interested in the lyrical qualities of the translations, he had still another agenda: he wanted clarity of content wherever content mattered to him. His meddling with the translation of Grade's "Elegy" is a case in point.

The fairly long poem (twelve stanzas of sixteen lines each) commemorates the murder of the Soviet Jewish intellectual elite by Stalin's henchmen on 12 August 1952.[37] More specifically, Grade's poem mourned the Yiddish writer Aaron Kushnirov, who died in 1949, having suffered a stroke while speaking on Jewish literature before the Assembly of Soviet Writers; the Yiddish actor Solomon Mikhoels, brutally killed in a car accident engineered by the Soviet secret police in 1948; and the executed Yiddish writers Dovid Bergelson, Dovid Hofshteyn, Leib Kvitko, Itsik Feffer, and Peretz Markish.[38] Grade exposed their self-deluding trust that the Communist Revolution would bring forth "the New Enlightened Man," when, in fact, it reproduced precisely the reign of terror, persecution, and slaughter from which so few Jews had just escaped. Throughout the poem the backdrop for Stalin's assault on the remaining Jewish elite is the Nazi annihilation of the Jews. Grade's despair at the suicidal idealism of the Jews, blinding them to the similarities between fascist and communist dictatorships, is channeled into the ineffectual outcry of Der Nister (that is, Pinkhas Kaganovich), a writer who was arrested a bit later than his colleagues and died in a camp hospital in 1950.[39]

> Dobrushin speaks: "The world is all Hitler! Cursed, a snare!
> Blessed be our Soviet land, and sacred Socialism!"
> Only *der Nister* warned: "Children, beware,
> run away!" He alone ran off, old man, into the ground.

At the climax of the poem in stanzas 8 and 9, the dead Markish appears to the poet. Having described the wild nature of Markish's person and poetry in stanza 8, Grade ties up in stanza 9 all of his leitmotives: the Jewish fate under German occupation, the Jews' vain hope for a better life in the Soviet Union, and his own relation to the Soviet Yiddish writers:

> Remember the poet who had no legs!
> The Germans hurled his wooden pegs

after him, onto the pile of dead. Vilna townsmen both,
Gradzenski and I. They threw his legs with a jeer. And I am loath,
Markish, mourning you, to pierce your pride with grisly metaphor
made to mourn your song: but it was a god of wood
flung after you into the grave—that poem where with a roar
of rage you paid violent tribute to the dead.
"Who can sleep? The horror!" you used to gasp. "The German dregs,
hangmen! To throw at a legless man his legs!"
Since then your mouth is numb and dumb. And since you fell,
I have no sleep or praise for God for any miracle,
though I came safe away. The miracle you waited for—
that the Revolution's poets might not become its prey—
vanished with the verdict on that fearful day:
"Slay the Jewish poet, slay his Lenin medal, slay, slay, slay!"[40]

At the outset of the stanza Grade reminds Markish of the death of the Yiddish writer Aharon-Yitzhak Gradzenski. Having lost his legs in a trolley accident in 1916, he had since then moved around on wooden ones. Like Grade a resident of Vilna, Gradzenski was caught there by the Germans, interned in the ghetto, and brutally killed in 1941. Grade's two-line narrative—

Dermon zikh dem poet fun vilne oyf di fis fun holts!
Der daytsh hot zey im nokhgevorfn oyfn toytn-vogn.[41]

—is based on Shmerke Kaczerginski's recollection of the events. Resisting his arrest by the Germans, Gradzenski was beaten, "aroysge trogn fun shtub, arayngevorfn in a farmakhtn oyto, vos hot avekgefirt oyf Ponar di alte un kranke, velkhe hobn tsufus nit gekent geyn" [Carried out of the room, and thrown onto a closed truck that carted away to Ponar the old, the sick, and those who could not walk on their own].[42] Ozick's translation is more layered with allusions than is the original. Her rendition of Gradzenski's fate as being thrown onto a "pile of dead" and his legs after him, alludes to Markish's poem *Di kupe* (the pile, heap), a long, furious work of mourning about the anti-Jewish pogroms in the Ukraine in the early 1920s. Markish, who was traveling in the area at the time, was thought to have gotten killed there. Rumors of his death began circulating and obituary notices appeared in the Yiddish press.[43] But Markish miraculously emerged unscathed from "the pile of dead" to publish his poem *Di kupe* in Warsaw in 1922. Choosing an allusion to Markish's poem over a wording more faithful to the original serves Ozick three purposes. First, it strengthens the theme of the miraculous escape, articulated by Grade more fully later in the stanza. Second, it reinforces Grade's leitmotiv of the sameness of Jewish fate. The uncanny similarity of the names Grade and Gradzenski, underscored by Ozick's translation of "mayn ben-ir Grodzenski" as "Vilna townsmen both, / Gradzenski and I," as if Grade's name and fate were engulfed by Gradzenski's, alerts readers to the fact of how easily Gradzenski's fate could have been Grade's own, just as Markish could easily have shared the death of the Ukrainian Jews. But while Grade's miraculous escape sufficed him as a warning, Markish's did not. And finally, Ozick's allusive translation intensifies Grade's main point, which he makes rather more bluntly than Ozick:

> Vi mayn ben-ir Grodzenski, der poet un invalid,
> vos s'hot a daytsh im nokhgevorfn zayne fis mit khoysek,
> hot oykh dayn opgot nokhgevorfn in dayn grub—dayn lid
> vu du host mit a shturm-vint fun reyt geloybt im broyzik.

As invitations to gestures of cynicism and derision, Grade compares the cripple's wooden legs, flung by a German after his bloody corpse, to Markish's poem, praising his political idol in stormy rhetoric, flung after him into the grave by that very idol. What Grade has in mind here is most likely Markish's twenty-thousand-line epic *Milkhome* (war), written in the 1940s, which abounds in praise of Stalin. The tenor of Ozick's translation is completely different from that of Grade's original. Her earlier allusion to *Di kupe* reverberates in her line (not found in Grade's poem) "where with a roar / of rage you paid violent tribute to the dead." This poem, written after the killings in the Ukraine, and the poetry Markish wrote during the forties, in which he expressed his Soviet patriotism along with his sorrow over the annihilation of the Jews, Grade compares, in Ozick's translation, in their absurd uselessness to Gradzenski's wooden legs (in the original *invalid* [cripple] rhymes with *lid* [poem]). Cunningly Ozick translates Grade's (ironic) representation of Markish's delayed recognition of the reality of Jewish fate in Eastern Europe with an allusion to Kurtz's final insight into the heart of darkness, "'The horror!' you used to gasp."[44]

In the last third of the stanza Grade relents somewhat in his critique of Markish. In Ozick's translation Grade even concedes that from the moment Markish was shocked into recognition his mouth was "numb and dumb."[45] In fact, however, Markish was exceptionally productive from the beginning of the Russian-German war in 1941 until his arrest in 1949.

In the Yiddish poem Grade's emphasis is on the similarity between the Jewish fate under Nazi and Soviet rule. Quoting Markish as saying that he can no longer fall asleep (presumably after having learned about the slaughter of the Jews), Grade adds that having learned of Markish's death, he too cannot sleep any longer, nor can he praise God for the miracle of his own escape. Grade's modest half-verse, "vos ikh bin gants aroys," one of the simplest in the poem, reflects his stunned awe at the miracle wrought in him. Ozick's elegant rendition, "though I came safe away," keeps Grade's meter, three iambic feet, in an allusion to the traditional iambic elegiac meter (alternating hexameter and pentameter lines). The half-verse itself conceals a triple miracle, Grade's triple escape: first from the delusion that the Communist party's social promises also extended to the Jews (the Moscow trials of 1937 were warning enough for Grade), then from German-occupied Vilna (Grade got away with the retreating Soviet forces in 1941), and, finally, from Stalin's domain. (Grade left the Soviet Union in 1946 for Poland; he continued on to Paris, and in 1948 settled in New York).

By contrast, Markish's very natural expectation, "as s'vet di revolutsye ir bazingers nit dermordn" [that the Revolution will not kill those who sing its praises], which Grade with superb irony likens to waiting for a miracle, is of course sorely disappointed. Grade drives the point home when in the stanza's last line, conveying the death sentence of his farcical trial, he chose "lenin ordn," the Lenin Medal given to Markish in 1939, as the perfect rhyme for "dermordn" (to murder). The poem itself ends after three more elegiac stanzas with Grade's acceptance of the bitter legacy left him by the Soviet Yiddish writers:

> You left
> me your language, lilted with joy. But oh, I am bereft—
> I wear your Yiddish like a drowned man's shirt,
> wearing out the hurt.

To Irving Howe this particular poem must have meant a great deal. That he would argue for changes in Ozick's translation that were "on the side of prose," that would prefer prosaic clarity to poetic diction, seems entirely understandable in light of the poem's allusiveness and Grade's heightened rhetoric. Mani Leib, quite possibly America's preeminent Yiddish poet, who welcomed Grade's arrival in New York and located him as a poet in the tradition of "'Rosenfeld, Yehoash, Frug, Peretz, Bialik, Liessin, and Abraham Reisin,'" privately expressed reservations about Grade's style. "Grade's rhetoric and his inflated attempt to describe the national Jewish sorrow represented for Mani Leib the worst tendencies in modern Yiddish verse—'*fat* exaggerated metaphors,' 'forced rhymes,' 'superfluous repetition'—all introduced to swell the importance of *khurbn,* the subject of the Holocaust."[46] On a subject as important as the murder of the Soviet Yiddish writers Howe may have preferred that the translation not be the original's poetic equivalent because English readers would, for the most part, not know the poem's historical context. On other subjects, Howe let Ozick's versions stand.

In her essay on the translation project, Ozick records her exchanges with Howe about David Einhorn's poem "Geshtorbn der letster bal tfile" (the last *bal tfile* is dead). Initially Howe insisted that *bal tfile* be rendered as "prayer leader." In the end, Ozick's version began with an elegant pentameter, "The last to sing before the ark is dead," despite the fact that a strong argument could be made against substituting for *bal tfile,* connoting a communal function, a term signaling individuality and joyful exuberance. But Howe acquiesced to Ozick's version.[47] Ozick took the greatest—and in my view poetically most successful—liberties with the poems of H. Leivick, especially with "Oyf di vegn sibirer," which begins like this:

Oyf di vegn sibirer
ken emets nokh itster gefinen a knepl, a shtrikl
fun mayns a tserisenem shukh,
a rimenem pas, fun leymenem krigl a shtikl,
a bletl fun heylikn bukh.

Even now
on the roads of Siberia
you can find
a button,
a shred of one of my shoelaces,
a belt,
a bit of broken cup,
a leaf of Scripture.[48]

Leivick's two five-verse stanzas both break into a gallop of dactyls after a calmly scanning first verse, indicating the running pace at which those condemned to hard labor, like Leivick, travel the roads and rivers of Siberia. Ozick's English version, by contrast, with its emphatic use of enjambements and radical shortening of Leivick's lines, brings into focus the austerity of the Siberian landscape, the isolation and deprivation of the prisoners, the few traces their suffering left. Ozick's translation works as a poem because its form expresses its content. However, her poetic choices also result in a toughening of the original poem. By sacrificing Leivick's galloping dactyls Ozick eliminates any sense of movement and thereby any trace of a human presence. Leivick's rapid meter, by contrast, creates the eerie illusion that those who once lost the button and left the footprint still haunt the place.

Ozick's deep immersion in a Yiddish poetry that consistently mourned the death of Jews in Eastern Europe,[49] and her own struggle to recover their culture from the brink of oblivion, led her to think about the fate of Yiddish in America and the human tragedies forged by its decline. In 1967 she wrote what has become one of her most famous stories, "Envy; or, Yiddish in America." "I put it in a drawer for a whole year," Ozick recalls, "because I regarded it as a bad story. I was ashamed of it. I remember calling it pedestrian. I had submitted it somewhere and it had been turned down. . . . And then one day I took it out of the drawer, thinking, what the hell, I'll send it to *Commentary* and see what happens." Norman Podhoretz, the magazine's young Hotspur editor, fell in love with it, but asked Ozick to rewrite the end. His objections were purely editorial, so she felt she could oblige. "This is the only time that I ever rewrote anything. I was not really publishing and I was old. I would have stood on my head if Norman Podhoretz told me to stand on my head. And then he published it [in the November 1969 issue] and the reaction was terrible. Unbelievable" *(TI)*.

The story caused an outcry of pain and fury to rip through the Yiddish community. In the eyes of the Yiddish writers the story was a *scandale.* Its protagonists are two poets, Edelshtein and Baumzweig, who have no audience for their works because the Yiddish-speaking community has shriveled to a few aging souls. "Yiddish dead, vanished. Perished. Sent into darkness. . . . To speak of Yiddish was to preside over a funeral. [Edelshtein] was a rabbi who had survived his whole congregation. Those for whom his tongue was no riddle were specters."[50] Edelshtein and Baumzweig believe fervently in the literary quality of their poetry and insist that if they could find a translator, they would become famous like Yankel Ostrover, a "writer of stories" (*Envy* 46).

> Ostrover's glory was exactly in this: that he required translators. Though he wrote only in Yiddish, his fame was American, national, international. They considered him a "modern." Ostrover was free of the prison of Yiddish! Out, out—he had burst out, he was in the world of reality.
>
> And how had he begun? The same as anybody, a columnist for one of the Yiddish dailies, a humorist, a cheap fast article-writer, a squeezer-out of real-life tales. Like anybody else, he saved up a few dollars, put a paper clip over his stories, and hired a Yiddish press to print up a hundred copies. A book. Twenty-five copies he gave to people he counted as relatives, another twenty-five he sent to enemies and rivals, the rest he kept under his bed in the original cartons. Like anybody else, his literary gods were Chekhov and Tolstoy, Peretz and Sholem Aleichem. From this, how did he come to *The New Yorker,* to *Playboy,* to big lecture fees, invitations to Yale and M.I.T. and Vassar, to the Midwest, to Buenos Aires, to a literary agent, to a publisher on Madison Avenue? (*Envy* 47–48)

The rest of the story deals with Edelshtein's and Baumzweig's desperate envy of Ostrover and their efforts, Edelshtein's in particular, to duplicate his success. Believing the secret to lie in translation, Edelshtein woos Hannah, a young woman, literate in Yiddish, whom he gets to know through her uncle, Ostrover's crazy translator Vorovsky. Edelshtein begs Hannah to take on his work. But Hannah rejects Edelshtein as outdated. And Ostrover? Edelshtein asks: "'. . . even in Yiddish Ostrover is not in the ghetto. Even in Yiddish he's not like you people,'" is Hannah's reply. They continue to quarrel until Edelshtein bursts out:

> "Very good, he's achieved it, Ostrover's the world. A pantheist, a pagan, a goy."
>
> "That's it. You've nailed it. A Freudian, a Jungian, a sensibility. No little love stories. A contemporary. He speaks for everybody."
>
> "Aha. Sounds familiar already. For humanity he speaks? Humanity?"
>
> "Humanity," she said.
>
> "And to speak for Jews isn't to speak for humanity? We're not human? We're not present on the face of the earth? We don't suffer? In Russia they let us live? In Egypt they don't want to murder us?"
>
> "Suffer suffer," she said. "I like devils best. They don't think only about themselves and they don't suffer." (*Envy* 95)

Turned off by Edelshtein's insistence on Jewish suffering, the young American denies his request. Seeing in Hannah his last chance to escape oblivion, Edelshtein continues to plead with her. But her final answer is incontrovertible: "She said desolately, 'You don't interest me. I would have to be interested'" (*Envy* 99). The story ends with a still uncomprehending Edelshtein caught in the fury that precedes the work of mourning, lashing out at all anti-Semites from the Amalekites to Nasr, and concluding, "On account of you children become corrupted! On account of you I lost everything, my whole life! On account of you I have no translator" (*Envy* 100).

Ozick's story touched a raw nerve in the insular community of Yiddish writers. The character Ostrover was easily identified as Isaac Bashevis Singer. ("The Singer character is the Singer character"—*(TI)*. He had been catapulted into the world of modern American letters by Saul Bellow's translation, done at the insistence of Irving Howe, of "Gimpel the Fool," which appeared in the May 1953 issue of *Partisan Review*. It stood to reason that if Ostrover was so clearly I. B. Singer, that Baumzweig and Edelshtein also had their real-life counterparts—Chaim Grade and Jacob Glatstein thought of themselves as possibilities—whose vain hopes and petty quarrels Ozick had seemingly exposed. But the real source of pain lay elsewhere, Ozick surmised. "The story said that Yiddish was a dying language. That's really what killed them; because it was truthful and bitterly exposed. It was too painful. If people are alive and well and old and working as artists in the only language they have, which is for them both a source of art and an expression of art," how can they bear to hear their language pronounced dead?

The *Forward* came out with a long article by its editor, Shimon Weber, condemning Ozick as a wolf in sheep's clothing. The Yiddish idiomatic equivalent "*hasershde fiselakh* [pig's feet]," which Ozick remembers Weber using, is in fact much more insulting than the English image for inimical deceit. The proverbial phrase suggests that the true nature of a disgusting object cannot be disguised. If you try to cover up a pig, its feet will stick out and its cloven hoofs will give it away as *treyf* (non-Kosher). "That was a very powerful image. The idea was that I looked like somebody respectful of Jewish themes and Yiddish [literature], but if you looked again, I was definitely *treyf*. They said that the commissars in Moscow and Warsaw could not be more anti-Semitic. . . . And so I became the enemy of the Jewish people. It was my little Philip Roth adventure. Yet I think it was more painful, in a way, than Philip Roth's. His was much more public; mine was more private. Why was it more painful? Because his dealt essentially with more ignorant Jews" *(TI)*.

The bitter, grieved reaction of the Yiddish intellectuals, whom Ozick regarded as the Jewish cultural elite, came as an absolute shock to her. "I felt as if I had held a gift up to my mother and father, and in return they had struck me a blow on the skull."[51] She had written "Yiddish in America" ("Envy" had been Podhoretz's addition[52]) without the satirist's sharp ridicule and the detractor's scorn. Quite to the contrary:

> I wrote it as an elegy, a lamentation, a celebration, because six million Yiddish tongues were under the earth of Europe, and because here under American liberty and spaciousness my own generation, in its foolishness, stupidity, and self-disregard had, in an act tantamount to autolobotomy, disposed of the literature of its fathers. I thought of my own, now middle-aged generation of American Jewish writers as unwitting collaborators in the Nazi extirpation of Yiddish.[53]

Clearly the story came out of the intellectual and emotional turmoil caused by Ozick's immersion in Yiddish poetry. She was ashamed that her generation had been so incurious about their parents' culture. She was pained by its brutal death in Eastern Europe, and yet she had been carried into the story by the "bliss of alphabet," as well as by her discovery of an artistically and morally sophisticated literature. Although Ozick had developed a good grasp of Yiddish poetry in the course of her work for Irving Howe, she had written the story in complete ignorance of the ins and outs of the living Yiddish writers' community in New York. "I had no gossip about their lives or their relation to each other. I did not know these people personally. What I remembered from my childhood was this tiny group called the Hebrew Poetry Association of America. It was my uncle [Abraham Regelson] and the American Hebraists. I remembered *their* meetings and *their* schisms and factions, and *their* bitterness and spite. I based the story on the Hebrew Poetry Society of America—that was its official name. They had a magazine of which my uncle was the editor" *(TI)*.

The magazine was *Riv'on Katan le-Mahshava ve-Shira* (little quarterly of thought and poetry), founded in New York in 1944. Like Baumzweig, who published in his biannual Yiddish periodical *Bitterer Yam* "much of his own poetry and a little of Edelshtein's" (*Envy* 46), Regelson was the *Riv'on Katan's* sole editor and main contributor.[54] An accomplished Hebrew poet, Regelson created a surprising connection to the world of Yiddish letters. He was an ardent Zionist with socialist leanings, but being badly in need of money in the early 1940s, he began working as a journalist for the Yiddish daily *Morgen Freiheit,* an organ of the Jewish Communists. Through his work he got to know many of the Yiddish writers; and one fine day, in 1942, he found himself sharing the dais with a Yiddish poet in an awards ceremony at the *Forward.* In the audience was his niece, fourteen-year-old Cynthia Ozick, with her parents.

> What I remember best about that afternoon is a smoky crowded hall, and my aunt singing in Hebrew with her thin pure voice. And at last the hall grew quiet, and the prizes were given—one, for a book of poetry in Hebrew, to my uncle. . . . The other poet to receive a prize that day had written a book of Yiddish poetry. His name was Jacob Glatstein.[55]

It was, in fact, Glatstein who felt most deeply hurt and personally wounded by Ozick's story. From his perspective there could be little doubt that he was Edelshtein.[56] As Elaine Kauvar pointed out in her analysis of "Envy," it is possible to recognize in Edelshtein's poetic program the goal of the *Inzikhisten,* the Introspectivists, who included Glatstein among their ranks, "to bring Yiddish poetry into the mainstream of Modern Yiddish literature."[57] Moreover, the ill feelings of the Yiddish writers toward Singer as a literary celebrity were notorious. In 1965, Glatstein had even written an essay against Singer in which he couched his objections in literary terms. The "fortuitous growth of Bashevis' fame," Glatstein charged, was due to the depraved taste of his English readers. The Yiddish reader, Glatstein claimed, was much "less enthusiastic over Bashevis' tales of horror and eroticism" and less attuned to his "distasteful blend of superstition and shoddy mysticism." Yiddish literature, Glatstein declared, "did not commit any wild and perverse crimes against its heroes." But Bashevis dehumanized his "so-called heroes . . . forcing them to commit the most ugly deeds." In short, to a Yiddish reader, "Bashevis' superstitious stories savor of a warmed-over stew of hoary old wives' tales, made alien by villainy, brutality, and cynicism." To make things worse, the decadent content was not compensated by literary artistry, since Bashevis lacked "an ear for language and a sense of style" and had "no artistic breath of his own." His autobiographical writings were "trivial, common-place and egocentric effusions," and his most recent stories showed a wasted talent in decline. "Bashevis, the once facile and competent story-teller, has become weary, prolix, and written-out."[58]

In Ozick's story, Edelshtein and Baumzweig also articulate their dislike of Ostrover by way of literary analysis:

> They hated him for the amazing thing that had happened to him—his fame—but this they never referred to. Instead they discussed his style: his Yiddish was impure, his sentences lacked grace and sweep, his paragraph transitions were amateur, vile. Or else they raged against his subject matter, which was insanely sexual, pornographic, paranoid, freakish—men who embraced men, women who caressed women, sodomists of every variety, boys copulating with hens, butchers who drank blood for strength behind the knife. All the stories were set in an imaginary Polish village, Zwrdl, and by now there was almost no American literary intellectual alive who had not learned to say Zwrdl when he meant lewd. (*Envy* 47)

The differences between Glatstein's critique and Ozick's fiction are obvious enough, but these were of no moment to the Yiddish writers. Rather, the uncanny similarities between Glatstein's essay and the complaints of Ozick's characters were simply taken as further evidence that Edelshtein was based on Glatstein. And yet the similarities were coincidental. "[Edelshtein] was not based on him at all," Ozick explained. "He was made up! I did not know, when I wrote that story—just think of my ignorance!—that there had been a great fight between Glatstein and Singer, and that Glatstein had written this essay against Singer. I had no idea. I didn't know anything about their gossip. I didn't read their papers. I couldn't. It is hard for me to read Yiddish. Each paragraph is a major labor. So it's impossible" *(TI)*.

There was no chance to make up with Glatstein, to explain that he had misunderstood "sorrowing love for hatred, and mourning for self-hatred."[59] Glatstein died in 1971. The remaining Yiddish community eventually understood. In 1972 Ozick was presented with the Jewish Heritage Award by the B'nai Brith for her story collection *The Pagan Rabbi,* which contained "Envy; or, Yiddish in America." At the same ceremony an award for excellence in literature was posthumously given to Glatstein. Ozick titled her acceptance speech "A Bintel Brief for Jacob Glatstein," sending after him the explanation he may (or may not) have needed in life.

A decade later, however, the opportunity for fuller restitution presented itself. Irving Howe, Ruth Wisse, and Khone Shmeruk were beginning to put together what became *The Penguin Book of Modern Yiddish Verse* (1987), and they invited Ozick to participate. Again, the task was "to create an English poem for every Yiddish original." They would reprint two of her Leivick translations since her rendering coincided with the editors' sense that "in order to capture for a culture of greater emotional restraint the same passion that Leivick carries in Yiddish, we [needed to present] him through a selection of poems that was all sinew, tight lines, spare diction, emotion controlled."[60] Ozick's Leivick fit the bill.

For fresh translation the editors sent her new batches of poems by two other writers, Jacob Glatstein and Abraham Sutzkever. In the early 1980s, when the project got really under way, Ozick was no longer unknown. Through her stories collected in *The Pagan Rabbi* (1971), *Bloodshed* (1976), *Levitation* (1982), her novels *Trust* (1966) and *The Cannibal Galaxy* (1983), and her essays, assembled in *Art and Ardor* (1983), she had established herself as a superior English stylist and as one of the "new Jewish writers." The latter Wisse defined as "writers who self-consciously define themselves as Jews and attempt to express their artistic vision in Jewish terms. Their interest is not in the sociological or even the psychological legacy of a Jewish background, but in the national design and religious destiny of Judaism, in its workable myths."[61]

Despite Wisse's own firm commitment to Jewish literature—she had turned from the study of English to research on Yiddish—her first reaction to Ozick as a fiction writer was far from favorable. Although Wisse considered "Envy; or, Yiddish in America," "a masterpiece of contemporary fiction," she found Ozick "not on the whole successful at creating autonomous characters whose destiny will tantalize or move the reader." But Wisse responded strongly to the intellectual force in Ozick's work, leading her to conclude, "Miss Ozick is, in fact, an intellectual writer whose works are the fictional realization of ideas."[62] And Wisse recognized clearly, despite her misgivings about Ozick's "cockamamie idea"[63] of creating a "centrally Jewish" or "liturgical" literature in English, that here was a writer who was deeply at home in Jewish and gentile literary high culture, yet able to articulate movingly the immigrant artist's anxieties. Above all, she was surprisingly ready to make her stories "Jewish assaults on fields of Gentile influence."[64]

In fact, Ozick's fictions even went a step further and indicted the gentile world for the indignities to which it had subjected the Jews. Wisse concluded that Ozick would be able to relate to the "anti-Gentile outburst" in Glatstein's poetry and could be trusted to solve the difficult problem of conveying fury with poetic subtlety. Indeed, Ozick's translation of Glatstein's "Mozart," in which the speaker "imagines himself the apostle of what is sublime in western civilization, the St. Paul of its desecrated culture," is witty and playful, without softening the poem's bitter sarcasm.[65] The other nine poems Ozick was given to translate, with subjects ranging from "Genesis" to "Old Age," made equally great demands on her verbal skills, contextual knowledge, and poetic judgment. As the translations progressed, Ozick received encouraging letters from Wisse, who served as "the overseer of the language." In the end, Ozick could say with confidence, "I got good at it" *(TI)*. She had retrieved what she had once mourned as lost.

Perhaps the strongest sign of how much Wisse trusted Ozick as a translator was that she sent her poems by Abraham Sutzkever, the living poet who, personally and artistically, meant most to Wisse.[66] Born near Vilna in 1913, Sutzkever belonged to the exclusive literary circle *Yung Vilne*. The left-leaning group was highly political, and the poems Sutzkever submitted when he sought admission to the group ("ballads about Kirghisian horsemen") seemed to the group "irresponsibly asocial and naive."[67] Recognizing Sutzkever's great talent, however, the members relented and Sutzkever became part of an artistic circle that included Shmerke Kaczerginski (who recorded Gradzenski's death) and Chaim Grade. When the Second World War erupted in September 1939, the Soviet Army invaded Vilna and ceded it to Lithuania two months later. The city was flooded with Jewish refugees escaping from German-or Russian-occupied Poland, increasing Vilna's Jewish population from sixty to eighty thousand. On 24 June 1941, German troops marched into the city; the persecution and execution of the Jews began immediately.[68] Sutzkever not only continued to write poetry but also insisted with growing fervor on aesthetic perfection. Survival, he believed, hung on the precision with which each Yiddish word was chosen. "In the face of so much degradation," Wisse explained, "Sutzkever's passion for the exactitude of every word and every syllable is the highest restorative measure of dignity."[69]

On 6 September 1941, the Jews of Vilna were herded into two

ghettos of which the smaller was liquidated forty-six days later. In January 1942, the various political groups in the ghetto created a unified fighting organization, the F.P.O. (Fareynigte Partizaner Organizatsye). Sutzkever, his wife, and Kaczerginski joined. Total liquidation of the Vilna ghetto began in August 1943 and concluded on 2 September 1943. The Sutzkevers and Kaczerginski left the ghetto through sewers eleven days before the final deportations and broke through to a Byelorussian partisan group that operated in the forests and swamps around Vilna. German troops combing the area forced the Sutzkevers to hide in freezing water. Sutzkever continued to write scrupulously perfected poems even in the intolerable conditions the partisans endured in the winter of 1943 to 1944. In March 1944, the Anti-Fascist Committee of the USSR airlifted Sutzkever from German-occupied territory to Moscow because his poetic summons to cultural and physical resistance had made him a symbol of heroism.[70]

The Sutzkevers lived through the war in Moscow but went to Israel as illegal immigrants at their first opportunity in 1947. In 1948 Sutzkever became the editor of what is now the most distinguished Yiddish quarterly, *Di goldene keyt,* in which he brought together what remained of Yiddish culture in Europe, the Americas, and Israel. Sutzkever's life comprises all major aspects of the Jewish experience in modernity. By a fortunate accident of chronology his poetry concluded *The Penguin Book of Modern Yiddish Verse,* thus ending the book on an "artistic peak"[71] that testified to the continued vitality and sophistication of Yiddish letters after the war.

For this anthology, Ozick translated a highly formal poem of twelve rhyming couplets and intricate meter, written in Moscow in July 1944, in which the poet is suddenly overwhelmed in the summer heat by his remembrance of "frozen Jews, row on row." But Ozick was also given Sutzkever's latest poems, written between 1975 and 1981. In the most recent and final poem of the anthology, simply titled "1981," the poet receives a letter from "mayn heymshtot in der lite," his hometown in Lithuania. The poet is haunted by the letter's enclosure, which dissolves the speaker's real world in remembrance and becomes the poem's steady refrain: a blade of grass from Ponar.

Ponar is a lovely wooded country retreat about ten miles from Vilna. In the summer of 1941, prior to the establishment of the Vilna ghetto, the Germans murdered some thirty-five thousand Jews there and buried them in a gigantic mass grave. Ponar is the anthology's final word. Although Wisse was right to point out that with Sutzkever the book did not peter out but ended on an artistic high note, Ponar *is* the final word in Yiddish poetry. While it is not the final theme in Yiddish poetry—in the Shoah's aftermath "Baumzweig wrote mostly of Death, Edelshtein of Love" (*Envy,* 46)—there is no reader of Yiddish poetry who is not at any moment aware of the culture's violent death.

To read Yiddish is to become inescapably engulfed in the hum of Ponar. In the first stanza of "1981" Sutzkever presents a fitting metaphor for Yiddish poetry. All that remains of Yiddish culture, he seems to say, is a letter arriving from the poet's home town, sent by someone whose appeal as a young woman still holds the poet in its grip (*lite* [Lithuania] rhymes with *shlite* [obsession, idée fixe]). But enclosed in the letter, conveying inseparably affection and sorrow, he finds a blade of grass from Ponar. In the poem's last stanza, the poet allies himself with the dead. In a gesture invoking the questioning of God's justice from Hiob to Tevye, the poet intends to bring "a matone farn har: / dos grezl fun Ponar" ("to the Lord my oblation at last: / the blade of grass from Ponar").[72]

Sustained immersion in Yiddish poetry creates a singularly eery effect: it drives home the finality of the German Final Solution and transforms what one has self-protectively come to think of as mechanical mass murder back into what it was at the time: the utterly unexpected slaughter of individuals. Just as Sutzkever, after thirty years in Israel, is still obsessed with his "heymshtot in der lite," so Ozick would never be free again, after her deep immersion in Yiddish poetry, of the maddening knowledge of its bloody death. What had died were real people. She went on to write about happier topics in Yiddish letters. A long essay on Sholom Aleichem, for instance, appeared in 1988.[73] But the brutal liquidation of his audience has become one of the most vibrant and prominent themes in Cynthia Ozick's writing.

NOTES

1. Cynthia Ozick, panel presentation on American Jewish writing, New York Public Library, May 1994.

2. Virginia Woolf, "Women and Fiction," reprinted in *In Depth: Essayists for Our Time,* ed. Carl Klaus, Chris Anderson, and Rebecca Faery 2d ed. (Fort Worth, Tex.: Harcourt Brace Jovanovich College Publishers, 1993), 792–93.

3. Cynthia Ozick, "Literature and Politics of Sex: A Dissent" (1977), in her *Art and Ardor: Essays* (New York: E. P. Dutton, 1984), 285–86. In an interview by Toni Teicholz Ozick said, "I think of the imagination as a place of utter

freedom. There one can do whatever one wants." See "The Art of Fiction XCV: Cynthia Ozick," *Paris Review* 29 (Spring 1987): 178.

4. Cynthia Ozick to author, [31] May 1994. The renaissance of Jewish American writing was the subject of an interview with Cynthia Ozick conducted by Elaine Kauvar and reprinted in *Contemporary Literature* 34 (Fall 1993): 359–94.

5. Ozick, presentation at the New York Public Library, May 1994.

6. The most notable critical endeavors include Elaine Kauvar, *Cynthia Ozick's Fiction: Tradition and Invention* (Bloomington: Indiana University Press, 1993); Sarah Blacher Cohen, *Cynthia Ozick's Comic Art: From Levity to Liturgy* (Bloomington: Indiana University Press, 1994); Victor Strandberg, *Greek Mind, Jewish Soul: The Conflicted Art of Cynthia Ozick* (Madison: University of Wisconsin Press, 1994); Gislar Donnenberg, *Innovation und Orthodoxie: Cynthia Ozick und der Versuch eines neuen amerikanisch-jüdischen Romans* (Ph.D. diss., 1993, University of Innsbruck, Austria); Norman Finkelstein, *The Ritual of New Creation: Jewish Tradition and Contemporary Literature* (Albany: State University of New York Press, 1992); Rosellen Brown, "The Ozick-Bloom Controversy: Anxiety of Influence, Usurpation as Idolatry, and the Identity of Jewish American Literature," *Studies in American Jewish Literature* 11 (Spring 1992): 62–82; Mark Krupnick, "Cynthia Ozick as the Jewish T. S. Eliot," *Soundings* 74 (Fall-Winter 1991): 351–68; Michael Greenstein, "Ozick, Roth, and Postmodernism," *Studies in American Jewish Literature* 19 (Spring 1991): 54–64. Two collections of essays continue to be interesting: Daniel Walden, ed., "The World of Cynthia Ozick," *Studies in American Jewish Literature* 6 (Fall 1987), and Harold Bloom, ed., *Modern Critical Views: Cynthia Ozick* (New York: Chelsea House Publishers, 1986).

7. Other Jewish aspects, covered in an earlier and much longer version of this essay, were Ozick's attitude toward ritual observance, Israel, Hebrew, Germany, and the Holocaust.

8. Ozick, interview by Teicholz, 172. In a 1979 essay on Harold Bloom Ozick speculated that "if there *can* be such a chimera as a 'Jewish writer,' it must be the kind of sphinx or gryphon (part one thing, part another) Bloom himself is, sometimes purifying like Abraham, more often conjuring like Terach, and always knowing that the two are icily, elegiacally, at war." In *Art and Ardor*, 198.

9. Cynthia Ozick, "Bech, Passing" (1970), in *Art and Ardor*, 123.

10. Ozick, interview by Elaine Kauvar, in *Contemporary Literature* 26 (Winter 1985): 375–401.

11. Cynthia Ozick, "Toward a New Yiddish" (1970), in *Art and Ardor*, 164.

12. Cynthia Ozick, interview by Catherine Rainwater and William J. Scheick, *Texas Studies in Literature and Language* 25 (1983): 259.

13. Ozick, interview by Teicholz, 188.

14. Cynthia Ozick, *The Messiah of Stockholm* (New York: Alfred Knopf, 1987), 8. Further references to this novel are cited in the text as *Messiah*.

15. Ozick, "Toward a New Yiddish," 165–66.

16. Cynthia Ozick, "The Suitcase," in her *The Pagan Rabbi and Other Stories* (1971; reprint, New York: Schocken, 1976), 108.

17. Cynthia Ozick, "Bloodshed," in her *Bloodshed and Three Novellas* (New York: Alfred Knopf, 1976), 69–71.

18. Ozick, interview by Rainwater and Scheick, 258.

19. "Debate: Ozick vs. Schulweis," *Moment* 1 (May–June 1976): 78.

20. Cynthia Ozick, quoted in Elaine Kauvar's introductory remarks to her 1993 interview with Cynthia Ozick, 359.

21. Cynthia Ozick, "Of Polished Mirrors," presentation at the conference "The Writer in the Jewish Community," Berkeley, Calif., 23–25 October 1988, distributed by the National Foundation for Jewish Culture.

22. Ozick, "Imagining the Other," proceedings of the conference "The Writer in the Jewish Community," Berkeley, Calif, 23–25 October 1988, distributed by the National Foundation for Jewish Culture. The last quote is taken from Ozick, "Hadrian and Hebrew," 77.

23. Ozick, "Toward a New Yiddish," 172.

24. Cynthia Ozick, telephone interview by author, 2 February 1995; all further references to this source will be cited in the text as *TI*.

25. Cynthia Ozick, "Mrs. Virginia Woolf: A Madwoman and Her Nurse," in *Art and Ardor*, 54.

26. Virginia Woolf, "Women and Fiction," 792.

27. This is the title of the first chapter in Kauvar's study *Cynthia Ozick's Fiction* (1993).

28. Ozick has never bothered to collect her poetry. However, forty-seven of her poems were made available in a bibliophile edition, accompanied by prints by Sidney Chafetz, in *Cynthia Ozick, Epodes: First Poems* (Columbus: Logan Elms Press and Paper Mill at Ohio State University, 1992).

29. Strandberg, *Greek Mind/Jewish Soul*, 57. Strandberg's is the only study I know of that considers Ozick's poetry at some length.

30. Harold Bloom, "The Sorrows of American-Jewish Poetry," *Commentary* 53 (March 1972): 73.

31. Cynthia Ozick, "A Bintel Brief for Jacob Glatstein," *Jewish Heritage* (14 September 1972): 58.

32. Ozick, "A Bintel Brief," 59. How the world of books and literary high art became the focal point of Ozick's intellectual life she described in a series of personal essays that includes "A Drugstore in Winter" (1982), in *Art and Ardor*, 298–305; "Washington Square, 1946" (1985), in her *Metaphor and Memory* (New York: Alfred Knopf, 1989), 112–19; and "Alfred Chester's Wig," *New Yorker* 68 (30 March 1992): 79–98.

33. Ozick, "A Drugstore in Winter," in *Art and Ardor*, 304. About Ozick's mother see Cynthia Ozick, "Passage to the New World," *Ms* 6 (2 August 1977): 70–74, 87.

34. Ozick, "A Drugstore in Winter," 300.

35. Ozick, "A Bintel Brief," 59–60.

36. Cynthia Ozick, "A Translator's Monologue" (1983), *Metaphor and Memory*, 201. The essay describes her work on the translations for *A Treasury of Yiddish Poetry*.

37. About this event the historian Nora Levin writes: "The writers Markish, Feffer, Bergelson, Kvitko, Hofshteyn, and Halkin, who had been arrested in 1948–49, languished in prison until the summer of 1952 and were among the twenty-five Jews brought to trial on July 11, after going through Beria's inquisition cells. They were charged with being enemies of the USSR, agents of American imperialism, guilty of bourgeois national Zionism, and trying to sever the Crimea from the Soviet Union. It is believed that there was a secret trial from July 11 to 18, at which twenty-five Yiddish writers, actors, cultural activists were tried, including Bergelson, Feffer, Hofshteyn, Kvitko, Lozovsky, Markish, Nusinov, Persov, Spivak, and Zuskin. . . . Dr. Lina Shtern, a gifted

scientist, was also among the twenty-five defendants, and the only one among them who survived. The others were executed on August 12, 1952, in the cellar of Moscow's Lubyanka prison." Nora Levin, *The Jews in the Soviet Union Since 1917: Paradox of Survival* (London: I. B. Tauris, 1988), 2: 527–29.

38. Short biographies, compiled by Mendl Pyekasz, can be found in Khone Shmeruk, ed., *A shpigl oyf a shteyn: Antologye poezye un prose fun tsvelf farshnitene yidishe shraybers in ratn-farband* [A mirror on a stone: An anthology of poetry and prose by twelve murdered Yiddish authors in the Soviet Union] (Tel Aviv: J. L. Peretz Publishing House, 1964).

39. Ibid., 740.

40. Chaim Grade, "Elegy for the Soviet Yiddish Writers," trans. Cynthia Ozick, in *A Treasury of Yiddish Poetry,* ed. Irving Howe and Eliezer Greenberg (New York: Holt, Rinehart and Winston, 1969), 341, 343.

41. Chaim Grade, "Ikh vayn oyf aykh mit ale oysyes fun dem alef-bet," *Der mentsh fun fayer: lider un poemes* [I weep for you with all the letters of the alphabet, The man of fire: Songs and Poems] (New York: CYCO, 1962), 107.

42. "Grodzenski, Aron-Yitskhak," *Leksikon fun der nayer yidisher literatur* (New York: Congress for Jewish Culture, 1958), 2: 335.

43. Shmeruk, ed., *A shpigl oyf a shteyn,* 752.

44. Howe, Greenberg, eds., *A Treasury of Yiddish Poetry,* 343.

45. Ozick reads Grade's verse "un sint du host a fal geton mit a farglivert moyl" metaphorically as referring to the death of the poet shocked into muteness by his recognition of the fate of the Jews symbolized by Gradzenski's death. I read Grade's verse literally. Only as he is being shot and collapses does Markish's mouth congeal.

46. Ruth R. Wisse, *A Little Love in Big Manhattan* (Cambridge: Harvard University Press, 1988), 228.

47. Ozick, "A Translator's Monologue," 203–7.

48. H. Leivick, "Oyf di vegn sibirer," trans. Cynthia Ozick, in *The Penguin Book of Modern Yiddish Verse,* ed. Irving Howe, Ruth R. Wisse, and Khone Shmeruk (New York: Viking, 1987), 228–30.

49. In addition to the translations printed by Howe (three poems by Einhorn, six by Leivick, and two by Grade), Ozick had also done Itsik Manger, "A Song about Elijah the Prophet," *Congress Bi-Weekly* 36 (28 April 1969): 13; and H. Leivick, "Father Legend," *Midstream* 17 (April 1971): 29–32. A few years later Howe asked her to translate an essay by A. Tabachnik, "Tradition and Revolt in Yiddish Poetry," for *Voices from the Yiddish: Essays, Memoirs, Diaries* (Ann Arbor: University of Michigan Press, 1972), edited with Eliezer Greenberg.

50. Cynthia Ozick, "Envy; or, Yiddish in America," in *The Pagan Rabbi,* 42–44. All further references to this story are cited in the text as *Envy.*

51. Ozick, "A Bintel Brief," 60.

52. Cohen, *Cynthia Ozick's Comic Art,* 62.

53. Ozick, "A Bintel Brief," 60.

54. Steven P. Hudson, *Fragmentation and Restoration: The Tikkun Ha-Olam Theme in the Metaphysical Poetry of Abraham Regelson* (Chicago: Adams Press, 1988), 8.

55. Ozick, "A Bintel Brief," 59.

56. Nor did anyone else doubt the identification very much, as Ozick was to learn. "When I went to see Gershom Scholem for the first time and I was ready to fall on my knees to him in homage and I walked in the door on

Barbanel Street and the first thing he said to me [was], 'So tell me, Ms. Ozick, is Edelshtein Glatstein?' I almost fell through the floor. It amazed me" *(TI)*.

57. Kauvar, *Cynthia Ozick's Fiction,* 58. In her reading of "Envy" Kauvar persists in identifying Edelshtein with Glatstein, basing her argument to a great extent on Ozick's translation of Glatstein's poetry. These translations, however, were not undertaken until the early eighties, almost two decades after the conception of the story.

58. Jacob Glatstein, "The Fame of Bashevis Singer," *Congress Bi-Weekly* 32 (27 December 1965): 17–18.

59. Ozick, "A Bintel Brief," 60. Irving Howe relates that he once argued with Glatstein about Ozick's story, "which he read as an assault on Yiddish writers at a moment when they were all but defenseless. I suggested the story was really written out of affection, and eyes blazing, he turned to me, 'Do you think it is *affection* we need?'" Irving Howe, "Journey of a Poet," *Commentary* 53 (January 1972): 77.

60. Ruth R. Wisse, "What Shall Live and What Shall Die: The Makings of a Yiddish Anthology," Twelfth Annual Rabbi Louis Feinberg Memorial Lecture in Judaic Studies, Judaic Studies Program, University of Cincinnati, 3 May 1989, 8, 12.

61. Ruth R. Wisse, "American-Jewish Writing, Act II," *Commentary* 61 (June 1976): 41. Ozick's response to this article was reprinted in "Writers and Critics," *Commentary* 62 (September 1976): 8–10.

62. Wisse, "American-Jewish Writing, Act II," 42, 43.

63. Ruth R. Wisse, interview by author, Cambridge, Mass., 18 July 1994.

64. Wisse, "American-Jewish Writing, Act II," 41.

65. Wisse, "What Shall Live," 19–20; for Wisse's analysis of the poem and Ozick's translation see 19–21.

66. See the chapter on Ruth Wisse in my forthcoming study, *Enlarging America: The Cultural Work of Jewish Literary Scholars, 1930–1990* (Syracuse: Syracuse University Press).

67. Ruth R. Wisse, introduction to *Burnt Pearls: Ghetto Poems of Abraham Sutzkever,* trans. Seymour Mayne (Oakville, Ont.: Mosaic Press, 1981), 10.

68. Abraham Foxman, *Encyclopedia Judaica,* s.v. "Vilna—Holocaust Period," (Jerusalem: Keter, 1972), 16: 148.

69. Ruth R. Wisse, "Abraham Sutzkever the Storyteller," introduction to Abraham Sutzkever, *Di nevue fun shvarteaplen: dertseylungn / The Prophecy of the Inner Eye* (Jerusalem: The Magnes Press of the Hebrew University, 1989), xix.

70. Wisse, Introduction to *Burnt Pearls,* 16; Benjamin Harshav introduction to Abraham Sutzkever, *Selected Prose and Poetry,* trans. Barbara and Benjamin Harshav (Berkeley: University of California Press, 1991), 20.

71. Wisse, "What Shall Live," 26.

72. Howe, Wisse, eds., *The Penguin Book of Modern Yiddish Verse,* 702–3.

73. Cynthia Ozick, "Sholem Aleichem's Revolution," *The New Yorker* (28 March 1988): 99–109; reprinted in *Metaphor and Memory,* 173–98.

"Daughters of Refugees of the Ongoing-Universal-Endless-Upheaval": Anne Roiphe and the Quest for Narrative Power in Jewish American Women's Fiction

MIRIYAM GLAZER

DRIVING across the continental United States to Juarez, Mexico, for a divorce, the narrator of Anne Roiphe's 1972 novel *Long Division*[1] reaches the midwestern heartland, the "great bowel of the countrytisofthee" (41), and comes across a monument named "Madonna of the Trail" (69). She parks her car, alights, and walks into the woods to see it: a "stone lady standing in the middle of nowhere . . . a pioneer woman . . . the stone embalmment of a basic American truth" (70). In the imagination of Emily Brimberg Johnson, the Madonna of the Trail emblematizes the women who went west, the women who endured dire hardships as they breathed and panted and heaved their children into the future in service to an historic purpose" (71). Emily feels "a love, a surge of worship" (70), but she also feels jealous: compared to those pioneer women, the "great-great grandmothers of the present Daughters of the American Revolution" (71), her own life is merely that of

> a wandering Jewess, covering the globe, belonging only peripherally to one culture or another, a grandmother who collected china, knowing alien boots could and would smash it all to bits a week, a century later. Perhaps contemporary Jewish women should form their own society, Daughters of Refugees of the Ongoing-Universal-Endless-Upheaval. We could meet on boats, three miles out to sea, and not allow anyone whose ancestors had lived in less than four countries to join. (71–73)

Emily feels isolated from the mythic American quest, even diminished by it, as she herself adventures across the continent. Like Hélène Cixous, who grew up in Algeria where "the routine our ancestors, the Gauls' was pulled on me [by the colonizing French],"[2] Emily knows the pioneer story is not her story. Like the colonized, she experiences herself not as an agent of history, but rather as being buffeted by history. Every shelter, every national identity, is a mere *sukkah*—that is, a temporary dwelling—in what becomes another wilderness, to be smashed and destroyed imminently or eventually, until the only "safe" space is not a land or a national identity at all, nor even the open horizons of oceans on which she might imagine herself a voyager. Instead, the generative symbolic locus of consciousness, the source of narrativity, is a boat (not even a ship) "three miles out to sea," anchored in dispossession, dislocation, and permanent exile.

Emily's boat is not alone. The "wandering Jewess" as Roiphe portrays her is a recurrent figure in contemporary Jewish American women's fiction, though her male counterpart, that archetype of Western literature, has long gone out of literary fashion. In her various guises she is, for example, Sarah of Nessa Rapoport's "The Woman Who Lost Her Names,"[3] whose kindergarten teacher sends home a note that "we have decided to call the child Sally for the purpose of school as it will help integrate her and make the adjustment easier" (229). She is Rita of Lynn Sharon Schwartz's "The Melting Pot," unable to place herself culturally and thus to love fully; Rachel, in Joanna Spiro's "Three Thousand Years of Your History . . . Take One Year for Yourself," who painfully grapples with her sense of alienation as a Jew and a woman in Israel and returns to America to find herself now problematically "white." She is Mara of Tova Reich's novel of the same name or the women characters who gather together as a straggly band of penitents in her *Master of the Return;* the women in Esther Broner's *A Weave of Women,* who all lack family names, as if they are dehistoricized, dislocated orphans all.[4] The "Daughters of the Refugees of the Ongoing-Universal-Endless-Upheaval" live in Grace Paley's New York tenements or on a mountaintop refuge in Colorado in Rhoda Lerman's *God's Ear,* where Lillywhite sings out with such loneliness her voice is like "a wolf cry in the wilderness" (118).[5] Marked by cultural transience, at home neither in time nor in space, their personal identities unstable or erased, these "Daughters of the Refugees of Ongoing-Universal-Endless-Upheaval" are fragmented characters, riven by their own sense of Otherness, marginality, and incompletion.[6]

When Hélène Cixous probes the meaning of Otherness that

has characterized her life and work, she locates the source in the nexus of her personal history with the collective expulsions, dispersions, and displacements of the Jews throughout the history of the West:

> I learned to read, to write, to scream, and to vomit in Algeria. . . . The routine "our ancestors, the Gauls" was pulled on me. But I was born in Algeria, and my ancestors lived in Spain, Morocco, Austria, Hungary, Czechoslovakia, Germany, my brothers by birth are Arab. So where are we in history? . . . Who am I? I am "doing" French history. I am a Jewish woman. In which ghetto was I penned up during your wars and revolutions? I want to fight. What is my name? I want to change life. Who is this "I"? Where is my place? . . . Who spoke for me throughout the generations? (71)

As Jew and as Algerian, an emblem of cultural hybridity, Cixous lived through revolution and war from the ambiguous subject position occupied by Algerian Jews toward both the French colonialists and the Algerian colonized, as well as the simultaneously problematic position(s) of woman and of Jewish woman. On the other hand, however, no such cultural upheavals were directly endured by the Jewish American women writers whose narratives—written in the 1970s and 1980s—inscribe the same instabilities of identity, history, place, and are marked by the same pervasive sense of cultural rootlessness and restiveness that characterizes Cixous. With the exception of Canadian-born Nessa Rapoport, they are nonimmigrant (and nonrefugee) Americans residing in the country of their birth. Literal historical destablizations and dispossessions, revolutions and wars have not been the source of their story. Nor can one attribute the profound unsettledness of their narratives to a kind of compulsive inscription and re-inscription of "Jewish memory" unless one also asks why, in the American cultural context, it might be so. Why the internalization of permanent impermanence? Why the fragility of self? What is *their* story?

Clearly, for women writers engaged in questions of Jewish identity and womanhood, the quest for female narrative power in contemporary Jewish American literature has been a complex enterprise involving intricate negotiation among multiple interpenetrating and conflicted cultural realities. This essay will address the terms of that negotiation and, in the process, consider how it has been particularly inscribed in the early novels of Anne Roiphe, whose narratives are possessed and obsessed by the consequent entangled questions of Jewishness, Americanness, and womanhood.

The drive to discover, name, and voice what has been hidden, muted, and silenced within androcentric American culture is shared by women writers across the lines of ethnicity, race, and class.[7] But there are unique aspects to the subject position of Jewish American women. Foremost is the unsettled and unsettling, problematic, and multivalent relationship of "Jewish" and "American," which in turn possesses its own complicated existential dynamics of gender. Unraveling the meanings of the ever-changing interplay of "Jewish" and "American" also involves a consideration that, as many studies since 1976 have documented,[8] "Jewish" implies a religious tradition ambivalent at best, exclusionary at the worst, toward females in general. What has been less recognized is that in marginalizing the Jew and perceiving/portraying the male as the exemplary Jew-to-be-marginalized, the dominant Western, androcentric, gentile culture has also inscribed an existential equation: the Jewish male has been to the gentile male as the female is to the male. That is, particularly, in the racist and masculinist theories arising in nineteenth-century Europe, the (male) Jew, positioned as the alien, weak, and passive Other, prone to hysteria, was encoded in gentile consciousness as female. The Jews, says D. H. Lawrence, for example, "kept his body always like the body of a bride ready to serve the bridegroom. He had become the servant of his God, the female, passive."[9]

That gender encoding had its Jewish counterpart. Within modern Jewish history, efforts ranging from the Zionist mission to transform the Jew from the passive victim to the active generator of history, to the drive for a rational, secular, modernity within the diaspora, have also been encoded as male. In Zionist texts, the passive diaspora Jew is feminized, associated with "the weeping mother Rachel, or the belief that it is the Shekhinah, God's female presence, that goes into exile with the Jewish people," as Susannah Heschel has commented.[10] In the diaspora literature of secular modernity, on the other hand, she points out, "from Spinoza to such as Otto Weininger and Philip Roth, religious observance has traditionally been viewed as emasculating. To be religious is to be a woman, or effeminate" (135).

But if the "Jew" is equated with Jewish male and coded as female in gentile consciousness and simultaneously within Jewish culture, despite women's marginality within the "classical religious system of Judaism,"

> femininity is identified with religious observance and diaspora ghetto life . . . while modernity, secularism, and especially, the new Israeli Jews are identified as masculine, where are Jewish women supposed to find themselves at home? Moreover, how are women—in the confusion and ambivalence of modern opportunity and traditional coding—to perceive redemption itself? (135)

No wonder, then, that the only home for the "Daughters of Refugees of the Ongoing-Universal-Endless-Upheaval" is out of the "colonized" land of masculinist consciousness: on boats "three miles out to sea." Without that uncertain refuge, they are apparently lost altogether. Thus, for example, the Jewish American women narrators of Anne Roiphe's early novels are unable "to find themselves at home" anywhere at all. Laura Smith, the narrator of Roiphe's first novel, *Digging Out* (1966),[11] whose "name," she tells us, "tells you nothing. A nice clean Anglo-Saxon name entered in the birth certificate at Doctor's Hospital" (7), ends her narrative with the declaration, "Somewhere I must find a place" (181). Reminiscing about the Sunday School lessons of her childhood, the relentless litany of Jewish suffering throughout the ages, the orphaned narrator Emily Brimberg Johnson of *Long Division* (1972) cries out now, "Rachel, Rachel, the wait is too long. Weep, Leah, weep . . . powerless to choose. . . . Weep because your sons will feel sanctified only in places their mother is forbidden. Weep for centuries of pain, none of your choosing:

> always you are cleaning pots, lighting candles, or putting away the linen when the pogrom starts—the Cossacks, the Turks, the Romans, the Germans, the Gentiles come and pulverize you and yours, while your men with long shawls kiss the hem of God's thought. In the end you believe nothing at all (58)

Emily describes herself "as a Jewess. I'm only an American until they decide to move again—cremating, gassing, crating in boxcars . . ." (8). She is "a Jewish woman so without tribe, so without clan, that I doubt if I will ever find a home, that my exile will ever end" (168–69).

And, finally, narrator Marjorie Weiss of *Torch Song* (1976) sees herself as "an anthropological impossibility, cultureless, defenseless, like an albino in the tropics" (89). Dismissive of a

Judaism that excludes her, because "If God was good he shouldn't mind a girl's hand in his ark" (88), she wonders, in her room at Barnard, if there was a "place, a space, a niche" where she could "live out [her] life" (89). The place space and niche cannot be within Judaism. Urged by her newly Orthodox brother to attend religious services with him, he explains that "You cannot sit near the Torah, or near the rabbi." "Men and women go differently to God. . . . Please believe me, it's good," he pleads. "You wouldn't think it was so good," she retorts, "if you had to go upstairs. If they hung a curtain in front of your face" (194). Like women throughout the generations thrust to the edges of rabbinic Judaism (off the land), Marjorie stands outside the service (a boat on the sea), and suddenly discovers that she has become the very embodiment of the *niddah*—that is, the ritually impure, untouchable woman. Her body inscribes the power of Jewish male projections; she gets the "curse" (195). But Marjorie fantasizes reversing the "curse"; huddled in the "ladies' room," she imagines wreaking a Gorgonlike revenge: pouring her menstrual blood on the altar, bleeding and bleeding until she and "all the unclean ones" see the Torah floating out" on an ocean of blood" while the women scream, "It's cleaner than you think. It goes deep into the pores and brings out all impurities" (197). The image is only fantasy, however, and it ends. She finds "some Kleenex" and is "temporarily saved from disgrace," pushing her way back into the street to wait for her brother. "I just can't join you," she tells him (197).

Depicting the isolation and loneliness of Jewish women, each of these novels thus becomes the story of a quest *for* home, conceived of not as a geographical locale, but rather as an end to spiritual, emotional, psychic, and physical exile, a locus of redemption, of liberation from a history of victimization. The quest for home is simultaneously a quest for narrative power—that is, for the right, the freedom, the space, to tell one's own story, distinct from the subject-position of victim. Writing becomes a recuperative strategy in the face of diminishments and erasures, a way of historicizing the de-historicized.[12]

In doing so, however, Roiphe's early narratives also inscribe the psychosocial and cultural biases of the era in which they were written. Dominated by the paradigm of the "melting pot" that was intrinsic to literature by Jews in this country, that time still both valorized minority assimilation into gentile (white) culture and lacked an acknowledged and sustained gendered critique either of Judaism or of the gentile culture into which

Jews sought assimilation. To read these texts today, however, is to perceive them from the very different socioideological and cultural matrix of our own era, which problematizes the intricate dynamics and implicit values of the process of assimilation and provides the tools of feminist criticism (and a wealth of women's narratives). That is, in 1994, as a Jew, a woman-Jew, and a Jewish American feminist critic, I know what neither Roiphe nor the narrators of her early novels could know. To begin, the passage of time alone allows *Digging Out, Long Division,* and *Torch Song* to be read intertextually: one can now perceive how the novels reflect back upon one another, revising the story, and can recognize how the quests declared by Laura Smith are lived out by Emily Brimberg Johnson and Marjorie Weiss. In the next decade it evolves into that of Annie Johnson of *Lovingkindness* (1987) and we can see how all of these novels relate to contemporary narratives by other women.[13] Tracing the quest of Roiphe's narrators to "find a place" thus involves negotiating the intricacies of consciousness inherent in being a woman in America, Jew in the diaspora, woman-Jew within Judaism, and Jewish American within what was once a prefeminist "melting pot" culture emphasizing assimilation and has recently been reconceived as a multicultural and gendered society endorsing the assertion of minority identity. Roiphe's novels form a uniquely Jewish American woman's version of the American quest-romance. They are of particular cultural value insofar as they are at the same time an intertextual critique of the "American Jewish" literary canon and a tortuous spiritual journey that culminates, in *Lovingkindness,* in an ambivalent deconstruction of the fundamental assumptions of the quest-romance announced in the very first novel. By focusing on how that quest-romance is initially launched in *Digging Out,* we can perceive just what those fundamentals are.

Like other titles of Anne Roiphe's novels, *Digging Out* is resonant with meaning. Clearly it is a way of describing narrator Laura Smith's decision, at the end of the novel, to break with the past, to free herself from the entrapments of family, people, "tribe." Laura's decision, however, is announced to the reader only as the body of her mother—whose slow death from cancer has been painstakingly mapped from the first page—is lowered into the ground. Doris Lessing's Martha Quest sees her mother as "the hungry earth," but Laura Smith is her mother.[14] The "secrets" Rose Tumarkin Smith told her daughter were deadly dissolutions of the boundaries between them: "We had spun between us a winding-sheet of words that made us not two but one" (107). The death of the one is thus the death of the other. In the hospital, says Laura, when "I saw her hair scattered on the pillow like the matted fur of a dead thing, I became numb as I pushed away the realization that I was dying" (63). "I felt faint. The source of my life . . . was fading. Would I be left when all the erasing was done? I would be cut loose from the mooring, floating out to sea—a message inside the bottle: "Elijah, where are you? My mother is dying'" (67).

But only as masquerade and angry graffiti does the prophet Elijah, promiser of redemption, appear in the novel. At a long-ago family Passover Seder, the door was opened to welcome him and the newly married Rose Tumarkin Smith, disguised in a sheet, rushed in crying "Whoo, whoo, boo, boo!" until the adults collapsed with laughter (70). Years later, in the hospital ladies' room, Laura takes her lipstick out of her bag and scrawls "Elijah was here!" on the mirror (67). Rose dies at home; after her corpse is removed, Laura looks in the mirror and sees "no reflection" (177). The mother's burial will be hers as well unless Laura separates herself, finds boundaries for the self, digs out of the hungry earth.

The narrative is the description of that digging. Seven chapters of the section "Primary Sources" relate Laura's entanglement in her mother's agonizing crawl toward death. Seemingly unrelated to these chronologically unfolding chapters, dated from the end of November to the end of December, are seven alternating chapters called "Secondary Sources: Kin" that unearth the history of the extended family. They begin with the story of family progenitor, Jacob Tumarkin, who, in the "rolling hills of peasant Russia . . . the village of Haddid" (12), in exchange for "money to travel across the border and guaranty of safe passage," guiltlessly betrays his mother and "his lovely young wife" to the rabid attacking Cossacks (18). The two narratives converge at Rose Tumarkin Smith's funeral, as the family gathers in the funeral home and later at the grave site. And it is there, as the family watches Rose's body being lowered into the earth, that Laura makes her bid for life. But it not only comes at a shocking moment, it comes in a shocking away.

At the funeral home, the cantor, says Laura, talked of "the sweetness of the life that had been lost and about the nature of the love between men and God and of the fine family of the lady departed," tendentious words spoken "in the phrases of a bureaucrat anxious to please his superiors" (179). But his tone alters radically at the grave site. Before Rose's body is lowered into the earth, the cantor speaks again, this time quoting lines, without comment, from Isaiah's bitter denunciation of the proud, bedecked, sensual "daughters of Zion" (Isaiah 3:16–24): these women clearly foreshadow the affluent Rose Tumarkin Smith, "who had learned to endure hair dye, hair dryers, eyebrow plucking, leg waxing, mud packs—all in the name of feminine beauty" (64). Laura herself, "heir apparent" (91), rummages through her mother's drawers to find perfumes and powder compacts, pearls and gold, rings and necklaces, monogrammed handkerchiefs, "gloves, pocketbooks and shoes too small to fit my feet" (91).

> Because the daughters of Zion are haughty
> And walk with stretched forth neck and wanton eyes
> Walking and mincing as they go
> And making a tinkling with their feet
> Therefore the Lord will smite with a scab
> The crown of the head of the daughters of Zion
> And the Lord will discover their secret parts.
> In that day the Lord will take away
> The bravery of their tinkling ornaments about their feet
> And their cauls and their round tires like the moon
> The chains and the bracelets and the mufflers
> And the head bands and the tablets and the earrings
> The rings and nose jewels
> The changeable sands of apparel
> And the mantels and the whimple and the crisping pin
> The glasses and the fine linens and the hoods and veils
> And it shall come to pass
> That instead of a sweet smell there shall be stink.

"As I heard the well-known threats of the Lord to destroy the daughters of Zion among whom without choice I stood," says Laura, "I plotted my own escape":

> The Lord, of course, was no real threat. He, before whom I had said a million words of obeisance and devotion, was nothing to me. But there were graver dangers. I stood isolated from the tribe, that tribe . . . tied by blood and upbringing to continue through suffering someone else's atonement. The tribe does not take kindly to defection, but now that my mother was going into the ground I could leave them chanting in the temple, forming businesses with each other and exchanging magic words. I could go alone. I could go no

> other way. I would become the first American in my family. To be American one must have no root, no family, perhaps a few hastily covered graves along the freeway. One must move without history, without a past commitment and find somewhere like Columbus, like Henry Hudson, like Cortez, like Lewis and Clark, a universe to claim in the name of one's self, a land to mark for one's own.
>
> Somewhere I must find a place to bear my American children, whom I will mother, and who in turn will leave me to find their own Americas. Sweet Jesus, has anyone the strength for such exploring? (179–81)

The final "Sweet Jesus" is intentional, for the chronological narrative of Rose Tumarkin's death culminates during "Christmas Week," and the endpaper of the novel tells us that the author was born "on Christmas Day, 1935." In the prefeminist era of the "melting pot," the only route to liberation —from the prophetic curse that uses the female body as the site of national corruption and warns of punishment; from the legacy of betrayal of women by males, ancient (Isaiah) and more immediate (Jacob Tumarkin, the cantor); and from, finally, emotional burial—is imagined not as mere assimilation, but rather as what the process of assimilation actually encodes: *gentilization.* The Jewish biblical prophetic tradition is thus inscribed in this narrative with a self-reflexive contempt. That is to say, rupturing the funeral by its inappropriate expression of contempt, it also erupts in the narrative to justify contempt for the very tradition that defines Laura. For Laura Smith, as presumably for Roiphe at this stage of her career, freedom from the legacy of victimization as "daughter of Zion" and the realization of autonomous selfhood—the realization of narrative voice—are conceivable only if she/they radically severs herself/themselves from family and people. Laura will light out alone on the great American—or gentile—quest-romance.

Both the fact that, in Roiphe's imagination, Laura, though born in this country, feels she must "become" an American and that (as the denouement of the book during "Christmas Week" and as its endpaper also imply) becoming an American means being Christianized reflect upon the impulses driving much of the "American Jewish" literature of the era. At the same time, the very construction of the declared quest underlines the unawareness at that time of the gendered issues involved. It will be left to Emily and Marjorie to get entangled in them as they live out the imagined quest.

For like Roiphe, the canonized "American Jewish" writers of

the post-World War II prefeminist era were negotiating the psychosocial processes of estrangement/assimilation through and in their fiction. Such writers as Saul Bellow, Bernard Malamud, and Philip Roth idealized male alienation, as Roiphe valorized female, but it was the Jewish male who came to be perceived as exemplifying an age that romanticized, as Heschel has argued, "the alienated spirit as heroic" (132). Paradoxically, then, writing about male alienation served as a "positive strategy" for Jewish men (132); it functioned to assure their belonging. The alienated Jewish male protagonist succeeded in fleeing from the confines of American Jewish culture into his psychosocial and literary niche: he melded with the antihero of the quintessentially American quest-romance.

"Judging from the prominent position occupied by questing male protagonists in the American canon," Dana A. Heller has noted, we would appear to be a nation obsessed "with masculine images of ritualized flight and self-exploration."[15] Driven by "restless wanderlust," the American hero or antihero was a man

> [whose] vision of personal achievement may be unholy in the eyes of his community, but through rituals of heroic initiation, the toils of conflict, the shaking off of demons bent on obstructing his path . . . he may still succeed in attaining heroic status. Social power and autonomy is the reward granted the hero who successfully completes the quest and survives the process of male initiation. However . . . if his efforts do not lead to successful social integration, he becomes our admired American anti-hero, our Huck Finn, on the lam from civilization, or our Holden Caulfield, who "lights out" for an inward territory, the field of the restless, solitary psyche. (7–8)

What Roiphe's cohorts, midcentury "American Jewish" male writers, succeeded so brilliantly in doing was to prove, as Lenny Bruce might have said, that Huckleberry Finn is Jewish.[16]

He is Jewish, but—despite his penchant for cross-dressing—he is not a woman. What the narrative of *Digging Out* does not take into account is that the literary mythography of "America" in which Laura Smith's quest is founded is, in the cultural matrix of her era, no more hospitable to either Jewish women, however rejecting of their Judaism, or to women seeking autonomy, than the androcentric misogynist landscape that she is determined to leave behind.

For while Huckleberry Finn is "Jewish," male Jewish writers could become Huckleberry Finn only by paying two sorts of interrelated, sociopsychological initiation dues. The first had to do with their Jewishness. In a culture where American Jews' main question was *how* to melt into the American pot, the concomitant question asked what, if any, remnants of Jewishness survived, such as a perennial lack of ease, compulsive self-doubt, neurotic guilt, or simply a "fishy" marriage broker ("The Magic Barrel") or the Patimkin wedding *(Goodbye, Columbus)*. "Jewishness" rather than Judaism prevailed, for beginning early in this century, Jewish religious—as distinct from cultural or ethnic—issues were presented, less explicitly than in *Digging Out,* as the province of the irrelevant, the annoying, the aged, the dying, the superseded or to-be-superseded generation: in other words, the province of the past. The late 1950s and 1960s witnessed what Philip Roth has cleverly called the "pasteurization of the faith,"[17] a world in which his character Eli, aware of the shame attached to an obvious Judaism, becomes a "fanatic," and Herman Wouk's Uncle Samson Aaron, that vestigial organ of religious observance, keels over with a heart attack the very moment Marjorie Morgenstern is about to "lose her virginity" to the persona non grata of American Jewish life, the bohemian Noel Airman. Even as they claimed alienation, the canonized "American Jewish" male writers were implicitly eliminating the prickly source of true difference: not the "Jewishness," which could be bleached into apparent "universality," but rather the Judaism, which, as Roiphe's narrator boldly represents, could not. In this sense, Marjorie Morgenstern Morningstar's cover on *Time* magazine was made possible by Uncle Samson Aaron's death. The subtle de-Judaicizing of the Jewish became a sluice-gate through which the male literature could flow into the deceptively inclusive American gentile sea.[18]

Roth has also called the age one in which "Brenda Patimkin dethrones Anne Frank" (132); this is true only in *Goodbye, Columbus.* The metamorphosis of the Jewish male into what Leslie Fiedler has described as "the representative American" was also accompanied by the mythicization and cultural incorporation of that object of the Jewish male's fantasy, the simultaneously desired and denigrated trophy of successful Jewish-male-gentilization—the *shikseh,* embodiment of authorial "marrying out," as well as of the rejection of the past, Judaism, and the cultural encoding of the Jewish male as female. In this regard, too, Jewish male writers were inscribing their own male-bonded belonging, for the quest-romance of the androcentric gentile tradition, in asserting masculinity, cast aside the mother, separated from the wife, or chose a female to serve, psychologically, as the male's own *anima* (*Feminization of the Quest-Romance,* 2), as his muse, or what Roiphe calls in *Long Division* his "assistant visionary" (47). In its American version, the "restless wanderlust" is itself seen as manly; fleeing from community and social convention, the male heroes flee as well from "full genital (heterosexual) maturity, and the domesticating figure of woman" (*Feminization of the Quest-Romance,* 8). For Jewish male writers, the "domesticating figure of woman" is the *Jewish* woman. Brenda Patimkin might have been enthroned, but she was also abandoned in the nuptial bed.[19]

When Laura Smith imagines herself taking off into the American mythography, leaving the tribe and tribal family behind, she is attempting to live the quest-romance of the gentile Huck Finn and his Jewish fellow-travelers. More than the latter, she knows that the underbelly of "assimilation" is gentilization, and she embraces it wholeheartedly. What she fails to acknowledge, however, is that there is no place, space, or niche for her on that great American literary frontier. Gentile heroes left autonomous women behind, and Jewish antiheroes were redeeming their own manhood from a "feminine" Judaism and from the cultural encoding of the Jewish male as female by romancing the *shikseh.* Put another way, there was no room at the saloon for the Jewish woman who internalized their values as if those values were gender-blind; Jewish or gentile, women were to seek incorporation into these male psyches, not a questing autonomy for themselves. The Jewish male strategy of "marrying out" to Americanization was gender-biased; *shikse* is included in Webster's Collegiate Dictionary, but *shagetz* (male gentile) does not appear.

Like Margaret Atwood's *Lady Oracle,* Francine Du Plessix Gray's *Lovers and Tyrants,* and Lisa Alther's *Kinflicks, Digging Out* thus ends with the promise of an escape from the past, but imagines "no future activities for the liberated self."[20] For the woman whose only available models are males such as Columbus, Henry Hudson, Cortez, and Lewis and Clark, the quest-romance will be thwarted. Emily Brimberg Johnson will drive across America, but as an orphan; she will be haunted by the victimizations of the Jewish past, self-destructively seek access to the hidden secrets of men, and experience repeated betrayal as she does so. On the road to Mexico to file for divorce, she will face the failure of her own attempt to overcome victimization by "marrying out" to a gentile artist-husband; she will have to face that it does not work to hide her own soul, as "artists' wives" do, "under the mantle of service for their menfolk . . . a godhead to a female whose own hands have frozen like ice mountains, and whose brain despises its own tormented small capacities" (88). When she comes across the monument to pioneer women that opened this essay, she will be aware only of her own utter foreignness, her own separate history, her own difference. She will imagine only the "boat." "I am without," she admits (169).

The gentile artist-husband of *Long Division* becomes the gentile writer-husband of *Torch Song*. Rather than imagining a future, however, Marjorie Weiss, a through-the-glass-darkly version of her predecessor Marjorie Morningstar, will reflect back through the "fog" of the present with which *Torch Song* begins to tell the story of the past. The narrative recounts her own fury at, and flight from a Judaism that both excludes her as a woman and that honors a God "who would crush whatever remaining Jews he found clinging to his fingertips" (195) and also from a mother who, like Rose Tumarkin Smith, "embalmed herself while still breathing" (118), and whose body had been "cramped by corsets, high heels, and hair that had been carefully set and dyed [and who] could move only cautiously, awkwardly" (71). A "compulsive romantic" (14), Marjorie tells us that she ran "for her life" (109) away from Judaism, away from the mother, and right into the arms of Roiphe's version of Noel Airman, unveiled in this novel as an unstable, fame-obsessed, sadistic, and eternally restless man who rejects genital heterosexuality in favor of fetishized masturbation and whose "assistant visionary" she sought to become. "I didn't understand then," she admits, "that behind a Gentile lunatic was not a safe place to hide" (195). By the end of the novel, Marjorie has surrendered her romanticism, her questing self, and like Marjorie Morgenstern in her suburbia, has married not a dentist but a pediatrician. She has achieved domestic happiness and a motherhood of her own; with the air of someone older but wiser, however, she confesses that the emptiness left within her, which she was once desperate for her former husband to fill, "remains now and forever voids" (245). As in so many prefeminist era quest-romances, Roiphe's early narrators are forced to reconcile themselves to the limited landscape allotted to women's lives.[21]

Lovingkindness (1987) ends up wrestling with the failed quest-romance of the earlier novels. The "ur-text" is again rewritten, again revised: the same family pain and betrayals, the same defeated mother, the same rage at victimization, at Judaism, at the Jewish God. But the gentile writer-husband of *Lov-*

ingkindness is portrayed as a long-ago suicide—that is, as a self-destructive man who in the end destroyed himself, as if the old male-defined myth of the quest-romance, once regarded by Roiphe as a refuge, has by now imploded. Narrator Annie Johnson's adolescent daughter, Andrea, turns her back on the paradigm of gentilization that her mother—the older, "melting pot" generation—sought to live; she recognizes how the struggle to live out that paradigm wounds the body and wreaks havoc on the psyche. Through an act of "self-naming" that, as Carol Christ has suggested, for a woman calls a "new identity into being by transforming a relationship between her individual spirit and the world which she inhabits,"[22] Andrea re-names herself the prototypical "Sarai."

But Andrea/Sarai's strategy for ending the exile of the "Daughters of Refugees of the Ongoing-Universal Endless Upheaval" on their boats "three miles out to sea" is to ensconce herself in the all-embracing Orthodox "Yeshiva Rachel" in Jerusalem, celebrating the constraints it places on her as a woman. The gentile Madonna of the Trail, the Pioneer Woman as icon of a female historical purpose from which, as gentile, the Jewish American woman is forever alien, has turned into the eternal Judaic Mother weeping for her lost children.

But Annie Johnson stays in New York. For a woman bruised by the past and marked by secular feminism, the young Andrea/Sarai's solution cannot work. Even in the age of multiculturalism, honoring the assertion of minority identity, *Lovingkindness* implicitly suggests that the Jewish American woman who seeks to challenge and transform the conflicted matrix of diaspora, Judaism, Jewish American identity, and womanhood into a narrative vision of heroic selfhood is still at sea. Perhaps in the end coming home will be possible only when the fabled Elijah is revealed as a "Mother of Zion"—one released and redeemed from both the constricting corsets and the endless upheaval of the past.

Notes

1. Anne Roiphe, *Long Division* (New York: Simon and Schuster, 1972). Citations to this and other novels discussed in this essay will be made parenthetically in the text.

2. Helene Cixous, "Sorties: Out and Out: Attacks/Ways Out/Forays," in *The Newly Born Woman*, ed. Helene Cixous and Catherine Clement, trans. Betsy Wing (Minneapolis: University of Minnesota Press, 1986), 71.

3. The stories by Rapoport, Schwartz, and Spiro are included in *Writing Our Way Home: Contemporary Stories by American Jewish Writers,* ed. Ted Solotaroff and Nessa Rapoport (New York: Schocken Books, 1992).

4. Tova Reich, *Mara* (New York: Farrar Straus Giroux, 1978); E. M. Broner, *A Weave of Women* (New York: Holt, Rinehart and Winston, 1978). See my "Orphans of Culture and of History: Gender and Spirituality in Contemporary Jewish-American Women's Fiction," *Tulsa Studies in Womens' Literature* 13 (Spring 1994): 127–41.

5. Rhoda Lerman, *God's Ear* (New York: Henry Holt, 1989). On Grace Paley see Gloria L. Cronin, "Melodramas of Beset Womanhood: Resistance, Subversion, and Survival in the Fiction of Grace Paley," *Studies in American Jewish Literature: Contemporary Women Writers* 11 (Fall 1992): 140–49.

6. I borrow the language here of postcolonial critic Bill Ashcroft in "Excess: Post-colonialism and the Verandahs of Meaning," *De-Scribing Empire: Post-colonialism and Textuality,* ed. Chris Tiffin and Alan Lawson (New York: Routledge, 1994), 33–44.

7. For an eloquent discussion of this topic see Marilee Lindemann, "'This Woman Can Cross Any Line': Power and Authority in Contemporary Women's Fiction," in *Engendering the Word: Feminist Essays in Psychosexual Poetics,* ed. Temma F. Berg, Anna Shannon Elfenbein, Jeanne Larsen, and Elisa Kay Sparks (Urbana: University of Illionis Press, 1989), 105–24.

8. See, for example, *The Jewish Woman: New Perspectives,* ed. Elizabeth Koltun (New York: Schocken Books, 1976); *On Being a Jewish Feminist: A Reader,* ed. Susannah Heschel (New York: Schocken Books, 1983); Judith Plaskow, *Standing Again at Sinai: Judaism from a Feminist Perspective* (San Francisco: Harper and Row, 1990; Letty Cottin Pogrebin, *Deborah, Golda, and Me: Being Female and Jewish in America* (New York: Crown, 1991). For an autobiographical/literary analysis, see my "'Crazy, of Course': Spiritual Romanticism and the Redeeming of Female Spirituality in Contemporary Jewish-American Women's Fiction," in *People of the Book: Thirty Scholars Reflect on Their Jewish Identity,* ed. Jeffrey Rubin Dorsky and Shelley Fisher Fishkin (Madison: University of Wisconsin Press 1996).

9. In "The Study of Thomas Hardy," in *Phoenix* (London: Penguin, 1961), 450. See also Sander L. Gilman's study *Freud, Race, and Gender* (Princeton: Princeton University Press, 1983), esp. 31, 37, 39; Gilman, *The Jew's Body* (New York: Routledge, 1991), 207; and Jay Geller, "(G)nos(e)ology: The Cultural Construction of the Other," in *People of the Body: Jews and Judaism from an Embodied Perspective,* ed. Howard Eilberg-Schwartz (Albany: SUNY Press, 1992), 243–82.

10. In "A Response to Marc L. Raphael," *Jewish History 7,* no. 1 (Spring 1993): 135. See also Myra Glazer's introduction to *Burning Air and a Clear Mind: Contemporary Israeli Women Poets* (Athens: Ohio State University Press, 1981).

11. Anne Richardson, *Digging Out* (New York: McGraw-Hill, 1966). The subsequent novels referred to here, written as Anne Roiphe, are *Long Division* and *Torch Song* (New York: Signet, 1977).

12. I am drawing again on the helpful language of postcolonial theory, which, in engaging the erasure of difference, the dehistoricization of the colonized, is pertinent to the Jewish—and more particularly the Jewish woman's—experience in America. However, one must keep in mind differences between a forcibly colonized people and a more subtle—and to some extent self-chosen—

process, which was the Americanization of the Jews. See Fiona Giles, "'The Softest Disorder': Representing Cultural Indeterminacy," in *De-Scribing Empire,* 141–51.

13. In ways worthy of further consideration, the relation among the narratives by Roiphe (and perhaps by all novelists) suggested here parallels Daniel Boyarin's reading of the nature of Midrash. "Later texts interpret and rewrite . . . earlier ones to change the meaning of the entire canon," Boyarin argues; "recognizing the presence of the earlier texts in the later changes our understanding of the later texts as well. . . . This is what the Midrash refers to as 'string [like beads or pearls] the words of Torah together . . . from the Torah to the Prophets and from the Prophets to the Writings'" (Daniel Boyarin, *Intertextuality and the Reading of Midrash* [Bloomington: Indiana University Press, 1990], 16). One, of course, would have to consider the difference between the positionality of sacred, rather than secular, texts.

14. See the discussion in Katherine Fishburn, "The Nightmare Repetition: The Mother-Daughter Conflict in Doris Lessing's *Children of Violence,*" in *The Lost Tradition: Mothers and Daughters in Literature,* ed. Cathy N. Davidson and E. M. Broner (New York: Frederick Ungar, 1980), 207–16.

15. See Dana A. Heller, *The Feminization of Quest-Romance: Radical Departures* (Austin: University of Texas Press, 1990), 7.

16. Days after writing these words and wondering if perhaps they were far-fetched, I discovered Leslie Fiedler's 1957 essay, "Saul Bellow," in an aptly named collection of essays, *To the Gentiles.* The theme of *Augie March,* says Fiedler, is "the native theme of *Huckleberry Finn*"; speaking of the typical, lonely, Bellow protagonist—"essential man, man stripped of success and belongingness, even of failure . . . man disowned by his father, unrecognized by his son, *man without woman,* man face to face with himself" (my emphasis), Fiedler comments that "such a man is at once a Jew in perpetual exile and Huck Finn in whom are blended with perfect irony the twin American beliefs that the answer to all questions is always over the next horizon and that there is no answer now or ever." And I thought that it was my line. See "Saul Bellow," *To the Gentiles* (New York: Stein and Day, 1972), 61.

17. *Operation Shylock: A Confession* (New York: Simon and Schuster, 1993), 132.

18. For another aspect of this argument, see Leslie Fiedler's recent analysis, "Christian-ness of the Jewish-American Writer," in *Fiedler on the Roof* (Boston: David R. Godine, 1991), 58–71.

19. And still is. While Jewish males today may be leading characters on television, they are always ether married to, surrounded by, or courting non-Jewish women. See "Northern Exposure," for example, in the early 1990s.

20. See Bonnie Hoover Braendlin, "New Directions in the Contemporary Bildungsroman: Lisa Alther's *Kinflicks,*" in *Gender and Literary Voice,* ed. Janet Todd (New York: Holmes and Meier, 1980), 162.

21. See Heller, *Feminization of Quest-Romance,* 13–15.

22. Referred to in ibid., 18.

Anne Roiphe: Finding Her America

JAY L. HALIO

AT the end of Anne Roiphe's first novel, *Digging Out* (McGraw-Hill, 1966), Laura Smith says: "Somewhere I must find a place to bear my American children, whom I will mother, and who will in turn leave me to find their own Americas. Sweet Jesus, has anyone the strength for such exploring?" (181). Anne Roiphe has the strength, as she has proved in her writings and in her life ever since. But while her next three novels give ample evidence of this exploration, they also reveal another aspect of Roiphe's search—for her identity as a Jew in twentieth-century America.

The passage above occurs as Laura, Roiphe's principal character, attends her mother's funeral. She listens to the chant of the cantor reciting verses from Isaiah 3 on the vanity of the daughters of Zion, whom the Lord will bring low. "The Lord, of course, was no threat," she thinks to herself. "He, before whom I had said a million words of obeisance and devotion, was nothing to me. But there were graver dangers. I stood isolated from the tribe . . ." (180). And like her surrogate Laura, Roiphe indeed stood isolated from her tribe. Like Laura, she had rebelled against everything that her wealthy, middle-class Jewish family stood for. She married out of the faith (the novel was published under her first married name, Anne Richardson); she proclaimed herself a nonbeliever; and she became committed to a life diametrically opposed to the wealth and luxury that surrounded her mother and father. But even as her first marriage broke up after the birth of her child and she continued writing, her heritage was not forgotten. She remarried, this time to a Jewish psychiatrist who, like herself, espoused humanism, not religion, and with him had more children, while also caring for two daughters from her husband's first marriage. Leading a comfortable life and gaining increasing recognition as a writer, she nevertheless remained preoccupied with nagging questions concerning her identity as a Jew who, like her forebears, lived in a predominantly Christian society.

In *Generation without Memory: A Jewish Journey in Christian America* (Simon and Schuster, 1981) Roiphe seriously questions who and what she and her children are. Driving with them by a Congregational church in Connecticut during a New Year's Day service, she muses:

> The sweet lights in the church are like a campfire keeping away the wild beasts of imagination if not of reality. We cannot move toward that campfire. We cannot warm our feet or hands there, because we are Jews. Or are we still Jews? Do we dare call ourselves Jews? Do we dare not call ourselves Jews? (10)

The ambivalence Roiphe expresses is recurrent throughout much of her published work and reflects the uncertainty that many American Jews of her generation experience.[1] She offers no easy resolution, and her novel *Lovingkindness* (Summit Books, 1987) dramatizes the situation as powerfully and honestly as any contemporary fiction I know.

Her earlier novels draw heavily upon personal experience and juxtapose their protagonists' immediate experiences with either the past experience of growing up or the fantasies of a life not yet lived. In *Digging Out,* for example, chapters called "Primary Sources"—what is happening to Laura and her mother—alternate with "Secondary Sources" —the family's history in the near and distant past. Laura's mother is slowly dying of an inoperable brain tumor, and her at times comically grotesque situation contrasts strongly with the elegance of her Park Avenue apartment, in which she, far more than her daughter, has taken much pride. Despite their Anglo-Saxon surname, they are a rich Jewish family, whose origins in America, as the "Secondary Sources" reveal, go back only a couple of generations. Brought up to attend the "proper" schools and dancing classes and otherwise prepare herself for a good marriage to some doctor, lawyer, or wealthy businessman, Laura goes to college, studies history, and against her mother's wishes decides to pursue graduate education while living in a small Greenwich Village apartment. Her rebellion has already begun, although it is not until *Torch Song* (Farrar, Straus and Giroux, 1977), Roiphe's fourth novel, that we see in far greater detail the kind of a revolt it will be.

What this first novel presents is the kind of family life Laura wants to dig herself out of. Within their close, nearly stifling relationship, Laura at once pities and despises her mother and her indolent existence. Trapped in a loveless marriage, Rose tries vainly to steer her daughter to a better way of life, but it is hardly one Laura wishes to pursue. Laura's father, Paul, is more distant, removed. The son of Hungarian immigrants, he "developed into a close-mouthed, well-dressed, ambitious boy" (9) who met and married Rose Tumarkin as much for her connections to banking and business as for her unsure manner and diminutive size. Their marriage quickly degenerated into one of convenience or rather, as Laura describes it, one of "those fierce dependencies that rely on an expected toleration to pain" (10).

Much of the material in the "Secondary Sources" is greatly expanded in Roiphe's later novel, *The Pursuit of Happiness* (Summit Books, 1991), a long, sprawling family saga on the model of a Leon Uris epic. But despite numerous small differences, the essentials remain the same: the mother's origin in a Russian shtetl, Jacob Tumarkin's Orthodox upbringing, his marriage to Hinda, her death in a pogrom and his escape (through a dastardly betrayal) to America, where he eventually prospers while raising another family. Money and social position replace Old World values, and although the family still observes Jewish rituals—the children are married by rabbis, and synagogue attendance at High Holidays is mandatory—the quest for position and pleasure largely replaces faith and tradition. Laura and her cousins are cared for by German governesses—just as Roiphe herself was raised—while the mothers play golf and mah-jongg, lunch together at Schraffts, and otherwise spend their time and money in idle pursuits. Laura determines to live a far different life and some inklings of her future course (and certainly Roiphe's) appear in the four "Christmas Stories" she writes while her mother lies dying. At that time of year Laura finds herself "thinking in terms of parables" (48). The stories are all about love and loss or sacrifice and retribution. They are also about parents and their children, with Jews as the main characters, and are extremely poignant.

Digging Out ends with the funeral of Laura's mother, but most of Anne Roiphe's subsequent novels are involved with similar mother-daughter relationships and quests for identity. Like Philip Roth in his later novels, Roiphe seems to be interested in the idea of "counterlives."[2] *Up the Sandbox!* (Simon and Schuster, 1970) is the story of a Margaret Reynolds, a young married woman with two children whose husband, Paul, is a graduate student in social history. Margaret is not very good at housekeeping and hates being left alone all day while Paul works hard on his doctoral thesis. The chapters on her mundane existence alternate with chapters of her rich fantasy life—as a member of a terrorist gang who blow up the George Washington Bridge, the lover of Fidel Castro, an anthropologist in the Amazon who narrowly escapes death, and so on. But the fantasies finally prove no more fulfilling than Margaret's normal existence and leave her feeling as ambivalent about herself and her future as she was at the start.

While *Up the Sandbox!* ignores the search for a specific Jewish identity, it examines a rather commonplace kind of America whose actuality circumscribes several feminist fantasies. *Long Division* (Simon and Schuster, 1972) explores in somewhat surreal fashion a much greater swath of America. Emily Brimberg Johnson, another young mother, sets out in her station wagon from New York with her ten-year-old daughter, Sarah, to get a quickie Mexican divorce. Although she served and adored her husband, a painter, throughout their marriage (much like Marjorie Weiss Morrison in *Torch Song*), he abandons her for other women, leaving her with an unlooked-for but eagerly grasped freedom. She uses this liberty to scrutinize not only the vastness of America and much of the richness and grotesquerie it contains, but also her identity as a mother, a deserted housewife, and (to a more limited extent) as a once-pampered Jewish American daughter who had the audacity to marry out of the faith.

What Emily discovers is not very cheering, her romantic idealism notwithstanding. She is repeatedly victimized, and at one point she has to use all the wit she can muster to escape a retirement village in Texas whose residents, forgotten by their relatives and longing to love a grandchild, virtually imprison Emily and Sarah. Through their many adventures, mother and daughter find their relationship becoming closer but strained; Sarah understandably resents being the child of a broken family and spends much of her time playing jacks, like the school champion she recently was. Despite its surface attractions, the great American heartland turns out to be hardly more winning than the more densely populated environs of New York, where Emily and her family, like Margaret Reynolds and hers, lived.

Like Margaret, too, Emily has a vivid imagination. But unlike the earlier novels, *Long Division* enfolds Emily's creative memories, not in intercalary chapters but within the ongoing narrative, blending past and present in a more natural fashion. For example, during one night in a motel early in their trip, Emily recalls the vacation on St. Croix that she spent years ago with her husband, Alex, swimming and snorkeling and observing the beauty of the undersea universe or watching the relentless march of soldier crabs to and from the ocean. In that tropical paradise they conceived Sarah, "not planning a future, but not wanting to deny anything" (28). But Emily is denied. Although she becomes pregnant, only Alex gets to see the amazing green flash at sunset touted by the natives. It becomes emblematic of the many disappointed expectations that Emily, for all her zesty imagination, experiences in her life.

At other times Emily is reminded of her family and childhood, of going to Sunday school and studying the tragedies of Jewish history. After a couple of years she begins to question the point of it all, especially the pride in being victims that Mr. Birnbaum, the teacher, tries to instill in his pupils. It is then that Emily plans her escape—"a painless genocide, a pleasure-filled life that would guarantee the future would hold no terrors of persecution." The "painless genocide" involves "marrying out," abandoning the faith so that "the children might be safe and the terrible tale of Jewish history would be done" (57). Emily carries through her plan to "marry out," but although freed perhaps from terrors of persecution, her life is as much filled with disappointment, abuse, and humiliation as it ever was with dubious and fleeting pleasures.

Margaret's fantasies and Emily's hopes, like Laura's vision of becoming "the first American" in her family to "go it alone," to "move without history, without a past commitment" (180), culminate in Marjorie Weiss's experience in *Torch Song*. In Marjorie, Roiphe more than recapitulates Laura's early years; she extends and deepens that experience, especially the mother-daughter relationship, once again bound up in a tight knot of love and hate. At the same time, Roiphe appears to be examining and trying to work through certain concepts of what it means to be a Jew in contemporary America, brought up in privilege and luxury, burdened with a weight of history (whose meaning she can neither grasp nor accept), while also deprived of any kind of spiritual sustenance. Understandably, her protagonists' first reactions are to reject the past, to "go it alone," to find something new. But Marjorie's liaison with Jim Morrison, like Emily's marriage to Alex, shows that the alternatives she discovers and willfully chooses are no more fulfilling or sustaining than those she has rejected.

Enrolled at Barnard College in the 1950s, Marjorie increasingly rebels against the upper-middle-class Jewish culture that is her heritage. She emulates typical fifties bohemian dress and behavior and eventually meets Jim Morrison, an extremely neurotic but talented writer whose bizarre habits, including his strange sexual habits, she tolerates because of her growing infatuation. Jim is a fuller version of the artist Emily married, but much crazier. Apart from his sexual perversities, Jim has other habits that his lover also feels compelled to tolerate, such as heavy drinking, nightly prowls, gambling and consorting with prostitutes, and many other obsessions. Nevertheless, Marjorie believes in Jim's genius as a writer, a not unwarranted belief as events prove, but one that is insufficient finally to keep their relationship intact. After living together for a year in Europe, where her mother and uncle make them get married, they return to New York, but marriage scarcely alters the couple's life together.

In America Marjorie gets a job, though later she decides to quit and have a child. Forcing Jim to give her one turns out to be the beginning of the end of their marriage. Meanwhile, Jim has published a successful novel and is working on another. He craves recognition and praise quite beyond what his fiction merits, but Marjorie continues to reassure him. When their daughter, Faith, now in nursery school, develops first asthma and then a stutter, Marjorie recognizes that their family life, such as it is, is rotten. Her life with Jim hardly seems an acceptable alternative to that of her parents. She begins to think of leaving Jim, but he beats her to it, taking off for Palm Beach with a rich young woman. The novel ends fifteen years later, after Marjorie has married again, this time to a pediatrician, by whom she has two young sons. Jim too has remarried, more than once, has become a famous novelist, and continues to engage in his ruinous habit of gambling for large sums of money.[3]

Contrasting with but not unrelated to Marjorie's experience as an "emancipated" Jewish woman is her brother' commitment, immediately following his bar mitzvah, to Orthodox Judaism, which, following the training and ritual of his coming of age, he takes with unexpected seriousness. It was his way, Marjorie believes, of escaping "the family drama," embracing "the rules and regulations of the Orthodox Jewish system of belief with the purity of heart and fanaticism of the desperate" (100). Eating only kosher food and dressing like a Hasid, he waged his own rebellion against his parents, especially his father, who himself looked like "an advertisement in *Esquire,* the most assimilated, handsomest of melted Jewry" (101). For the elder Weisses, rabbis and Sunday-school teachers "were necessary to maintain Jewish identity and assuage guilt," Marjorie recalls. "But to be taken seriously? Never. My brother was among the first in his generation to practice downward social mobility" (102). Brother and sister thus react in radically divergent ways against the emptiness of their parents' existence, but the nature and quality of their achievements, as the novel presents them, indicate quite clearly Roiphe's continuing uncertainty and ambivalence and the need for further exploration.

Marjorie and her brother never got along as children, and if he grieved for her atheism, she taunted him with aspersions against a God who "shoved little children into gas ovens," proclaiming in her loud existentialist voice that "God is dead" (103). The Holocaust and the search for identity as a Jew without belief in a God that permitted such a catastrophe form one of Roiphe's major philosophical themes. In her next book, *Generation without Memory,* a work of nonfiction, she examines this theme and others developed in her novels, unveiling the autobiographical basis for much of what she has written. In it the reader learns about Roiphe's mother, her mother's family, the rejection of her mother's materialist values and those of her father (who closely resembles Marjorie's father in *Torch Song*), her brother and his early interest in Orthodox Judaism and *Yiddishkeit* (though he became a doctor, not a rabbi), her childhood German nanny, and many other aspects of her personal life. She writes about her schooling and her children, but very little about her first marriage. Her ideas and experiences all influenced her attitudes toward herself as a woman, an intellectual, and a Jew, and they go far to explain, though they do not resolve, the ambivalences that so frequently emerge in her writings.

For example, when Roiphe describes the shame she felt for her mother, whose clothes and manner were so different from those of her classmates' mothers in the predominantly gentile high school she attended, she also remembers the shame she felt for that shame; "even a child knows snobbery for what it is, and especially a child understands primary loyalties to group and tribe" (171). Her own children have an entirely different experience; thanks to their mother's membership in "the intellectual, left-wing, primarily Jewish (though for most the Jewish part is not very consciously relevant)," they are not "strangers in America" (171). They have not experienced anti-Semitism of any sort. Nevertheless they "share with me certain empty spaces where a sense of who they are and who they were and where they came from is thin, slippery and just possibly inadequate" (172).

What led Roiphe as an adolescent and young woman to reject much of her Jewish heritage, especially as it was expressed in her family's way of life, has a good deal to do with the attitude of contemporary women to Judaism. Emily in *Long Division* gives vehement, rhapsodic utterance to views many intelligent Jewish women have held:

> Rachel, Rachel, the wait is too long. Weep, Leah, weep for being first and ugly; both weep for being cattle traded two for one on the open market. Powerless to choose, to run away into the long desert, no god outside your father's house, helpless before your husband's pleasure or displeasure; breasts will sag, and infections gray your vaginal lips, but you must live according to the schedules of law and ritual and give the obedience demanded of any domestic animal. Weep far away from the Torah, weep away from the holy center of the men's world, because the Lord God, Jehovah, the nameless name of all names, does not like menstruating women whose blood is after all their own. Weep for being unclean, weep for being born Jewish. . . . Weep because your sons will feel sanctified only in places their mother is forbidden. Weep for centuries of pain, none of your choosing. . . . (58)

Roiphe recognizes that traditional attitudes may have a lot to do with why many Jewish women increasingly have engaged in intermarriage—what Emily calls "painless genocide"—but this may only be a momentary blip of history's radar.[4] "There are pulls, strong pulls, in the opposite direction," Roiphe says, "that mandate a return to Jewishness, to acceptance of oneself as a Jew" (*Generation without Memory,* 172). Forces are at work to change the position of women in the Jewish community, to improve their role within the Jewish framework so that many daughters and sisters may remain or return. In many synagogues that have broken from strict orthodoxy women may be counted in the *minyan* and engage fully in religious rituals together with men. "There is perhaps a Hegelian dialectic at work," Roiphe suggests, "where universalism stretched to its utmost will snap and rebound into its opposite and the nation will find itself welcoming back its prodigal sons and daughters" (ibid.).

Something like this "snap and rebound" occurs in Roiphe's next (and for many her best) novel, *Lovingkindness.* The narrative (typically, in Roiphe's fiction, told in the first-person singular) conveys the story of another mother-daughter relationship—more intense than any of those so far, but in the context of the previous novels, with an extremely ironic twist. For now the mother is not like Mrs. Smith or Mrs. Weiss or any of the other surrogates for Mrs. Blanche Roth, Roiphe's mother; she is much more like Roiphe herself—a well-educated, modern humanist, a professor in a New York City college, of Jewish descent and fully assimilated into the intellectual life of her profession and her social class. In fact, her name is Annie. But, highlighting the mother-daughter relationship, she is a widow with an only daughter, Andrea, who (like many young people and as Roiphe herself did) vigorously rebels against the older generation. There is, however, an important difference: whereas Roiphe and her surrogates reacted against their parents' materialism and shallow Judaism, substituting instead their own brands of intellectualism and secular humanism, Andrea drops out totally, is addicted to drugs, and worse. When she suddenly turns up at Yeshiva Rachel in Israel and commits herself to become an ultra-Orthodox Jewish woman, her mother is both astonished and deeply disturbed.

Annie has great difficulty in accepting her daughter's choice. The letters that pass between them eloquently express their conflicting values, especially as Andrea—renamed Sarai—describes them. Like Laura and Roiphe's other protagonists, Annie had early forsaken her mother's affluent world. As a graduate student in political science, she fell in love with a young poet of Yankee stock—Hilary Cabot Johnson, a shining representative of that "other America" that Roiphe's heroines seem inevitably attracted to, just as Philip Roth's heroes are attracted to shiksas, and for many of the same reasons. But the marriage ended during her pregnancy when during a party Hilary walked off the balcony of a friend's apartment to his death. Though Hilary's parents ignored her and their grandchild thereafter, Annie struggled on, creating a life for herself and her daughter that appeared to fulfill all of Annie's, if not Andrea's, needs and desires. She filled her house with books, took Andrea on protest marches in Washington against the Viet Nam war, tried to give her a good education, and after her daughter's rebellion began, even paid for her several abortions as well as her visits to a psychiatrist.

Though as a latter-day hippie Andrea deeply troubles her mother, Annie tolerates as gracefully as she can both Andrea's self-abuse (she has a tattoo on her back, puts a safety pin through her nostril, takes a variety of drugs, and is sexually promiscuous) and her repeated failures to change. Thus when she does drastically change, Annie is entirely unprepared and appeals to her daughter's erstwhile free spirit, her love of independence, her "appetite for life." She questions her daughter's sanity and wonders if Andrea is only fooling herself. She writes:

> I want you to be a shape, to carry a destiny of your own, to be responsible for yourself. I want you to go on learning new things. I don't want you frozen in a time warp that experienced its grandeur in the backwoods of Poland several centuries ago. . . . If you close yourself off in this Jewish particular, this walled city of convictions, you must renounce the universal. You can no longer feel yourself kin to all the spinning colors of the globe. Can you possibly see progress for human beings as retribalization, where each of our little clans turns inward and becomes absorbed in the details of ritual and refines its own method of conning the sun to rise each morning? (56–57)

As a statement of twentieth-century secular humanism opposing ancient ritual and tradition, Annie's letter can hardly be surpassed. It is written in response to Andrea/Sarai's letters describing the beauty and tranquillity of her new life under the guidance of Rabbi Cohen and his wife at Yeshiva Rachel. In her turn Andrea writes her mother:

> Sometimes I think of you left in New York with all the voices talking at once and wish you would come here and see my yeshiva. I believe now that Gd [*sic*] is good, that when He created the earth He intended man to be good, He intended His creation to be good, and He intended me to play my part. Can you, will you try to understand? You must understand because you are my mother. Gd is a God of Lovingkindness. He is the Master of Life and Death. He is the Redeemer. He brings flowers to the field and sweetness to the fruit. Rabbi Cohen tells me I am a good student. This is the first time you have heard that. Are you surprised? Mrs. Cohen is teaching us about the Mikvah and the laws that married women follow. I am so amazed. I thought my body didn't matter to anyone but me. Mrs. Cohen says that even the crevices, even the parts that get stained, can be cleansed and made good and serve their rightful purpose. . . . I know that you will think that purity laws are against women but that's because you don't understand. The truth is they bring us closer to Gd. (94–95)

To Annie her daughter suddenly sounded extremely young and innocent, like a virgin who knows nothing about real sex. And in a sense that is what Andrea's rebirth as Sarai signifies. Her very language is different, utterly changed from the sassy, rough talk she formerly used when addressing her mother, which Annie secretly enjoyed.

Events come to a head when Annie hears from Rabbi Cohen that a marriage is being arranged between her daughter and a young man at the yeshiva, an American like Andrea who has also been reclaimed by these Orthodox Jews in Jerusalem. In Rabbi Cohen's view, Sarai is "a very special person with a deep spiritual thirst. She has been reaching for the path, longing for the path, her entire life. Her inability to conform to your expectations was a sign of her real nature struggling to assert itself, searching in vain among the cleverness of the world for the truth that would nurture and cherish her, the place for her to dwell in righteousness and holiness" (75). When Rabbi Cohen says this place is "here among us," Annie Johnson cannot accept that. Her first reaction is outrage. But after calming down, she agrees to visit in the spring if her daughter is still at the yeshiva. Then Rabbi Cohen writes her about the arranged marriage.

It is testimony to Roiphe's art and integrity that she presents all sides of the quarrel, which soon involves the intended bridegroom's parents, with extraordinary sensitivity and conviction.[5] Here she is again like Philip Roth, who at his best, as in *The Counterlife,* also set partly in Israel, presents in persuasive detail the arguments of both the right and the left wing, the religious and the secular, regarding the occupation of the West Bank and Israel's role in the world.[6] The issues are difficult, complex, and far from easily resolved—if they can be settled at all. Micah Rose's parents in *Lovingkindness* handle them simply by abducting their son and bringing him back to Cleveland, and they try to get Annie to go along with their plan. They almost succeed. But by then Annie has become less skeptical of the changes in her daughter and warns Rabbi Cohen, who knows how to counter force with force.

What leads Annie to become more cooperative, not with Dr. and Mrs. Rose, but with Rabbi Cohen? Carole McKewin Weaver has argued that Annie's dreams of Rabbi Nachman of Bratslav (where her grandfather came from) are crucial insofar as they put her in closer touch with her own spiritual nature. To a large extent I think this is true.[7] They also contrast strikingly with the help Annie, secularist that she is, seeks in vain from Andrea's psychiatrist, Dr. Wolfert. The dreams begin early in the novel, soon after Andrea's phone call from Jerusalem, and recur frequently until nearly the end. As Weaver maintains, they are lessons about love. Couched in a peculiarly negative fashion, each of the tales Rabbi Nachman tells Annie are about dramatic failures in love, lessons "in reverse," or "antifables."[8] Some are about disastrous mother-child relationships; others are about married couples who terribly fail each other. Almost all of them end with Rabbi Nachman as a baby or small child crying "Mama" to Annie, who usually is repulsed, except in the last dream, when she takes the infant lovingly in her arms—until the Angel of Death comes and carries it off, still crying "Mama" (264).

McKewin relates this part of the dream to the parable Bruria tells her husband when their children suddenly die, comparing the little ones to a great treasure that must be returned to its owner. As an early Jewish feminist dating back to rabbinic times, Bruria interests Annie very early in the novel. Perhaps her loss of Andrea is similar to Bruria's loss of her children, a trial of love rather than a punishment, and her action in informing Rabbi Cohen of the Roses' plot to abduct Micah is Annie's act of "lovingkindness," or *chesed.* Perhaps. But as Sarai and Micah drive off to be married, Annie remains ambivalent, even as she wishes her daughter happiness in her new—but to Annie, still strange and alien—land.

If Annie Johnson found another America, one far different from her mother's and much closer to what Laura Smith seeks, it evidently fails to satisfy her child and her child's generation. Midway through the novel, when Annie confides to her best friend, Louise, what has happened, she recalls the plans they both had for their children's adulthood: "education, of course, but dedication to a cause also, beauty and comfort, but concern for others and love of music and books" (115). Louise, an expert in Asian art, wanted her son to know the Orient and to enjoy travel and "a capacity for sexual pleasure and decent affection," and both mothers confessed to each other that they hoped their children would "cast a small shadow over the planet, maybe build houses or design new methods of production or improve our healthcare delivery system." Like true liberal feminists, they wanted their children "to change the order of things, to fight it and improve it" (115). But Louise's son becomes a stockbroker, and Andrea converts to a religion that Annie believes suppresses women. Their mothers contemplate what happened to bring their children to fates so different from the ones they expected and hoped for. Did they do everything wrong? Or was it just the Zeitgeist—as if they were all sitting on a beach having a picnic (as Louise puts it) and a tidal wave came and washed their children out to sea?

In *The Pursuit of Happiness,* a long rambling saga about the Gruenbaum family, whose origins lie deep in central Europe, Roiphe explores a good number of possible "Americas" that Jews have discovered and, for one reason or several, appear unsatisfactory. Interestingly the novel begins and ends in Israel, where Hedy, a member of the present generation (a woman like Roiphe in background and history), has married and settled down—not in a religious community, but in an ordinary, secular Israeli lifestyle. Episodes of her childhood and life in America intersperse with those of many other family members, who include rich relatives and poor ones, scapegraces as well as successful business and professional people, devoutly religious Jews and nonbelieving hedonists. *The Pursuit of Happiness* chronicles four generations, juxtaposing episodes from one era and way of life against another, sometimes within an immediate family, sometimes between related family branches. For example, midway through the novel Roiphe recounts the scandal that befell the banker Julie Eisen, married to Isaac Gruenbaum's eldest daughter, Mildred. She describes not only the family's reactions, but also the general public's, which include outbreaks of anti-Semitism in the press and elsewhere (the time is 1932, a Depression year). The story immediately follows that of "Great-Uncle Max," the ne'er-do-well who was eased out of the Gruenbaum family business and who spends his time in New Jersey playing polo with stable boys and jockeys, since he is prevented from joining any of the exclusive clubs.[9] Shortly thereafter we hear about Eli Herzberg, Isaac's grandson, who becomes a pious Jew like his father—unlike his two older siblings: Sharie, who inherits the marvelous Herzberg voice but becomes a nightclub singer; and Meyer, who earns a Ph.D. in English at Johns Hopkins and becomes a City College professor, but is disgraced during the McCarthy years.

The Pursuit of Happiness is punctuated throughout by brief interludes concerning Hedy's anxious vigil while her daughter undergoes surgery in Hadassah Hospital for a gunshot wound suffered while working among children in the West Bank. It is also, unfortunately, interrupted by periodic admonitions and exhortations addressed directly to the reader—a curious throwback to an outmoded novelistic style. The abundant variety of

Jews and their *modi vivendi* in twentieth-century America, through which *The Pursuit of Happiness* explores issues of Jewish identity, still leaves open, however, the questions Roiphe asks early in *Generation with Memory.* These concern not only belief in God, identification with other Jews, and the relationship of Jews of the Diaspora to Israel, but also replacements in "the building of the soul" that are available if, by abandoning the synagogue, one leaves the "tight world of one's ancestors." A fifth question, moreover, intrudes (Roiphe deliberately breaks the tradition of the Four Questions by asking it): "Is it possible for a twentieth-century female, educated to have hopes of equality and justice, to accept the traditions of the past that have left her excluded from the law and prevented her from entering the sacred or the Halakah—how can a feminist feel about the Jewish religion?" (18).

In her novels as in her writings, including *A Season of Healing: Reflections on the Holocaust* (Summit Books, 1988), Roiphe has shown how at least one Jewish feminist feels about Judaism—its religion, history, and culture. With unfailing honesty and perseverance she has searched directly and indirectly through her fictional personae for a kind of Jewish identity that will provide satisfactory answers to her Five Questions. If none has so far clearly and firmly emerged, the quest has none the less been worth the effort, and the answer may lie in the searching. Interestingly, in her latest novel, *If You Only Knew Me* (Little, Brown, 1993), she drops almost every aspect of that search and concentrates mainly upon the problems of ordinary human relationships, or rather the difficulties informing a satisfactory human relationship between two lonely people moving into middle age, each having guilt, preoccupations, and more or less set ways. As neither of them is identifiably Jewish, and their problems are basic human problems rather than specifically Jewish ones, perhaps Roiphe has moved on beyond that quest, though to say that she has answered her Five Questions satisfactorily—at least for herself or for the time being—may be more than one can or should suggest.

Notes

1. Anne Roiphe was born in 1935 to Eugene and Blanche Phillips Roth. A third-generation American, she is in many ways typical of assimilated Jews who nevertheless have some experience of Jewish traditions, including religious observances.

2. See Roth's essay "After Eight Books," in *Reading Myself and Others* (New York: Farrar, Straus and Giroux, 1975), 105–13, and my chapter, "The Comedy of Counterlives: *The Counterlife* and *Deception,*" in *Philip Roth Revisited* (New York: Twayne, 1992), 181–201.

3. It would be dangerous to speculate how closely this novel parallels Roiphe's biography—her year in Europe and marriage to the gentile playwright Jack Richardson, their child and subsequent divorce. Though the general outline of events is similar, many details are very likely invented. In her memoir, *Generation without Memory,* Roiphe is almost entirely reticent about her first marriage.

4. Of course Jewish men also are engaging in intermarriage in increasing numbers. They too react against traditional attitudes and beliefs, though not quite the same ones, and like Roiphe's protagonists they seek to find their own Americas, as Philip Roth and other novelists have shown.

5. As Miriyam Glazer notes, not all critics agree with this position. Some, like Evelyn Avery, feel the novel is "deceptive," betraying both points of view. Others believe the novel depends upon a "crude dichotomy between religious and secular worlds." Glazer argues that these critics miss the point of the novel, failing to consider adequately the nonrational parts of her Annie Johnson's experience—her memories and dreams—as well as her intellect. See "Male and Female. King and Queen: The Theological Imagination of Anne Roiphe's *Lovingkindness,*" *Studies in American Jewish Literature* 10 (Spring 1991): 82.

6. Naomi Sokoloff analyzes in penetrating detail the significance of Israeli settings in both Roiphe's novel and Roth's. See "Imagining Israel in American Fiction: Anne Roiphe's *Lovingkindness* and Philip Roth's *The Counterlife,*" *Studies in American Jewish Literature* 10 (Spring 1991): 65–80. Israel is not only "a haven for mixed-up young Americans"; by its geographical distance from New York it also "underscores the spiritual distance between mother and daughter" in Roiphe's novel (71). Furthermore, the conflict between Annie and Andrea/Sarai reflects a similar conflict between secular and religious Jews in Israel, exacerbated by the growing numbers of *haredim,* although Roiphe does not emphasize this aspect of her theme. Instead, by focusing on an Israeli yeshiva instead of an American one, Roiphe "presents a simplified opposition of cultural outlooks" (72). She thus avoids treating many varieties of Jewishness between the extremes represented by Rabbi Cohen on the one hand and Annie Johnson on the other.

7. Carole McKewin Weaver, "Tasting the Stars: The Tales of Rabbi Nachman in Anne Roiphe's *Lovingkindness,*" in *Mother Puzzles: Daughters and Mothers in Contemporary American Literature,* ed. Mickey Pearlman (New York: Greenwood Press, 1989), 131–39.

8. Ibid., 138.

9. The story is identical to that of Roiphe's own great-uncle Max, who was "probably the first Jew from the Lower East Side, whose Yiddish was not yet dead in his mouth, to play polo" (*Generation without Memory,* 123).

Responding to an Old Story: Susan Fromberg Schaeffer, Lesléa Newman, and Francine Prose

Victoria Aarons

"'HE has the power to answer prayers because he writes.'"[1] So avows the protagonist in Susan Fromberg Schaeffer's short story "Homage to Isaac Bashevis Singer," as she fervently anoints Singer as God's "representative on earth": "He had suffered so that he could testify" ("Homage" 302). This aging protagonist, stricken with a fever of unknown origin, an illness that puzzles even the doctors in the hospital—"'We're sending you home next week,'" her doctor resolves, "'before something really happens to you'" ("Homage," 299)—takes the matter into her own hands. She finds, after reading Singer's stories, stories about people who "seemed crazy" but "no crazier than she," that they bring down her temperature, that, in fact, they make her well: "'First, I could do nothing. Now I can do next to nothing," Mrs. Klopstock tells her daughter ("Homage," 301). What she comes to believe in is the talismanic power of storytelling, the healing, curative abilities of the writer, an affirmation not unlike that made by Grace Paley's narrator in the short story "Debts," whose self-imposed sense of responsibility to her family and friends makes it incumbent on her "to tell their stories as simply as possible, in order, you might say, to save a few lives."[2]

Of course, this saving power of storytelling, though a commonplace in Jewish literature since Hebrew Scripture, is not here without its self-reflexive irony, a critical "writer's" eye, finally, that at once evokes the imperative of telling stories and at the same time undercuts their authority by suggesting the opposite—"he testified *so* that he could suffer." Storytelling is a given, a demand made on characters in Jewish fiction just as it is made by them. Storytelling bears witness to the past as well as to present conditions and future possibilities; it is both motive and intention. It provides both the impetus for action, if only the action of talk, and a hoped-for closure, the transferential effect of interaction among characters. And storytelling, however desired, indeed demanded by the characters of themselves and of others, carries the weight of the past, its heaviness and its prolonged grief, an accounting for the specifics of Jewish history, a connection to past events that cannot be exorcised or denied, however seductive that impulse may be. As Lesléa Newman's character Harry, in "A Letter to Harvey Milk," makes clear to the young teacher who wants him to write, to "preserve our history": "'the dead are gone. Talking about them won't bring them back. You want stories, go talk to somebody else. I ain't got no stories.'"[3] Refusing to tell can be a way of bearing witness, too, of bearing witness to the unimaginability of the Holocaust and to the dignity and realistic appraisal with which it must be engaged historically.

But of course, tell stories he finally does. "Stories she wants," Harry implicitly challenges his teacher, who means well but does not quite understand the force of history upon him, does not quite know what she is getting herself (and him) into: "Well, alright, now I'll tell her a story" ("Letter," 334). His consent is uneasy and portentous, suggestive of an acknowledged vulnerability on the part of both storyteller and listener, a vulnerability born of their mutual implication in and commitment to the catastrophic story about to be told. And indeed, the story Harry tells is, for him, a tortuous undertaking. "This is what I never told anyone," he begins ("Letter," 334). It is a story about his friend Izzie, who years ago told Harry a story about an experience he had in the camps, a story in which he reveals the horrors of witnessing the murder of a friend who had been accused of homosexual behavior, an activity not allowed in the camps, where any attempt at compassion and warmth, any human connection and exchange, was brutally denied. Izzie sees in his dying friend, who refuses to tell the authorities that it was, in fact, Izzie with whom he was involved, an emblem of the imperative felt but resisted by Harry: to "tell the world our story" ("Letter," 337). And here, typically, we find a layering or blurring of stories, one story becoming another story: stories within stories within stories, layers or currents of stories that, like history, would quell time. In this fiction, storytelling creates at once a stasis and extenuates time, so that the sharpened, intersecting grafting of past upon present creates an effect that is at once utterly fantastic and utterly real. In this way the authority of both the story and the storyteller gives way to the primacy of the process of telling stories, the collaborative effort among storytellers, dialogues held in the spaces between and among stories within any given narrative. No one person "owns" these stories; they are all part of a larger picture—in this case, the master narrative of the Holocaust and the specter of history repeating itself.

And although this is not directly Harry's story, he relays it to the writing teacher with an obstinacy that at once challenges her request and complies with it on his own terms. He feels committed to the transmission of the story, a complicitous act of futile catharsis made all the more cataclysmic by the suffering replayed in the telling: "I don't sleep so good at night, these stories are like a knife in my heart" ("Letter," 338). Storytelling thus becomes an often unwelcome compulsion, an urgency, a requirement not only for living but for dying as well: "Maybe now that I told, I can die in peace," Harry finally recognizes ("Letter," 338).

Newman's is very much a contemporary story, a story of the late twentieth century. It is a story dedicated to Harvey Milk, the homosexual councilman gunned down in San Francisco, a figure undeniably remote from the shtetl, from the "old country," from the Yiddish of the immigrants, the "boat ride to America" that the writing teacher to the narrator's puzzlement so insistently wants to hear about. And yet Newman's story, with its simultaneous references to past and present, is framed by the desire to know a mysterious past in order to make sense of the present. Harvey Milk, for example, first appears in the story in a flashback, in a fictitious letter written by Harry and addressed to his old friend Harvey, who shares with Harry a matter-of-fact taste for the "old ways"—"a good *kosher* butcher," "a piece of rye bread with *schmaltz.*" Murdered at forty-eight, Harvey was "a *mensh* with a heart of gold, too good for this rotten world. They just weren't ready for you" ("Letter," 328, 333, 327).

The "stories," lived and told—of Harvey Milk, of the young writing teacher, and of Izzie's friend in the camps—all intersect, grafted upon each other by a common history of oppression, acts of persecution that, for Newman's characters, are framed by Judaism as the testatory trope. For it is against the backdrop of Judaism that Barbara, the writing teacher, contextualizes her own sense of persecution, "Mogen David . . . around her neck . . . onto her bookbag an upside-down pink triangle" ("Letter," 325, 334). The connection between the two sources of persecution, viewing the one within the magnitude and historical significance of the other, legitimates Barbara's avowed lesbianism, at least for her: "'My parents haven't spoken to me since I told them I was gay,'" she reveals to Harry. "'How could you do this to us?' they said. I wasn't doing anything to them. I tried to explain I couldn't help being gay, like I couldn't help being a Jew, but that they didn't want to hear. So I haven't spoken to them in eight years'" ("Letter," 331). Judaism, for this character, becomes a symbol, a metaphor for survival, an antidote for the loneliness and isolation she obviously feels: "She has some sadness in her eyes, this teacher. Believe me I've known such sadness in my life, I can recognize it a hundred miles away" ("Letter," 329), acknowledges Harry.

Trying to understand his teacher's preoccupation with Judaism, with an idealized and romantic vision of a past that would seem to provide solace and shared identity, Harry explains her motives as a misunderstanding of the moral and emotional weight of Jewish experience:

> She tells us she wants to collect stories from old Jewish people. . . . She tells us she's learning Yiddish. For what, I wonder. I can't figure this teacher out. . . . Her grandparents won't tell her stories, she says, and she's worried that the Jews her age won't know nothing from the culture, about life in the *shtetls*. . . . She says that's why she wants the old people's stories so much, she doesn't know nothing about her own family history. She wants to know about her own people, maybe write a book. But it's hard to get the people to talk to her, she says, she doesn't understand. ("Letter," 325, 332)

She does not understand why people will not tell her stories about the past because she does not see how horrifying it really is to speak about it. The story thus reveals a gap between the invented past and the incomprehensible past. The writing teacher's desire to know is rivaled only by her inability to understand the difference between the comforts of ethnic identity and the horrors of this particular history, a "story" that, like Harry's notebook, "doesn't have nice stories in it, no love letters, no happy endings for a nice girl like you. A bestseller it ain't, I guarantee" ("Letter," 338). But understanding this difference is the key in the story to revitalizing individual identity for all the characters in terms of a collective Jewish past. Self-discovery will consist not only of knowing "the culture," but also of knowing one's distance from it and being able to see oneself as a Jew despite that distance. As Newman herself puts it, "I come from a long line of immigrants who came to America not by choice.

I don't know what would have happened to my writing if there hadn't been raging anti-Semitism."[4] We find, as a result, an uneasy but determined infusion of the old with the new, stories that embrace, and in doing so either willingly or unwittingly admit the past and carry it into the present.

In Susan Fromberg Schaeffer's "Homage to Isaac Bashevis Singer," a story of an aging protagonist's reprieve from fever by reading the stories of and praying to I. B. Singer, almost imperceptibly gives way to another story, a remembrance of her past: "'I used to make dolls,'" Mrs. Klopstock tells her daughter. "'Not the heads but the bodies. That's how you made them in those days. You bought the heads and hands and feet and made the bodies yourself.'" "'Let's change the subject,' said her daughter," who is both frightened and mesmerized by her mother's story of her unimaginable childhood ("Homage," 302–3). She is frightened because of what her mother's past may reveal about her own fate; she is fascinated by the story, however, because in it she may find the key to her mother's character and thus her own, a discovery she is not at all certain she wants to make.

In these stories, the resistance to telling and the resistance to hearing are overcome by the necessity to tell, the urgency to hear. For in most of the fiction by contemporary American Jewish women writers, stories are told, whether characters intend to or not, or even when characters protest against the value of stories. And the withholding of stories is often viewed as a denial of a common history, a denial that attempts to resist the desperate will to self-formation of an American-born generation.

In, for instance, Lynn Sharon Schwartz's short story "The Opiate of the People," the American-born daughter of Jewish immigrants sees in her father's often angry reticence to comply with her request to tell stories of his childhood a willful holding back of information essential to her sense of herself: "'Would it have cost you so much to tell me some of those things?,'" she demands of her father. "'Would it?'"[5] And, by his own admission, it would have. It would have cost him his tenuous hold on the present in the belief that it is a good enough present, if not to erase the past, at least to repress it. For if he does not maintain his vigilance, his tenacious resistance to the past, he fears an imagination that might return him there, just as it does when for one moment he projects his daughter out of the present and into his own past:

> She said something with a swift dramatic flick of her hand that suddenly brought his mother back to life. David . . . imagined she

was taking on their rough-edged foreign accents as well, her voice falling into a nasal, singsong intonation. He felt a chill: it was as if she were being transformed before his eyes, as if he had delivered her over to the very powers he had been shielding her from all these years, and she was all too willingly drawn in, drawn back. For a split second he glimpsed her not in her stylish silky dress but in heavy shapeless skirts and shawls, a dark scarf wrapped around her shaved head, her fine features coarsened by endless childrearing, scrubbing, cooking, and anxiety. When he blinked the image vanished. ("Opiate," 185)

He wants to eradicate the past, to relegate it to an historical fiction; he wants his children "new, untainted, bred without that ancient history" ("Opiate," 186). The irony is that it is precisely an enabling fiction that his children want, while his willed relegation of his own history to the trashbin of inconvenient fictions renews for his daughter its status as motivating truth. And the father, too, constructs his own "story"; America, the future, is his fiction, just as his daughter's fiction is a romanticized Jewish past. But Schwartz, like other American Jewish women writers, does not romanticize the past; nor does she idealize or sentimentalize traditional Judaism. On the contrary, these writers admit it as they admit the feared loss of identity that complicates one's criticism of the tradition, especially given the feminist concerns of American Jewish women writers. What we find here, more often than not, is a reconciliation of feminism and Judaism, an uneasy match perhaps, but one that is wedded by like concerns, particularly issues of identity, long concerns for both feminists and American Jews, both "immigrants" in the sense of perceived interlopers, claimants of territories institutionally belonging to others and made their own.[6] The self-conscious struggle to change and to bring about change, a struggle of self-transformation, is as fundamental to feminism as it is to at least liberal Judaism.[7]

"A Letter to Harvey Milk," like "Homage to Isaac Bashevis Singer," like any number of stories currently being written by American Jewish women, is a continuing response to an "old story," the attempt to develop new forms of expression to meet the requirements for living in America at the rapidly approaching close of the twentieth century. Lesléa Newman, in "Passover Poem," hears Judaism as a language through which to express her personal sense of difference: "Three years ago I came out as a lesbian / and came home / to my Jewishness. / All of a sudden Yiddish sprang from my lips / like leaves from a barren tree."[8] One form of identity gives root to another that, ironically, precedes it historically. These atemporal forms circle back to the centrality of the voice of the storyteller, of the arduous but no less compelling and compulsive process of telling stories. But this process of dredging up and organizing memory is infused with an interrogatory humor that does not veil the inherent threat, an implicit warning about the events of a tragic Jewish past.

So these stories, unexpected and unlikely conduits to the past, always return there. Peculiarly American stories, stories born of personal and cultural imperatives bearing their own sense of immediacy, end up as multiple contemporary versions of a history of defining Jewish catastrophe. In Newman's "A Letter to Harvey Milk," for example, improbable circumstances lend themselves to a resurgent fictive reenactment of the past in a fragmented, unpredictable present: the narrative frame of the young lesbian writing teacher at the Senior Center leads into the story of the homosexual relationship in the concentration camp. Harvey Milk's murder ("here in America, a man climbs through the window, kills the Mayor of San Francisco, kills Harvey Milk, and a couple years later he's walking around on the street? This I never thought I'd see in my whole life. But from a country that kills the Rosenbergs, I should expect something different?" ["Letter," 326]) provides the opening for the story Harry tells of the murder of the young man whose death can only be seen as a sacrifice for others. And the famous "twinkie" trial in defense of the murderer ("[t]he lawyer, that son of a bitch, said Dan White ate too many Twinkies . . . so his brain wasn't working right. Twinkies, *nu,* I ask you. My kids ate Twinkies when they were little, did they grow up to be murderers, God forbid? And now, do they take the Twinkies down from the shelf, somebody else shouldn't go a little crazy, climb through a window, and shoot somebody? No, they leave them right there next to the cupcakes and the donuts" ["Letter," 326]) underscores an irony not missed by the immigrant, who wants to believe the myth but finally cannot: "Better off we're here in America, the past is past" ("Letter," 325). But not so, we are reminded again and again, if only by the ominous undertones of the stories told, the uneasy understatement with which the stories are admitted into life and become reminders of the past that would be escaped but that repeats itself in a violent, intolerant, and traumatic present.

In this way, the narration in "A Letter to Harvey Milk" takes us back to earlier Jewish fiction; it intermingles humor with pathos. The unabashed astonishment and resigned understatement with which we have come to identify post-World-War-II American Jewish literature define a present unimagined, not only by the Eastern European shtetl Jews, but also by those orators and revolutionaries (as Tillie Olsen describes them in "Tell Me A Riddle"), the "advanced socialists," who come to America in Grace Paley's "The Immigrant Story." But its impassioned telling and ironic movement are remarkably the same. It is a tradition demarcated by characters and narrators who slip into the role of storyteller and who tell the stories of their seemingly ordinary lives, lives given meaning through the talk that extends them and the history that haunts them.

One might well argue that such stories, stories told by characters to narrators, to implied authors, to other characters, stories within stories, ambiguously layered stories, have characterized Jewish literature since Sholom Aleichem's "kleineh mentshele" told his stories to the quietly interested but no less humorously detached writer, Sholom Aleichem: "'Now listen to me,'" begins, in typical form, the narrator of one such story, "'I'll tell you a good one. . . . You'll like it.'"[9] And while we have come to know that such a challenge to the implied listener has an ominous ring to it, we also know that the act of telling stories becomes a communal experience. In Sholom Aleichem's "Baranovich Station," the characteristically manipulative storyteller within the frame story, one of the Jews sitting in the third-class compartment of the train, is cajoled by his fellow passengers to tell a story: "'You want to be asked to tell us a story? All right, we're asking! Tell us what happened . . . we're curious. Only what are you standing for? Why don't you have a seat? There aren't any, you say? Jews! Shove over a bit! Make room please.'"[10] Made the center of attraction and a character within the overall story, the narrator enlists the avid participation of his fellow passengers. For a time, his is the voice of authority; it is he who has a story—"Listen well, my dear friends, because what I'm about to tell you, I want you to know, is not some opera or fairy tale. It's a true story . . ."[11]—that brings with it the ambivalent promise of shared history, a shared sense of a uniformly threatening world.

And it is no less so for the characters who narrate their stories in the fiction of these contemporary American Jewish women writers. What seems to connect the "old" and the "new," the stories of American Jewish women writers such as Susan Fromberg Schaeffer and Lesléa Newman, with the monologues and feuilletons of Sholom Aleichem is the way in which the act of storytelling transforms ordinary life into an extraordinary moment of vision and transformation. In "Homage to Isaac Bashevis Singer," for instance, a story that makes literal the metaphorical transformation of a life through stories, Mrs. Klopstock, "more dead than alive," is miraculously cured, brought back to life, "healed" by the master storyteller himself ("Homage," 300, 302). And even Harry, for instance, the narrator-turned-writer (despite his protestations) in Lesléa Newman's "A Letter to Harvey Milk," is convinced that his ordinary life does not lend itself to the stuff of literature: "The teacher says we should write about our life, everything that happened today. So *nu,* what's there to tell? . . . I get up, I have myself a coffee, a little cottage cheese, half an English muffin. I get dressed. . . . *Nu,* for this somebody should give me a Pulitzer Prize?" ("Letter," 324–25). Thus a narrative metamorphosis takes place as the everyday events of his life give way to stories of an almost unspeakable past. The commonplace, quotidian lives of ordinary characters are reconfigured, reinvented, as authors turn the telling over to their characters, who are able to accommodate authorial unease by being placed into a wider historical context, one that frees them of temporal constraints if only for the dilatory space of a single narrative. It is the story they rely on.

And they rely on storytelling in ways that are both self-defining and defining of experience. Storytelling helps these characters to explain and account for the unbelievable, the seemingly inexplicable conditions of their lives, circumstances beyond their control that inevitably control them. In describing the fiction of Francine Prose, for example, Rena Potok argues that there is a relation between the characteristic layering of stories and the transformation of the ordinary into something else, something remarkable: ". . . stories within stories within stories. . . . replete with the tricks of the teller. . . . stories . . . told, then retracted, retold, then revealed . . . as a detour . . . the fantastic and the marvelous with the utterly mundane . . . conflating the everyday with the illusory."[12] In, for instance, Prose's short story "Electricity," Anita, in the throes of new motherhood and divorce, returns to her parents' home, only to find that the changes in their lives are as dramatic as her own. Her father, a man who in the past "never went to *shul,*" now spends his evenings downstairs in the basement, where he "claps his hands, leaps into the air, and sings hymns in praise of God and the Baal Shem Tov." A "born-again Hasid," protests

Anita's mother: "Only my Sam waits till he's fifty-seven to join a cult."[13] In response to his daughter's confused and suspicious queries, Sam can only tell her a story: "Her father took a deep breath. Then he said: 'Once upon a time, a jeweler was taking the subway home to East Flatbush from his shop on Forty-sixth Street . . .'" ("Electricity," 126). Sam tries to stand outside of the experience, to deflect it. He creates a story in which he becomes his own character, and thus as the "writer" of the story, Sam maintains seeming control over the cultural and historical dissonance that has apparently become his life.

But telling the story in which he refers to himself in the third person as if someone else (a jeweler taking the subway home, who witnesses youths with knives stealing money and jewelry from other passengers on the train, whose thieving is averted by a mysterious flashing of lights, an SOS signal that makes the youths run off the car at the next station) suggests much more than the storyteller's illusive but no less emphatic control over the interpretation of the events of his life. Sam, "head between his knees . . . trying to breathe," enormously relieved by this sudden and unexpected turn of events, is informed by a young Hasidic man who has been watching him that the blinking lights were no miracle; they were, rather, the work of the Hasid, who, after repeating the feat for Sam's benefit, hastens to add that "'It wasn't my doing. Everything is the rebbe's . . .'" ("Electricity," 128). Such events, witnessed by the incredulous but now believing Sam, are, however, all the while reinterpreted by Prose, whose ironic guiding voice directs us toward what we too may not want to see: that telling stories provides only a temporary stay against the inevitable confusions, complications, and isolation of everyday living and dying and against the material circumstances of attenuated Jewish faith.

In making his life a story, the narrating character validates his experience both to himself and others by contextualizing it in a tradition of stories and storytelling, "once upon a time." Essentially he tells us that "this has happened before . . . this will happen again," both the promise and the threat of continuity. He puts his experience in a long line of miracles, of near-disasters witnessed and averted, as a kind of antidote to a history of unmovable disasters. He takes his own personal experience out of its particular time and place, justifying the conditions that have altered the course of his life. After all, he is responding to something beyond him, something that existed before and without him, which, for him, makes the story true.

Like Sholom Aleichem's narrators, who begin their stories with a vow that "it's a true story, I should live so . . . what would I be doing with fiction,"[14] Francine Prose's character, Sam, constructs a story to validate his experience and his choice; as such he is both inside and outside the experience. He does not really understand what happened to him on the subway; he cannot comprehend his own motives in becoming a Hasidic Jew any more than his wife and daughter can. But he can tell a story about it, and the story, the act of storytelling, ironically becomes the link to the tradition that his "conversion" so desperately tries to attain. The story is enough for both Sam and his daughter, who "wanted to ask if his story really happened or if he'd made it up as a metaphor for what happened. She thought: *Something* must have happened. In the old days, her father didn't make up stories" ("Electricity," 128). The irony here is complete: characters who take other characters to task for fictionalizing lives are all the while given "life" themselves because they are fictionally contrived. The veracity of the story, of course, is incidental, beside the point. The story is a metonymy of the need for an enabling originary myth, no less authentic, no less real than the experience itself, since the experience becomes real in the telling, the reenactment of it.

I think this kind of self-validation, a justification of one's emotional responses and actions, really a demand to be heard and acknowledged, finds its roots or is patterned on an earlier tradition—in this case Sholom Aleichem's short stories and monologues of shtetl Jews who relate their tales of disasters and unexpected and unwelcome changes in an attempt to make sense of the catastrophic events of their lives. While in many instances part of the humor is in the overblown, hyperbolic assessment of the events, "catastrophes" brought on by the characters themselves, the feeling that they convey to the writer "Mr. Sholom Aleichem" is no less genuine for it in part because it is rooted in an historical background of very real catastrophe, of marginalization, of persecution, of annihilation.

In a story such as "Hodl," for instance, Tevye the Dairyman relates a story to Sholom Aleichem, a standard opening, in which he tries to make sense of his daughter's defection, her abandonment of the family for a young socialist sent to prison for his revolutionary activities. She will follow her husband, a man she has wed without matchmaker or her father's permission, and in all likelihood will never see her father again. These circumstances are too much for Tevye to bear, too complicated and foreign for him to begin to understand. And so, he reveals to Sholom Aleichem, "I tell her a story."[15]

There is a tradition of characters who become their own authors, in a sense characters who tell the stories of their lives while at the same time believing with absolute certainly in the capacity of the writer to help them (and it is this latter part that seems to me unique to the tradition of Jewish literature). "Isaac Bashevis Singer, save me!", cries Mrs. Klopstock in Susan Fromberg Schaeffer's "Homage to Isaac Bashevis Singer." "She prayed to him continually, out of habit, out of devout belief" ("Homage," 301), we are told, a belief in the storyteller's ability to understand, to identify, to recreate, to mystify, and thus make sense of individual experience. Not surprisingly, then, Mrs. Klopstock begins to write stories herself: "'Writing gives me strength" ("Homage," 302), she tells her daughter, the saving strength of self-expression and self-invention. But these are stories, we must remember, of ordinary suffering, of events unnoticed except in the lives of individual characters and their families and friends, but stories that, as Mrs. Klopstock ominously affirms, "are about something all right" ("Homage," 302).

The reconstruction of an individual life in a self-told story takes it out of the ordinary, magnifies it, making it an articulation of received history and an opportunity for modest transformation, or it becomes a recognition that a transformation has taken place and must be acknowledged. But these reconstitutions do so in a way that is painfully cognizant of shared suffering. In a self-parodic reference to another "old story," Harry, in "A Letter to Harvey Milk," asks, "Why should today be different than any other day?" ("Letter," 324). But it becomes so. The writing, the storytelling, makes the day different, a tenuous form of deliverance. The storytelling takes it out of this particular time and place and connects it to a history of shared suffering (by circumstance or by choice, an empathetically "felt" suffering) and thus a determined perseverance built upon a kind of collective wisdom and collective good humor in the face of misfortune, the seemingly impossible, the unpredictable, even the ridiculous.

This created community of memory depends upon a coming-to-terms with the past, a past that by necessity is comprised of the ethical choices and circumstances of others, choices that determine possibilities for the future. But they also set limitations, patterns that inevitably design and shape the future. In this way memory is not private. Experiences and portraits are only validated by making them public, by giving life to those individuals who constitute the fabric of the extendable historical community, a community currently being both rediscovered and redefined by contemporary Jewish American women writers.

NOTES

1. Susan Fromberg Schaeffer, "Homage to Isaac Bashevis Singer," in *America and I: Short Stories by American Jewish Women Writers,* ed. Joyce Antler (Boston: Beacon Press, 1990), 302. Subsequent references are from this edition, identified as "Homage" in the text.

2. Grace Paley, "Debts," in *Enormous Changes at the Last Minute* (1960; reprint, New York: Farrar, Straus and Giroux, 1983), 10.

3. Lesiéa Newman, "A Letter to Harvey Milk," in *"America and I,"* 332. Subsequent references are from this edition, identified as "Letter" in the text.

4. Gail Koplow, "Lesléa Newman: Writing from the Heart," *Sojourner* (August 1989): 8A.

5. Lynne Sharon Schwartz, "The Opiate of the People," in *Acquainted with the Night and Other Stories* (New York: Harper and Row, 1984), 188. Subsequent references are from this edition, identified as "Opiate" in the text.

6. Whether implicit or explicit, such a coupling is characteristic in much of the literature by Jewish women writers, for instance, Edna Ferber's "The Girl Who Went Right" or Anzia Yezierska's "America and I."

7. See, for example, Grace Paley's short story "Friends," in which her recurring character, Faith, refers to "an old discussion about feminism and Judaism" by insisting that "on the prism of isms, both of those do have to be looked at together once in a while," the one refracted through and in the other, both occasions in Paley's fiction for interpretive possibilities for self-expression. See also Victoria Aarons, "'The Tune of the Language': An Interview with Grace Paley," in which Paley comments on the relation between Judaism and feminism, how both inform her writing and her commitment to reform (*Studies in American Jewish Literature* 12 [1993]: 50–61).

8. Lesléa Newman, "Passover Poem," in *Love Me Like You Mean It* (Santa Cruz: HerBooks, 1987), 74.

9. Sholom Aleichem, "The Search," trans. Norbert Guterman, in *A Treasury of Yiddish Stories,* ed. Irving Howe and Eliezer Greenberg (New York: Schocken 1973), 182.

10. Sholom Aleichem, "Baranovich Station," in *Tevye the Dairyman and The Railroad Stories,* trans. Hillel Halkin (New York: Schocken, 1987), 153.

11. Ibid.

12. Rena Potok, "Francine Prose," in *Jewish American Women Writers: A Bio-Bibliographical and Critical Sourcebook* ed. Ann R. Shapiro, Sara R. Horowitz, Ellen Schiff, and Miriyam Glazer (Westport: Conn.: Greenwood Press, 1994), 308.

13. Francine Prose, "Electricity," in *Women and Children First* (New York: Pantheon, 1988), 122–23. Subsequent references are from this edition.

14. Sholom Aleichem, "On Account of a Hat," trans. Isaac Rosenfeld, in *Selected Stories of Sholom Aleichem,* ed. Alfred Kazin (New York: Modern Library, 1956), 4.

15. Sholom Aleichem, "Hodel," in *Tevye the Dairyman and The Railroad Stories,* trans. Hillel Halkin, 67.

Erica Jong: Becoming a Jewish Writer

Charlotte Templin

In a chapter entitled "How I Got to Be Jewish" in her book *Fear of Fifty: A Midlife Memoir,* Erica Jong writes, "The older we get, the more Jewish we become in my family."[1] The notion that one can become Jewish is somewhat paradoxical, but Jong goes on to describe how such an evolution comes about. Jong recounts a very secular upbringing, claiming a Communist grandfather on the maternal side. (Jong thus links herself to a strand of Jewish heritage important in this country.) Her parents were Seymour Mann (born Samuel Weisman), the son of Polish Jews with a German name, and Edith Mirsky, the daughter of Russian Jews from England, where Edith was born. (Edith was born Yehudit but became Edith as a result of the intervention of a clerk in the English registry office.) Seymour and Edith were married in city hall and raised a family of daughters who "never belonged to a synagogue or had bat mitzvahs" (59).

Jong's upbringing was secular. If there was a religion, it was devotion to the arts: painting and literature. For a time Jong aspired to be an artist like her maternal grandfather (a portrait painter and commercial artist) and her mother (who sacrificed her career to raise a family). Her father was a musician who played in resorts and for weddings before he gave up show business for a more secure career in business (the *tchotchke,* or gift wares, business). Jong attended the High School of Music and Art in New York City. As we know, she gave up painting for poetry and then the novel. (But she is writing poetry again now.)

In Jong's work we can trace a steady progress toward the discovery and acceptance of her Jewish identity, from realizing her Jewishness during her years in Heidelberg in early adulthood (described fictionally by the protagonist of *Fear of Flying,* in poems written during this time, and in *Fear of Fifty*) to her lament in *Fear of Fifty:*

> After fifty, I began to question my ambivalent relationship to my Jewish identity and the unexamined assimilationism I have written

> about earlier. It seems astonishing to me that a woman born at the height of the Holocaust should not have been trained to a stronger sense of Judaism. And I also began to regret not having raised Molly [Jong's daughter] more Jewishly, and not having had more Jewish children to replace those lost among the six million. Lately I have begun to yearn for solidarity with other Jewish feminists, to join the search for nonsexist Jewish rituals, to celebrate my Jewishness without shame, without internalized anti-Semitism, and to embrace my Jewishness as part of my search for truth in my writing. In this I have been inspired by African-American and Asian-American writers who have already overcome the false assimilationist stance. As a secular Jew, I will have to *invent* a heritage as much as rediscover it. For the first time, I am willing. My heart is open. (301)

There may be an even more marked Jewish character to Jong's future work. She stated at the panel on *Fear of Flying* at the Modern Language Association annual meeting in 1994 that she is working on a novel that has significant Jewish content.

Jong's relation to Judaism is similar to that of many Jewish women of her generation. Batya Bauman says in "Women-identified Women in Male-identified Judaism" (part of Susannah Heschel's collection *On Being a Jewish Feminist*) that it would seem entirely reasonable for Jewish women to abjure the self-negating (for women) structure of Judaism. She concedes, however, that even after the Jewish woman has fully grasped the position of women in Judaism, it is difficult to separate herself from Jewish tradition and community: "We feel that we are a link in Jewish history, a history in which so many women as well as men have suffered and died just because they were Jews and in order to remain Jews."[2] Noting especially the terrible sufferings of Jews in this century and the rebirth of Israel, Bauman asks, "How can we, after all that has come before us, break the chain? And, we do not want to stop being Jews."[3]

Jong illustrates another phenomenon noted by Bauman, who points out that as feminists Jewish women carry on important Jewish traditions of activism in the cause of freedom and justice. Carolyn Heilbrun agrees that feminism has been fostered by Jewish traditions. She writes in *Becoming Woman:* "To be a feminist one had to have an experience of being an outsider more extreme than merely being a woman. . . . Having been a Jew, however unobserved that identification was, however fiercely I had denied the adamant anti-Semitism all around me as I grew up—still having been a Jew had made me an outsider. It has permitted me to be a feminist."[4] When Jong came to be seen as the representative American feminist of the 1970s because of the popularity—or notoriety—of *Fear of Flying,* little was said about how her outsider status as a Jew enabled and facilitated her feminism, but that such was the case seems beyond doubt. Ted Solotaroff has noted that for American writers of this century, "their American rather than their Jewish interests were much more evident."[5] This could certainly be said of Jong, and it could also be said that her feminism is more evident than her Jewishness. Nevertheless, the amalgamation of all these identities—American, feminist, and Jew—may be the key to understanding Jong's work.

Though Jong's progressive embracing of her Jewish identity is a subject I will discuss in some detail, in some ways her writing has been informed by her Jewishness from the beginning. Certainly she has taken the life of the Jewish woman in the assimilated Jewish family as her subject. Though in some of her novels Jong's protagonists are not Jewish, most often they are, a factor that plays an important part in the story. Such is the case with the three Isadora novels—*Fear of Flying, How to Save Your Own Life,* and *Parachutes & Kisses*—and Jong's most recently published novel, *Any Woman's Blues.* Two other novels (*Fanny* and *Serenissima*) have gentile protagonists though *Serenissima* marks a stage of increased attention to Jewish content since the heroine, Jessica (a thorough WASP), time-travels to the Venetian ghetto of Shakespeare's day and becomes Shylock's daughter.[6]

In her novels Jong explores growing up and living one's life in American society within a secular Jewish family, but without making Jewishness her exclusive focus. In Jong's portrait of American society—and of a woman struggling to find a place in it—she has not had an axe to grind about American Jews. Norma Rosen's uneasiness about the negative images of Jews that pervade Jewish books was not provoked by Jong's novels.[7] Jong makes comedy of the full range of human experiences; she does not single out Jews for negative treatment. Often her main characters are Jews, but it could never be said of her, as Norma Rosen has said of some Jewish writers, that in portraying Americans as Jews they inadvertently suggested that "the faults of Americans or human beings in general were exclusively the faults of Jews."[8] In his well-known review of *Fear of Flying* John Updike comments, as others have done, on Jong's treatment of the "family slapstick of growing up," finding universal themes in the novel.[9]

Jong has not taken Arthur Miller's tack of refusing to use Jewish characters in her books because of the fear that faults he attributed to Jewish characters would somehow strengthen the forces of anti-Semitism.[10] Nor could Jong be classed with Philip Roth, whose candidly satiric portrait of Jews has sometimes been seen as exploitation or betrayal of his Jewish heritage. Jong has painted a canvas that is evenhandedly clear-sighted about Jews and non-Jews and that makes jokes about the failings and absurdities of both groups without losing sympathy for flawed humanity. This is not to say that Jong does not present some hilarious comedy around Jewish material—including Isadora's family, the White clan. Isadora's mother, while clearly Jewish, defies stereotypes à la *Portnoy's Complaint*. Brilliantly artistic, she turns her talents to nurturing daughters who are "not ordinary." Rebelling against—and loving—such a mother provides some of the warmest comedy in the novel. Isadora's sisters' marriages to non-Jews—one to an Arab and one to an African American who is more WASP than many WASPS—allow comic treatment of social climbing and chasing the dream of wealth and success.

Affectionate satire on psychoanalysts (practitioners of "the Jewish science") is one of the trademarks of *Fear of Flying,* much of which is set in Vienna during a psychoanalytic conference. On the whole the novel's satire is fairly distributed between Jews, including aspiring conductor Charlie Fielding, the heir of millions who lived on a trust fund created by a father who had "amputated half his nose" (217); and non-Jews, including Isadora's best friend at the age of five—an Episcopalian whose mother had told her that Jews "make wee-wee in the bath water" (53). In *Fear of Flying* Jong is not foregrounding the Jew so much as she is foregrounding women as second-class citizens. Her harshest satire is reserved for those who belittle and abuse women.

When one begins to look at Jong as a Jewish writer, evidence crops up everywhere. Certainly the fact that Jong has excelled in the comic mode is fitting for a Jewish writer. The antiheroic bias of comedy has attracted many Jews. Perhaps even more important evidence is that Jong comes from a culture that highly values the word and the book. "To sit at the feet of a sage is the act of a Jew," writes Bernard Sherman."[11] Jong's admiration for writers and intellectuals is evident in her abundant literary allusions and massive use of quotation. She is highly knowledgeable about such writers as Sartre, Neruda, Flaubert, Shelley, Byron, and many others. Jong majored in English at Barnard (where she was elected to Phi Beta Kappa) and went on to do graduate work in eighteenth-century literature at Columbia. She did intensive research for her imitation eighteenth-century novel, *Fanny,* and for *Serenissima,* set in part in sixteenth-century Venice.

Jong's tendency to use abundant quotation is part of her style and marks her work as aspiring to high-culture status. This device has often been harshly criticized, however. Of the many reviewers who have called attention to Jong's use of literary allusions and her many quotations, some have indicated that they find such devices inappropriate in novels that deal with sexuality and the body.[12] In a 1975 article entitled "The Writer as Sexual Show-Off: Or, Making Press Agents Unnecessary," Alfred Kazin criticizes Jong (along with Norman Mailer and Gore Vidal) as writers who use a sexual confessional mode for self-promotion. While Kazin suggests that Mailer, however shallow his work has become, began with promise as a writer and that Vidal is a "natural entertainer"—they are "pros with a respect for the intricacies of narrative"—he sees no redeeming qualities in Erica Jong, "as commonplace a mind as ever appeared on the best-seller lists, but a woman novelist who obviously speaks for all the oppressed women writers in this country." Kazin finds Jong vulgar and is incensed that she would employ voluminous literary quotation: "From now on, English majors will be able to give a high-class flavor to sexual reminiscences," he writes.[13] In a review of *Parachutes & Kisses,* a novel written twelve years later, Herbert Mitgang has a similar reaction. He counts the literary allusions, listing by name thirty-one authors cited by Jong and suggesting that such plentiful allusion is ridiculous, a form of name-dropping. Mitgang, who also criticizes the section of the novel dealing with the protagonist's search for her grandfather's spirit in Russia, says that the "philosophizing" does not belong in a category of fiction he has formulated: the humorous "raunchy" novel." According to Mitgang, Jong should forget the literary allusions and the discussion of ideas and stick to writing sexual fiction.[14] Another reviewer, Victoria Glendinning, remarks that Jong "scatters the names of major authors across the pages like referees."[15]

What grates on these reviewers is the use of literary allusions in the sexual fiction that is Jong's métier. As Henry Miller commented in a 17 August 1975 joint appearance with Jong on CBS's "Sixty Minutes," Jong did for women what he had done for men.

Jong liberated women writers to write freely about sex and the body, as he had done for male writers. In claiming sexuality for women, Jong followed in the path of Jewish forbears. C. Beth Burch traces the theme of sexuality in the writing of Jewish women to Emma Goldman (a woman Jong greatly admires), who listed her lovers and described her passion for them in her *Living My Life* (1931). Burch writes that "Jewish women are unashamed of and believe themselves entitled to sexual pleasure by virtue of Jewish law," while being further encouraged by the American notion of freedom.[16] Jong was not alone in her generation of women writers in choosing sexual fiction. Others, including Alix Kates-Shulman *(Memoirs of an Ex-prom Queen),* had done so before her. As Burch points out, Jewish lesbian writers (such as Adrienne Rich and Irena Klepfisz) have also explored sexuality and sexual choices.

Jong joined the fictional exploration of intellectual life and the life of the body and thereby provoked the attacks noted above. However, we should note that one group of readers welcomed the creation of a heroine who is both intellectual and sexual. Among the reviewers of *Fear of Flying,* feminists were the only ones who noticed that the protagonist of the novel is a poet. Molly Haskell, who wrote one of the most appreciative reviews of *Fear of Flying,* likes the wit and intelligence of the protagonist and notes with approval the sexual content of the novel, interpreting Jong's blunt sexual language as a parody of the language of pornography.[17] Judith Martin, the syndicated "Miss Manners," imitates the pseudo eighteenth-century language of Jong's novel *Fanny Hackabout Jones* in a review in the *Washington Post Book World.* Martin approves of Jong's Fanny because she has a "lusty Appetite," but also approves of the fact that "'tis not the whole of her." She is also a person of "Learning, Courage, Kindness, Wit, and good Chear."[18] Grace Lichtenstein, who reviewed *Parachutes & Kisses,* likes the balancing of "four-letter words with five-syllable ones."[19] In these reviewers some Jewish men are critical of Jong and some Jewish women approve of her (though there have also been Jewish men and women in the opposite camps).[20]

Jong came on the scene after the work of adjustment and adaptation of the first generations of Jews in America had been done. It was left for Jong and others of her generation to deal with the question of what it means to be Jewish—and a woman—in a secular world, specifically in America in the late twentieth century. If early in her career Jong did not make Jewishness her central concern, she discovered that the Jew will be taught by her culture that she is a Jew. Jong may have seemed the all-American blonde beauty when she started out as a poet and novelist in the late 1960s and early 1970s, but she quickly learned from the reviewers and journalists who spoke for the culture that she is a Jew. Vilified herself, she began to identify with the group that had been the subject of persecution. In *Fear of Fifty* Jong quotes Jean Paul Sartre's remark that one is created a Jew by anti-Semitism: "Jews are made by the existence of anti-Semitism—or so said Jean-Paul Sartre, who knew."[21]

As a matter of significant fact, many of Jong's first reviewers mention her Jewishness; hence it seems safe to assume it was a factor in her reception. Sometimes reviewers mention that there are numerous novels by and about Jewish women. Perhaps such references are not entirely innocent: one never hears the phrase "Here's another novel by a gentile or a Protestant." Daphne Patai has coined the term *surplus visibility* for the quality that makes members of a minority group particularly noticeable and casts them as representatives of the group. To Patai, *surplus visibility* is related to a lack of positive values associated with minorities and thus to their invisibility in circles of power and authority. Invisibility leads to heightened visibility when a member of one of these groups is noticed. A cheating stockbroker with a WASP pedigree may escape public scrutiny, while one with a Jewish name is sure to be noticed. A member of a minority is always viewed not as an individual but as a member of that group. Thus when one member of a minority is noticed, all of them are seen as taking over.[22]

One of the most appalling reviews Jong received was from D. Keith Mano in the *National Review*. The review is of Jong's second novel, *How to Save Your Own Life*.[23] This novel was generally negatively reviewed as a kind of backlash against the success of *Fear of Flying*—and as a backlash against feminism. Jong was frequently attacked as a stand-in for feminism at this time and in later years as well. (Mano says, for example, that Jong "has managed to make being a Ms. a big mistake.") Mano's review begins with a reference to Jong's Jewishness:

> I'm treed; it irks me no end. I have to—have to—ravage Erica Jong's new book. Irksome, because this is just what Erica wanted all along: the barracuda treatment. I mean, a man and a gentile blitzing her: oh pogromville and joy. . . . She'll relish this flop the way Al Goldstein secretly relishes going to Leavenworth for public lewd-

> ness. Discipline is love; American society has been too permissive. Erica, I love you. *How to Save Your Own Life* is Christ-awful. An aphid could have written it.

Mano, a novelist and contributing editor for the *National Review,* does not like Jong's subject matter: her treatment of the institution of marriage and her assertive sexuality. There are several points of interest in the review: the references to Jong's Jewishness, the idea that Jong will like being attacked, the repudiation of an active female sexuality, and the violence of the language. (Mano comments, "If I were Mr. Jong I would have decked her long ago, or gotten out a Tong contract.") This review may give us some insight into Jong's reference to having learned through experience what it means to be Jewish.[24]

Anti-Semitic overtones appear in the denigration of the persona in the Jong novel—usually seen as representing Jong herself—as a species of Jewish American Princess: a spoiled, self-centered, pleasure-seeking woman, rich but without taste, and dominated by her physicality. In an article in *Humor: International Journal of Humor Research,* Gary Spencer reports a very negative characterization of the so-called Jewish American Princess (JAP) on college campuses. She is a "loud, aggressive, whining, self-absorbed, materialistic, shallow, gaudy, clannish, nouveau riche bitch."[25] Spencer, who did a survey of student opinion, believes that the word "bitch" added at the end has the effect of masking the anti-Semitism, disguising it as mere sexism, which most students find socially acceptable. Of course the JAP is not associated with intelligence. It makes no difference to the students what her IQ is; she's still a JAP. Spencer's list of adjectives is reminiscent of the descriptions of Jong's persona or personae—and often of Jong herself—by a number of reviewers. The fact that the person—usually the Isadora character—has a tendency to align herself with high culture and a literary tradition calls more scorn upon her head from certain reviewers.[26] In a *Washington Post Book World* review of *How to Save Your Own Life,* Isa Kapp describes Isadora: "Clearly her cardinal sin, and the author's, is Gluttony—for food, fame, flattery, gratification. . . ."[27] Another reviewer, Maureen Freely, gives us the following description of Jessica Pruitt of *Serenissima:*

> She spends the first 100 pages strutting around the Excelsior in Zandra Rhode's ballgown and futuristic Thierry Mugler jumpsuit "absolutely festooned with zippers," alternately spurning and yielding to mercurial men with mesmeric gazes.

> But despite the obvious pleasure she takes in designer art, hotel furniture, real champagne, and very important people, all is not well with Jessica the private person.[28]

It is not surprising that Jong began to make wry jokes about anti-Semitism in her novels. *Any Woman's Blues* has the following exchange between protagonist Leila Sand and her (gentile) boyfriend's father during a dinner conversation in which the elder man has been discussing his own ability to triple sums of money by shrewd investments:

> "Jews never got rich worrying about good taste," said Mr. Donegal. He looked at me. "I mean," he said, "Hebrews."
> "'Jews' is not a dirty word, Mr. Donegal," I said. (43)

I detect in this exchange a different tonality—a more biting satirical edge—than in the jokes about anti-Semitism in *Fear of Flying,* which mainly concern Adrian Goodlove's comments on how he finds Jewish girls sexy.

Jong meditates on Jewishness and anti-Semitism in *Fear of Fifty.* Summarizing her own history, she writes:

> A woman poet *is* a hunted Jew, eternally the outsider. She is asked at first to disguise her sex, change her name, blend into the approved poetry of male supremacy. People who suffer discrimination make up new names, bleach their skin, bob their noses, deny who they are in order to survive. That was, I realized, what I had done in college and graduate school. (100)

In her midlife memoir, Jong speaks frankly and fully of her realization of her own Jewishness. She tells how this came about in Germany, where she went with her second husband, psychologist Allan Jong, who was drafted and sent to Heidelberg in 1966. In Heidelberg, Jong dug deep within herself and discovered the identity—woman and Jew—that enabled her to become a writer. As she read the poetry quarterlies and discovered Sylvia Plath and Anne Sexton, her own voice began to emerge. She was also exploring the Nazi past in books and in landmarks around Heidelberg. In *Fear of Flying,* Jong describes how Isadora suddenly began to feel profoundly Jewish and extremely paranoid as soon as she arrived in Heidelberg:

> Suddenly, people on buses were going home to houses where they treasured clever little collections of gold teeth and wedding rings. . . .

> The lampshades in the Hotel Europa were suspiciously finely grained. . . . The soap in the restroom of the Silberner Hirsch smelled funny." (55)

As Isadora penetrates more deeply into the history of the Third Reich, she realizes that any protestation that she is not a Jew but an agnostic or a "pantheist" would not save her from anti-Semitism.

In one of the early poems, "By Train from Berlin," published for the first time in *Becoming Light: Poems, New and Selected,*[29] the speaker is riding in a train with an American G.I., who speaks of the cheapness of life in Asia (presumably in reference to the Viet Nam War). As they pull beside an old car with the letters "Reichsbahn" on its side, the speaker has an instinctive reaction:

> Thirty years sheer away leaving bare cliff.
>
> This is a country I don't recognize.
> Bone-pale girls who have nothing to do with home.
> Everyone's taller than me, everyone's naked.
> "Life's cheap there," he says.
>
> But why are we screaming over a track
> which runs between a barbed wire corridor?
> And why has it grown so dark outside,
> so bright in here
>
> that even the pared moon is invisible?
>
> In the window we can only see ourselves,
> America we carry with us,
> two scared people talking death
> on a train which can't stop.
>
> (80)

In her next novel, *Parachutes & Kisses,* Jong delves into her Jewish heritage once more, this time on a more personal level as she writes a fictional reminiscence of her grandfather's death. Isadora honors her painter grandfather for his devotion to art and Western culture. Toward the end of the novel she goes to Russia with a delegation of writers who have been invited to a conference in Kiev. She visits Babi Yar and mourns the deaths of Jews. She visits Odessa, "the most Jewish city in Russia," and the home of her grandfather in his youth, searching for "the spirit of the place, the *Geist,* the breath of the Black Sea air which her grandfather had breathed into her own lungs" (449). In the night she feels the spirit of her grandfather near her, and "She understood that she was not Russian, but American, and that she was rooted not in Odessa, but in her own soul" (457).

Jong's fifth novel, *Serenissima,* marks an important stage in her relation to being Jewish. Here Jong moves beyond the concern with her vulnerability as a Jew to an exploration of the inner life of a Jew and a Jewish community, albeit one of sixteenth-century Jews in the Venetian ghetto. Jong writes in *Fear of Fifty* of her long-standing love of Venice. Visiting Venice in 1983, she began to research the ghetto. In the later novel, Jong created a twentieth-century WASP woman who becomes a Jewish woman of the sixteenth century. Jessica Pruitt is an actress who has come to Venice for the Film Festival and in anticipation of playing the role of Shakespeare's Jessica in a movie to be directed by a famous Swedish director. While suffering from the flu, she is transported to the sixteenth century. Jong evokes the sights and sounds—and smells—of old Venice: the synagogue, the market, the costumes of the day, including the red hat that Jews were forced to wear. She creates a convincing character in Shalach, Jessica's father. Shades of Shakespeare's *The Merchant of Venice* (still to be written, according to the date of the fictional setting) begin to emerge. Will appears—drawn to the ghetto to pawn a silver mirror—and falls in love with Jessica.

Jong uses a sizeable chunk of the history of the Jews in Venice, evoking their pride and love for the city and their people. We learn that Jessica's mother's family is as old as the doge's. The threats that hang over Jews are dramatized: expulsion, being walled up in the ghetto, having their children stolen and baptized.

Jessica inhabits two minds and bodies at once, made easier by her theatrical training: "To hold two characters in my mind at once, one's self and one's not-self, this is my art" (258). For the author it can be seen as an exercise in discovering one's Jewish identity, while also asserting the universality of human life. Jessica and Will flee in an attempt to save the life of a Christian baby born in a convent and thus threatened with death to protect the reputation of the convent, and deliver him to a Jewish couple to be circumcised and raised as a Jew. It is at this point that Jessica must answer a question about her identity. Asked if she is a Jew, she hesitates:

> I swear I don't know what to answer. Jew, Christian, man, woman—what am I truly? Just one burning human soul, one flame, one puff of white smoke—who wears different disguises in different times—seeking to ascend to heaven. And yet, if it is most difficult of all things on this earth to be (and most perilous), then I shall choose to be a Jew. For a Jew is one who goes willingly into the flames rather than renounce her burning faith, and such heroism would I choose.
>
> "I am a Jew," I say, pleased enough with the words to repeat them. "I am a Jew," I reiterate, "and my friend is a poet." (290)

Throughout this novel, Jong's admiration—even adoration—of Shakespeare is evident. It is clear that she wants to associate herself with the tradition of high art and great beauty that Shakespeare represents for her. At one point Jessica remarks: "If only I could bring my world and Will's together! That he might know my Antonia [Jessica's daughter]—and I might know his babes as well. Perhaps I could save Hamlet's life were *I* his mother!" (340). Let me note here also that Shakespeare is portrayed as having transcended his Englishness (while also asserting it). He is powerfully drawn to Jessica, and he supports her attempt to save the infant by providing him with Jewish parents. Jong also shows that Shakespeare reveals a unique understanding of the Jew through his portrayal of Shylock in *The Merchant of Venice:* "Oh, dear Will Shakespeare, when he finally came to write his Jewish play, was unerring about Shylock! For all his grumbling and bitterness, he remains the most interesting character in the story—a tragic hero like Lear, a great soul despite his defects" (361–62).

An important theme for Jong in this novel is the search for identity that acknowledges Jewish roots, joined with allegiance to an idea of worth and beauty that is not Jewish—presumably universal but also gentile in this example. How does one embrace Jewishness and transcend it at the same time? That is at the heart of *Serenissima,* and it is, in some sense, the burden of the Jew in the secular world and in America.

Much of *Fear of Fifty* explores what it means to be a Jew in America. In this role one must appear American enough to throw persecutors off the scent. All Americans are obsessed with defining identity, Jong says, but Jews are even more obsessed. Jong writes convincingly about the problem of class for the American Jew. Born Jewish, one cannot be an Episcopalian WASP. One cannot have the unquestioned acceptance reserved for the descendants of those who came over on the Mayflower.

Jong believes that it is the desire to find a class that made her a writer:

> Do you ever wonder why Jews are such relentless scribes? You may have thought it was because we are people of the book. You may have thought it was because we come from homes where reading was stressed. You may have thought it was repressed sexuality. All that is true. But I submit the *real* reason is our need to constantly define our class. By writing, we reinvent ourselves. By writing we create pedigrees. (67)

Celebrity becomes a way to achieve distinction in a society that has closed off certain other ways. The search for identity and class sums up much about Jong as a writer. It is an interesting fact that Jong largely welcomed her celebrity status. Of course, she did not welcome the attacks that necessarily come with fame, and she probably knows better than anyone the ways in which celebrity is meaningless. She discusses her views in an interview:

> In a society that recognizes only three ways of treating people—routine contempt (this is reserved for most of us, the unfamous), fawning adulation alternating with savage attacks (these two treatments are applied to the famous, in turn, like hot and cold compresses)—being famous requires the hide of an elephant, the studied indifference of a Zen Master. . . . In fact, I hate both words "success" *and* "failure," because both states come down to precisely the same thing in the end and are virtually interchangeable.[30]

On the other hand, Jong has welcomed fame and its monetary rewards because it has also brought freedom.[31] Celebrity and fame have given Jong a clear sense of who she is, as well as providing her a public voice. They have conferred a status of importance.[32]

Jong is woman, Jew, American. The realization of her place in the world as a female gave the first impetus to her writing. A search for her identity as a Jew became an integral part of her writing, and the self-knowledge she has gained of herself as an American Jew is a sign of the maturity she has reached in her exploration of who she is.

Notes

1. New York: HarperCollins, 1994, 59. All subsequent quotations are from this edition and will be cited parenthetically in the text.

2. Batya Bauman, "Women-identified Women in Male-identified Judaism," in *On Being a Jewish Feminist: A Reader*, ed. Susannah Heschel (New York: Schocken, 1983), 94.

3. Ibid. Anne Roiphe's *Generation without Memory: A Jewish Journey in Christian America* (New York: Simon and Schuster, 1981) explores the same problem: how to embrace Jewish identity in America as a nonobservant Jew. Roiphe's account is a more anguished discussion of loss than Jong's.

4. Quoted in Susannah Heschel, "Forging New Identities," in her *On Being a Jewish Feminist*, 117–18.

5. Ted Solotaroff, "Marginality Revisited," in *The Writer in the Jewish Community: An Israeli-American Dialogue*, ed. Richard Siegel and Tamar Sofer (Rutherford, N.J.: Fairleigh Dickinson University Press, 1993), 60.

6. *Fear of Flying* (New York: Holt, Rinehart and Winston, 1973); *How to Save Your Own Life* (New York: Holt, Rinehart and Winston, 1977); *Parachutes & Kisses* (New York: New American Library, 1984); *Any Woman's Blues* (New York: Harper and Row, 1990); *Fanny: Being the True History of the Adventures of Fanny Hackabout-Jones* (New York: New American Library, 1980); *Serenissima: A Novel of Venice* (Boston: Houghton Mifflin, 1987).

7. Norma Rosen, "The Literature of Contempt," in her *Accidents of Influence: Writing as a Woman and a Jew in America* (Albany: SUNY Press, 1992), 41–46.

8. Rosen, *Accidents of Influence*, 7.

9. John Updike, "Jong Love," review of *Fear of Flying*, by Erica Jong, *New Yorker*, 17 December 1973, 149.

10. Rosen, *Accidents of Influence*, 7.

11. Bernard Sherman, *The Invention of the Jew: Jewish-American Education Novels* (New York: T. Yoseloff, 1969), 143.

12. My *Feminism and the Politics of Literary Reputation: The Example of Erica Jong* (Lawrence: University Press of Kansas, 1995) analyzes the production of literary reputation, using Jong as a case study. The work contains an extended analysis of Jong's reception and reputation and cites numerous book reviews.

13. *New York*, 9 June 1975, 36–40.

14. "Books of the Times," review of *Parachutes & Kisses*, by Erica Jong, *New York Times*, 10 October 1984, C23.

15. "Dreams of Fair Women," review of *Serenissima*, by Erica Jong (and other novels), *(London) Sunday Times*, 25 November 1984, 42. See also the review of *Fanny* by playwright James Goldman in the *Chicago Tribune Book World*, "Jong's *Fanny*: A Heroine Too Far Ahead of Her Time," 10 August 1980, 1.

16. C. Beth Burch, "Jewish-American Writing: Fiction," in *The Oxford Companion to Women's Writing in the United States*, ed. Cathy Davidson and Linda Wagner-Martin (New York: Oxford University Press, 1995), 441.

17. Molly Haskell, review of *Fear of Flying*, in *Village Voice Literary Supplement*, 22 November 1973, 27. Susan Rubin Suleiman makes much the same point in "(Re)Writing the Female Body: The Politics and Poetics of Female Eroticism" in her important book, *The Female Body in Western Culture: Contemporary Perspectives* (Cambridge: Harvard University Press, 1985), 7–29. Calling attention to the element of parody in *Fear of Flying*, she writes: "what is involved here is a reversal of roles *and* of language, in which the docile and/or bestial but always silent, objectified woman of male pornographic fiction

suddenly usurps both the pornographer's language and his way of looking at the opposite sex" (9).

18. Judith Martin, "The Pleasure of Her Company," review of *Fanny,* by Erica Jong, *Washington Post Book World,* 17 August 1980, 4.

19. Grace Lichtenstein, "Fear of Landing," review of *Parachutes & Kisses,* by Erica Jong, *Washington Post Book World,* 21 October 1984, 9.

20. Jong comments about the attitude of Jewish men to Jewish women writers in *Fear of Fifty:* "Sexism is practiced perhaps most fiercely by Jewish intellectual men who chronically suffer from the Annie Hall syndrome. And, curiously, the literary discrimination against Jewish women has gotten worse, not better, in the last few decades" (79).

21. *Fear of Fifty,* 60. Anne Roiphe and others have identified anti-Semitism as one of the forces that have worked to preserve Jewish community and tradition. Roiphe writes: "A double force has preserved Jewry. The isolating marks of Jewish life . . . together with the brutality and viciousness of the peoples of the non-Jewish world . . ." (*Generation without Memory,* 39).

22. See Patai's article "The View from Elsewhere: Utopian Construction of Difference" in *"Turning the Century": Feminist Theory in the 1990s,* ed. Glynis Carr (Lewisburg, Penn.: Bucknell University Press, 1992), 132–50.

23. D. Keith Mano, "The Authoress as Aphid," review of *How to Save Your Own Life,* by Erica Jong, *National Review,* 29 April 1977, 498.

24. Interestingly, Jong and Mano were in college together, he at Columbia and she at Barnard. Jong reports that they knew each other slightly since they both frequented literary circles. In the early 1970s, Mano took on the role of denouncing the women's liberation movement (as it was then called). See "Lib on the Rocks," *National Review,* 15 March 1974, 326–27.

25. "An Analysis of JAP-Baiting Humor on the College Campus," *Humor,* 2, no. 4 (1989): 334.

26. The JAP is also usually described as sexually withholding. This characteristic does not fit the Jong persona.

27. "And Erica," review of *How to Save Your Own Life,* by Erica Jong, *Washington Post Book World,* 20 March 1977, H4.

28. "Unzipping Shakespeare," review of *Serenissima,* by Erica Jong, *Observer Review,* 13 September 1987, 27.

29. New York: HarperCollins, 1991.

30. Interview by Mary Cantwell, *Mademoiselle,* June 1976, 125, 96, 98.

31. Jong said to Mary Cantwell, "I'm sorry I have to fight against that image [created by paperback book covers] but it sells books and that enables me to do my thing. It means freedom" (181).

32. In *Fear of Fifty,* Jong describes a number of incidents in which family members and relatives proudly introduce her as a famous writer and a celebrity.

The "Pin with which to Stick Yourself": The Holocaust in Jewish American Women's Writing

Sara R. Horowitz

"MUST we tell stories that reflect the Holocaust . . . ? Can't we just leave it out?" Norma Rosen asks rhetorically in her 1974 essay, "The Holocaust and the American-Jewish Novelist,"[1] posing a question that informs the work of contemporaneous Jewish American women writers as well. Rosen's own novels, *Touching Evil*[2] and *At the Center*,[3] give an indication of her own answer to that question—that "The Holocaust is the central occurrence of the twentieth century. . . . the central human occurrence" ("The Holocaust," 8–9), that the murder of European Jewry ought shake the souls of American Jewish writers "with pity, with awe, with empathy and identification, and with the desire to know what it was that had been lost" ("The Holocaust," 9). With the Holocaust at its center, Rosen's novels look back at the Jewish past and ahead at the effect of the genocide on subsequent generations of Americans, Jews and non-Jews.

Other Jewish American women writers—survivors who made their way to the United States and women born elsewhere or later—similarly bring the murder of Europe's Jews into their imaginative work. Jewish-American women's writing about the Shoah centers on three issues. First, in works by survivors and others, the Holocaust itself is explored, along with its traumatic effect on Jewish continuity, practice, and community. The impact of the experience or knowledge of the extremities of evil on those of us who come after is also probed through the vehicle of fictional narrative, memoir, and poetry. In *Probing the Limits of Representation,* Saul Friedlander speaks of "the difficulty in establishing the elements" of "some sort of 'master-narrative'" of the Holocaust. While Friedlander does not consider the question of gender in his extended discussion of what does or should comprise the "necessary components . . . of such a master-narrative," the term itself suggests that women's reflections on the Shoah require special attention by scholars lest the gendering of experience, memory, and interpretation be written out of whatever master-narrative eventually becomes the dominant way we record and remember this past.

Second, the Shoah figures centrally in the construction of identities—American, Jewish, female—as Jewish American women writers imagine themselves into the unimaginable. The Nazi genocide functions as the degree zero point for the dual axes of Jewish and American identity. Ultimately, and in increasingly complicated ways, the Holocaust becomes crucial to thinking about Jewish identity in America, functioning in the capacity of what Francine Prose refers to as the "pin with which to stick yourself" when assimilation threatens. Similarly, Jane DeLynn refers to the Holocaust as "the instrument of my return" to Judaism. Marge Piercy promises her grandmother to honor the memory of the murdered Jews of Europe by remaining Jewish herself. Piercy calls this "one of the first commitments of my real, my adult life." For many Jewish American women writers, then, the memory of the Nazi genocide serves also as a reminder of present Jewish identity, seen sometimes as inescapable, sometimes as freely elected.

Third, as Jewish American women construct their multiple identities, the Holocaust becomes the means by which to explore other issues. Piercy explains, "the Holocaust made me feel that being political is a necessity." Jewish American women writers, whether born here or elsewhere, frequently connect Jewish oppression in Europe with racial oppression in this country. Further, the Shoah—historical atrocity predicated on racial or religious difference—comes to represent by metaphor or analogy the atrocities of sexual abuse and incest, predicated on gender difference. Taken together, Jewish women writers in America have evolved a body of letters in English that recollects and interprets the experiences of women in the Shoah. As women develop theoretical and pragmatic approaches to specifically Jewish feminism, they claim the historical experience of Jewish victimization as their own and utilize it to acknowledge, define, and resist other victimizations.

Literature as Testimony

In 1953, under the tutelage of Archibald MacLeish, a twenty-three-year-old immigrant and Radcliffe student named Ilona

Karmel published her first novel, *Stephania,*[4] drawing on but not elaborating aspects of her experiences less than a decade earlier at Starzysko Kamienna and other labor camps. Like the author, the protagonist of *Stephania* survives Nazi atrocity, but emerges from the war physically marked. In the novel Stephania does not articulate her actual memories of Nazi atrocity. Rather, she grapples with the effect of survival on her sense of self. Physically deformed by the brutal conditions she endured, Stephania's hunchback becomes a metaphor to explore the possibility of deformations of the spirit or psyche. In contrast to a sister who survived the war in better conditions under false Aryan papers, and who later marries and has a child, Stephania finds that her own experience intrudes upon her sense of herself as a woman. She imagines that no man will want her deformed body and ignores the letters of her prewar fiance, who has also survived the war.

In *Stephania* Karmel probes the process by which people struggle to know themselves and to make moral choices. Voluntarily subjecting herself to painful medical procedures in the unlikely hopes of correcting her deformity, Stephania enters the closed world of hospital confinement. The physical disabilities of three hospital roommates throw into sharp relief the ways in which one's body limits and shapes but does not wholly define oneself. Stephania's deformity—a hunchback exacerbated by the harsh wartime conditions and by Nazi brutality—alienates her from herself. "Here something happens to your body, and you just sit back and watch and can't do a thing about it. It's as if your body were not yours at all, as if someone else was telling it what to do" (48). Although physicians repeatedly tell her that they cannot ameliorate her condition, she attempts to undo the damage to her spine by sheer will power. Stephania berates her hospital roommates for giving in to their disabilities without a comparable struggle. For example, she blames one roommate's self-indulgent obesity, which impedes the healing of her leg's fragile bones. When their third roommate, a paralyzed adolescent, struggles vainly to move her fingers, Stephania tells her "it is your fault. . . . You've talked yourself into believing that you can't do it" (243).

In this novel Karmel utilizes the tension between destiny and self-determination, as acted out on one's physical being, to explore the deeper issue, agency, and impotence, in making moral choices. Truthfulness, rather than self-delusion, constitutes the necessary precondition for all meaningful actions. Stephania scorns the fantasies of a fabricated past that one roommate constructs to comfort herself in her current deprivations. Stephania's harsh but honest words propel her companions from self-indulgence, helping them overcome their impediments. One woman moves her fingers, the other loses weight, and both are eventually released from the hospital. Ultimately—and ironically—it is Stephania who makes the least progress in her recovery.

Worse than her roommates' real or imagined shortcomings, Stephania blames herself for the death of her parents, both murdered in the Nazi genocide. With what has come to be termed survivor guilt, she blames herself for abandoning her father, who had grown increasingly helpless as conditions worsened. Stephania confesses her guilty memory to her roommates. Made wise by their own struggles against intractable circumstances, they point out the limitations to moral responsibility, not unlike those of physical self-determination. Stephania eventually realizes that she could no more save her father than she can undo her hunchback.

With the overwhelming suffering and losses of the Holocaust as backdrop, the novel asks about the meaning of life. Rather than asserting an eloquent philosophy that justifies human existence, it indicates that human connection alone is meaningful in and of itself. In the midst of her own despair, searching for a distraction or an escape, Stephania begins helping other patients in the hospital. To her surprise, she finds that this soothes her. "[I]f we could, can mean so much to each other . . . then that shows something; it must. It means that it was not just senseless, that year in here, not just doing nothing, but there was something . . ." (352).

In *Stephania* the hospital routine and personalities increasingly define the parameters of life for the young survivor and her roommates. Stephania's bedside window is a palpable marker of the intractable barriers dividing the infirm from the healthy. This in turn serves as the novel's metaphor for the difficulties survivors face when they attempt to articulate their memories and experiences to those not personally a part of the Nazi genocide. For example, Stephania is shocked by the naiveté of her Swedish roommates, who simply cannot comprehend that her father was shot because he was a Jew.

In Karmel's final novel, *An Estate of Memory,*[5] she writes directly about the experience of the concentration camps. One of the few novels—American or European—set almost entirely within the boundaries of a camp, *Estate* depicts the daily life and death of Jewish women under Nazi atrocity. Karmel examines the social structures that developed among women—hierarchies based upon physical and emotional stamina, access to needed resources, and assigned work. The women form "makeshift camp families—women, young girls, whom loneliness unaccustomed and sudden had brought together" (7). Within these surrogate families, they help one another endure.

I will not elaborate at length on this novel, which has already been written about extensively.[6] I will note that the plot of *An Estate of Memory* centers on the hidden pregnancy of one woman—a condition that, if known in the nightmarish order of concentration camps, would mark her for immediate death. Three other women—her camp "family"—conspire to protect her secret and, out of their own meager rations, to support her, feed her, and enable her to carry her child to term and smuggle it out to freedom. Through the interactions of these four women in extreme circumstances, Karmel explores the way people make difficult ethical choices, weighing the needs of the self against the needs of others and the needs of community. The acute and painful circumstances of women and children introduced here find expression in other works by or about women in the Holocaust—developed in different ways, for example, by Cynthia Ozick in "The Shawl" and "Rosa,"[7] by William Styron in *Sophie's Choice*,[8] and by Sara Nomberg-Przytyk in *Auschwitz: True Tales from a Grotesque Land*.[9]

In both novels, Karmel reverses the conventional war narrative wherein heroic men protect endangered women. In many male Holocaust narratives, women figure peripherally as helpless victims or as rescued ones. Without developing a narrative of false heroics, Karmel puts women's suffering, struggles, and triumphs at the center of her writing. Men, on the other hand, frequently appear passive, weak, and childlike, wholly reliant upon women for survival in the extreme conditions of the Holocaust. In both novels, men face death by pathetically seeking the reassurances of a vanished domesticity from their wives and daughters. In an almost identical moment in each novel, men turn helplessly to their wives on the eve of a roundup or murder, asking "Myrele, what should I put on?" (*Stephanie,* 270), or "Aurelia, should I have tomorrow?" (*Estate,* 160).

By exploring the behavior and choices of a group of women in extremis, Karmel explores ideas about the self, survival, and ethics. Because of the Nazis' deliberate effort to dehumanize their victims, to lacerate communities and families, to remove the victims from their social milieu, to force them to live in filth and hunger amid the constant presence of death, the women in *An Estate of Memory* do things they once regarded as unthinkable. Stripped of most of the conventional benchmarks of identity, the women in camps felt themselves connected only tenuously at best to the self they remembered before the war. This sense of inner discontinuity led Karmel to observe that "the self is more fluid than Western thought has imagined."[10]

Ilona Karmel and her sister, Henia Karmel-Wolfe, managed to stay together during the war.[11] Together with their mother, who perished at the war's end, the sisters survived three labor camps. Like her younger sister, Henia Karmel-Wolfe transmuted her Holocaust memories into fictional narrative, writing in the American English of her postwar home. *The Baders of Jacob Street*[12] follows the struggles of the Bader family and their neighbors to survive the war in the Crakow ghetto. The novel plays upon the ironic tension that history creates between the characters, who only gradually learn what awaits them and other Jews in the Nazi genocide, and the reader, who knows all along about the final solution. The poignancy of the Crakow Jews' unknowingness shapes the novel, as the characters struggle to make ethical decisions, to protect their families, and to hold on to their Jewish identity in circumstances that make that identity dangerous. One family grapples with a decision about whether to circumcise their newborn son, thereby visibly marking him as a Jew—and possibly, marking him for death—or to settle him in a Polish family, under the protection of a false Christian birth certificate. Halina Bader, the adolescent protagonist, begins to absorb the dominant culture's anti-Semitic attitudes and feels ashamed of her Jewishness. She escapes the ghetto by assuming a non-Jewish identity. As she is forced to witness the humiliation of the Crakow Jews, however, she comes to realize the price exacted by such inner denial.

In a later novel, *Marek and Lisa,*[13] Wolfe-Karmel focuses on the relationship of a young Jewish Crakow couple separated by the war. The novel centers on the aftermath of the Holocaust, and is marked by absence, bereavement, the search for loved ones, and the survivor's hope of rebuilding a life.

Karmel-Wolfe's novels chart the gradual but inexorable encroachment of the Nazi anti-Semitic measures on the everyday life of Cracow Jews and the intrusion of the Holocaust into one's intimate connections. Like *An Estate of Memory, The Baders of*

Jacob Street and *Marek and Lisa* explore strategies for survival—physical, psychological, and moral. Wolfe-Karmel's depiction of ghetto life in *The Baders of Jacob Street* exposes the murky moral ambiguities of the Judenrat, the Jewish Council responsible for administering civil law, and thus for meting out life and death by way of ration cards, jobs, and transport lists. Moreover, the novel's ethical challenge looks not only backward at the European past, but also ahead, to the American context of writing. When one character asks, "Could it be possible that the world . . . didn't care?" the novel implicates its American readership. The novel's political activist asks the ghetto Jews, not without irony, "What were you doing a year ago? . . . People were being killed all over. . . . And you didn't lose any sleep over it." The questions resonate years later as a clarion call to the reader's ethical responsibility for the world we inhabit.

Imaginative Reconstructions

Three American-born writers—Cynthia Ozick, Norma Rosen, and Marcie Hershman—whose work concerns the Holocaust and its aftermath, have adopted distinctly different narrative tactics for approaching their subject. Cynthia Ozick, long convinced that nonsurvivors dare not approach the concentrationary universe directly, wrote about the Holocaust by indirection until "The Shawl," which was situated within the boundaries of a camp. Norma Rosen filters perceptions of Holocaust atrocity through the consciousness of the two non-Jewish American protagonists of *Touching Evil*[14] who measure its horrors and implications through its resonances in their own lives. In *Tales of the Master Race,*[15] Marcie Hershman revisits the Shoah not through the eyes of its victims or survivors, but through the perceptions of its perpetrators, the ordinary people of Kreiswald, an imaginary German town in the Third Reich. Sherri Szeman takes perhaps the most daring tactic in *The Commandant's Mistress,*[16] measuring the perceptions of perpetrator against those of victim, by juxtaposing the erotic memories of a concentration camp kommandant with the recollections of the Jewish prisoner forced to trade sexual services for survival.

Much of Ozick's writing approaches the subject of the Shoah indirectly by focusing on the memories of survivors in America, or on the attempts of American Jews and non-Jews to reconstruct or evade the European catastrophe. For example, in

Trust,[17] Ozick's first published novel, and in "Levitation,"[18] a later story, Jewish and non-Jewish spouses differ in their attitudes towards Holocaust remembrance. Chicago-born Enoch Vand finds himself haunted by "the *dybbuk* of the slaughtered six millions" (*Trust,* 236), his developing obsession fueled his role as witness during the war, in the American military, and rekindled by a pleasure trip to Europe, and by encounters with traces of the Jewish past. His Christian wife, Allegra, however, feels oppressed by so much memory. "Maidenek, Auschwitz, Chelmno, Dachau, Treblinka, Buchenwald, Mauthausen, Sovibar—tolling like a chorus of some unidentifiable opera of which I could remember the music but not the import" (76), she reflects. Enoch's presence in Europe during the war, "confidante of corpses" (66), allows for vivid Holocaust memories in the narrative, while Allegra's ultimate indifference to past atrocity is subtly linked with pervasive Christian anti-Semitism. In "Levitation" Lucy converts to Judaism when she marries Jim Feingold, but remains aloof from his intense interest in Jewish history, most notably Jewish martyrdom. Although connected by their passion for writing and scholarship and by their involvement in the world of New York literati, this "pair of novelists" (3), Lucy and Jim (like Enoch and Allegra), finally stare at each other across the great divide engendered by the long history of Jewish catastrophe. During a gathering of literary friends, Lucy realizes she has become "jaded by atrocity . . . bored by the shootings, and the gas, and the camps" (19) as a group of Jewish writers and scholars, immersed in the recollections of a Holocaust survivor, levitate above her, growing "smaller and smaller, more and more remote" (15) in the distance.

In juxtaposing the memories of Jewish survivors of the Holocaust with those of their non-Jewish spouses, however, Ozick does not mean to imply that only Jews may carry these memories, or even that all Jews understand what they commemorate. Her stories look ironically at the way Jews misuse or misperceive the catastrophic past. Jim Feingold, for example, retains a lasting fascination with episodes of Jewish martyrdom, but not with Jewish life, marrying Lucy "because he had always known he did not want a Jewish wife" (3). This dilution of the content of Jewish life in America is explored in *The Cannibal Galaxy,*[19] where the school started by Joseph Brill, a Holocaust survivor, to promulgate the lofty ideals of a "dual curriculum"—Jewish and Western cultures—fails because its teachers care little about education, imagination, ideas, the human spirit. In this novel it is the European-born and American-born Jewish spouses who speak across the chasm created by the cataclysmic past that one has experienced and the other has safely eluded. Thus Ozick locates her second cultural divide between European-born Jews who have immigrated to the United States after experiencing the upheaval of the Nazi genocide and American-born Jews who learn about the catastrophe from afar. Moreover, a shared past does not unify the novel's two survivors, Brill and Hester Lilt, who remember and understand in radically different ways.

More important, in "Levitation," Ozick attributes to the Christian Lucy the central challenge in writing about the Holocaust: how to describe Nazi atrocity without its sounding like "only a movie" (14). Lucy correctly perceives the danger in repeated tellings of similarly brutal narratives that sound "exactly like the movies." She realizes that "Cruelty came out of the imagination, and had to be witnessed by the imagination" (14). Lucy's reflections on Holocaust remembrance, evoked in the presence of a survivor testifying, indicates the limitations of her imaginative and empathic capacities—she can picture only endless simultaneous crucifixions, crosses, and "big bloody nails" (14). At the same time, it articulates the strategy Ozick herself adopts in recounting the Holocaust through fictional narrative. In *The Cannibal Galaxy* she imaginatively reconstructs the French Jewish childhood of Joseph Brill, the steady encroachment of anti-Semitism on his life, and his struggle to survive and make sense of his losses.

Not until "The Shawl," however, does Ozick situate the narrative in a concentration camp, rather than in memory alone. The narrative intensifies its power by paring down the action to the relationship between Rosa and Magda, a mother and her suckling child, who perishes in the camp. The novel's pivotal moment rehearses a recurrent scene in Holocaust fiction—the mother, paralyzed by fear and helplessness, who witnesses the death of her child without intervening. By focusing on the mother's feelings—her determination to feed baby Magda although starvation has dried up Rosa's breasts; her resolution to hide Magda, thus saving her from murder; her anguished indecision as "she saw that Magda was going to die" (8)—Ozick exposes the horror of the Nazi genocidal machinery, which turns even a mother's love into an instrument of torture.

In "Rosa," the more extensive sequel to "The Shawl," Ozick explores survivor trauma. As Rosa explains to a retired Jewish dentist who wonders why she still lives in fear, "Thirty-nine years ago I was someone else" (19). Living and aging in Florida many years after the war, Rosa cannot relinquish her daughter, cannot acknowledge the finality of death. In her mind and in the letters she endlessly composes, she imagines a living Magda and extends for her daughter the future that was so brutally truncated by the Nazi genocide. On one level, her on-going act of imagination comprises a form of resistance against the genocide that, in actuality, ended Magda's brief life. At the same time, however, the ceaseless psychic effort to retain the fiction of a living Magda cuts off Rosa from living connections. Indeed, as she softens to the romantic advances of the retired dentist, she realizes that "Magda was not there. . . . Magda was away" (69). While the narrative looks at Rosa's traumatic loss with compassion, Ozick does not romanticize the survivor. Just as she presents the limitations and failures of Joseph Brill in *The Cannibal Galaxy,* his bitter experiences as a young Jew in Vichy France notwithstanding, Ozick depicts Rosa as an embittered woman, spiteful towards the niece she blames for Magda's death.

Through Rosa's consciousness, Ozick also examines the growing academic concern with the Holocaust in America, where enthusiasm for the details of research may inadvertently lead a researcher to dehumanize the victim once again. Rosa receives many "university letters" that seek to use her memory as "data" (37). The scientific language, devoid of empathy, strikes Rosa as "excitement over other people's suffering" (36). In reading the letters, she herself feels diminished:

> Consider also the special word they used: *survivor.* Something new. As long as they didn't have to say *human being.* It used to be *refugee,* but by now there was no such creature, no more refugees, only survivors. A name like a number. . . . Blue digits on the arm, what difference. They don't call you a woman anyhow. *Survivor.* . . . Who made up these words, parasites on the throat of suffering! (*Rosa,* 36–37)

For Rosa, being the subject of academic research is powerfully reminiscent of her initial experience of being a subject of genocidal practice. This suggests a critique of academic memory work that, Ozick indicates, may miss the mark entirely even as it compiles more and more data. One might say that while we all agree on the importance of remembrance, we are not quite sure how to understand that memory, what to do with it.

Like Ozick, Norma Rosen recognizes the importance of fictional discourse in transmitting Holocaust remembrances:

"Witness-through-the-imagination could be the only role for the American writer" ("The Holocaust," 10). Rosen utilizes a different strategy, however, to represent Holocaust atrocity in *Touching Evil.* For Rosen, the Shoah represents not only the central and cataclysmic event in Jewish history, the event that should reside at the center of Jewish writing. Rather, the knowledge of the Nazi genocide—the extremities of evil—should exert a strong impact on all who encounter it. Rosen explains, in "The Second Life of Holocaust Imagery,"[20] that this does not entail "universalizing" the Holocaust, a movement that "implies a weakening of the specific Jewish experience by broadening it to include what all people experience of suffering." To the contrary, insists Rosen, "the Holocaust experience is so intense that it radiates out to affect non-Jews who then experience it through the imagination. . . . that is not universalizing, not generalizing, a spreading and thinning-out of the Jewish trauma, it is the opposite: a bringing of the non-Jew into Jewish experience" ("Second Life," 51).

Both to describe that radiating-out process and to create a vehicle to accomplish it, Rosen invents a central consciousness for *Touching Evil* in the person of Jean Lamb. Jean and her friend Hattie Mews, two non-Jewish American women, have "been stricken by knowledge of the Holocaust" ("Second Life," 51). Once Jean learns of the Holocaust, she cannot shake it from her mind, from the core of her being. Jean comes upon this knowledge when the sociology professor with whom she is having an affair shows her photographs of the camp. Rosen explains elsewhere, "I made the moment of discovery the precise moment of sexual seduction, almost of intercourse itself, so that everything should be open and the appearance of penetration complete" ("Holocaust," 12). Thus, just as the Edenic couple tastes of the tree of knowledge of good and evil and finds that the world has irrevocably changed, Jean encounters simultaneously sexuality and the knowledge of evil, and for her the world changes as well. For Hattie, the impact of the Holocaust comes about through watching the Eichmann trial on television.

Both women experience the mark of Holocaust knowledge specifically in their reproductive capacities. As a result of "touching evil"—that is, of absorbing the knowledge of Nazi atrocity—Jean decides not to have children. In contrast, Hattie, pregnant during the Eichmann trial, sees in the Holocaust a threat to the life of her unborn child. For each woman a particular image symbolizes the entire horror. For Jean it is a woman survivor, digging her way up from a mound of murdered corpses; for Hattie, a pregnant woman in labor, under the gaze of a concentration camp guard. These images provide each woman with her own point of access to the Holocaust, her own point of vulnerability—and hence her own point of empathy. Elsewhere, Rosen reflects, "can someone else's suffering be felt? . . . only through one's own suffering" ("Second Life," 50).

While Ozick and others focus on the vast chasm separating those who have personally experienced Nazi atrocity from all others, Rosen's novel affirms the possibility for transmitting meaningful knowledge about the Holocaust. Rosen herself touched evil through her husband, a Vienna-born Jew who escaped the genocide that murdered his parents by reaching the safety of England on the *kindertransport.* Like Jean, Rosen watches the Eichmann trial and asks herself, "How can we live now?" Then pregnant, like Hattie, Rosen internalizes this knowledge and makes the encounter the subject of her art.[21] For Rosen, Americans not only can but also must take account of the Holocaust and its implications. Moreover, for those not part of atrocity, the only path to understanding resides in an empathic imagining.

More startling, Marcie Hershman imagines herself not into the psyche of the victim, but into the heart and mind of the perpetrators. In *Tales of the Master Race,* she creates an imaginary German town during the Nazi regime. The interlocking stories of its different people—petty bureaucrats, police, wives, girlfriends, opportunists, and a few (a very few) dissidents—probe the inner mechanisms that allow a regime of atrocity to be actualized. The willed ignorance, denial, greed, and prejudice of the people of Kreiswald illustrate the way the "unimaginable" was not only imagined but also actually transpired. As the inhabitants of Kreiswald scheme, struggle, and manipulate one another, the murder of the Jews of Europe occurs quietly in the background. Commander Terskan, for example, successfully woos the beautiful wife of a file clerk by plying her with gifts and by assigning her husband to participate in torture and interrogations. The husband does "body recording" of the torture victims—that is, he weighs and measures their naked bodies prior to interrogation. These sessions unsettle the young man and distance him from his wife, who does not wish to hear of them. "Sometimes talking is a mistake," she tells him (11). Against the backdrop of these interrogations, Terskan and Gerda exchange gifts and romance one another. Another Kreiswald inhabitant, a draftsman, finds he can run a more competitive mapmaking business by finding Jewish printers to handle his orders, since, desperate for work, they give him "a good price" (68). The draftsman dutifully calls the printer "Israel" and his secretary "Sarah," although each flinches at being called a name not his or her own. According to "the new laws all German Jews had been given special first names. Males were assigned the name Israel, females Sarah" (68).

A pair of interviews brackets the interlocking stories that comprise the narrative. Ostensibly occurring years after the war, each interview presents only the words of the questioner, not the responses of the two Kreiswald inhabitants being questioned about the past. From the words of the interviewer, who clearly repeats some of what he is told, it is apparent that both interviewees still deny the events of the war. The first refers to Holocaust remembrance—whether in newspapers, politicians' speeches, or elsewhere—as "lies" and "rubbish" (3), insisting that "the winners wrote the articles" (4). Although he admits to knowing "secrets" during the war, he believes "everything found was made up of lies" (3), but also, in retrospect, that Nazis lied about Jews. He recollects knowing that people "were taken away" during the war (5), but not what befell them. The second interviewee insists that he knew no one who "was taken away" during the war (218), and only learned of Nazi atrocity and murder after the war. Reluctant to discuss the war, he recollects hearing of German citizens forced to dig up a mass grave and rebury the bodies, "one by one" in a "decent" grave (221). Yet he himself had never visited these graves, on the outskirts of Kreiswald, and wants only "to live a good life" and to care for his loved ones (219).[22]

While Rosen suggests that we understand, even feel, another's suffering only through its resonances in our own suffering, Hershman implies that we can understand the perpetrator of and bystander to racism also by looking into ourselves. Rather than identifying with the Holocaust victim, Hershman's narrative pushes its reader to acknowledge a connection with the culpable. While the novel is set safely in the European past, the shifting and multiple consciousnesses of the individual stories ultimately unsettle the reader, demanding that he or she examine instances of personal complicity with racism and prejudice—one's own willed ignorance.

Past and Present

Poet and essayist Irena Klepfisz survived the Holocaust by hiding, with her mother, as a Christian child in the Aryan side of Warsaw. Klepfisz's father perished in the Warsaw ghetto uprising, with the rubble serving as his grave. In 1949 Klepfisz and her mother immigrated to the United States. These experiences and memories form the center of her artistic oeuvre, dominating her earlier works and long poem, "Bashert," Yiddish for destiny or predestined.[23] Because only a stroke of fate separates her from the vast majority of other European Jewish children murdered by the Nazis, something stronger than empathy connects her life with the deaths of murdered Jewish infants, whom Germans would

> pick up . . .
> by their feet
> swing them through the air
> and smash their heads
> against plaster walls.
>
> somehow
> i managed
> to escape that fate.
>
> (43)

This poem and others function as testimony, describing the poet's own experience in hiding and her father's death, as well as what befell the murdered Jews of Europe—a fact she learned years after the Holocaust.

Taking stock of her adopted home, Klepfisz uses her own sensibilities as a survivor and child of a survivor to understand the contemporary situations of other oppressed minorities, her own feminism, lesbianism, and childlessness, other sources of marginalization. She imagines with intimate detail the experience of dying women during the Holocaust, noting their "sagging breasts sparse / pubic hairs" ("death camp," 47) or linking the sexual violation of women during the Holocaust with earlier pogroms ("herr captain," 45–46). "Bashert" meditates on the relationship between the world she survived and the one she now inhabits. Reflecting on the impediments facing her Brooklyn students in the early 1970s, all black or Puerto Rican, she first catalogues the Yiddish names intoned during a Holocaust memorial ceremony years earlier—names whose very sounds distinguish the otherness of their murdered bearers: *"Surele. Moyshele. Channele. Rivkele. Yankele. Shayndele. Rayzel. Benyomin. Chavele. Miriam. Chaim"* (195). Those foreign-sounding names are then juxtaposed with the names she reads daily as she takes attendance: *"James. Reggie. Marie. Simone. Joy. Christine. Alvarez. Ashcroft. Basile. Colon. Corbitt. White. Raphael. Dennis. Juan. Carissa. Lamont. Andrea"* (195–96). As she "balance[s] the heritage, the histories of two continents" (197), she realizes that even in the country that offered her haven, "safety . . . is only temporary" (197). In America, "the present dangers" are less visible; they comprise "the dangers of the void, of the American hollowness." Klepfisz calls our era "the Holocaust without smoke" (193).

While Klepfisz writes in English, her acquired tongue, she incorporates Yiddish words and phrases—her native tongue—into her poetry. Her collection of poetry, *A Few Words in the Mother Tongue,* for example, is written in English but contains Yiddish. By foregrounding in her title the few instances of Yiddish, Klepfisz suggests that the large portion of the poetry—the many, many words in English—matter in the final analysis because they serve as the container for the few words in the language of childhood, the language of memory. In evoking Yiddish, the *mame loshen* (or mother tongue), she links her own writing with the interrupted tradition of women's poetry and prayer in that language. However, Yiddish serves not only as a nostalgic trace of the lost world of the poet's childhood, the destroyed world of the European Jew, but also as an assertion of Klepfisz's radical politics. The use of Yiddish, a marginalized language, marks her alliance with all marginalized cultures; it also distances her from Israel, whose treatment of Palestinians disturbs her.[24]

American-born novelists such as Rosen, Ozick, and Hershman imagine the Holocaust both as a cataclysmic event in the recent Jewish past and as a context in which to confront evil, immorality, empathy, and altruism. Some contemporary Jewish American women writers, like Klepfisz, link radical politics with collective memory of the Holocaust. For them, the memory of the Nazi genocide links Jews with other racial minorities. But as women develop theoretical and pragmatic approaches to specifically Jewish feminism, they claim the historical experience of Jewish victimization as their own, using it to acknowledge, define, and resist other victimizations. Lore Segal, who witnessed Krystallnacht as a young child in Vienna before joining the first children's transport to England, reflects that as a survivor "It is my business to imagine the oppressions that are done under the sun." Often, remembering the Holocaust separates Jewish American women from other colleagues in radical politics. As women writers, not themselves survivors, imagine themselves into the unimaginable, the Shoah—historical atrocity predicated on racial or religious difference—comes to represent by metaphor or analogy the atrocities of sexual abuse and incest, predicated on gender difference.

Melanie Kaye/Kantrowitz, for example, begins her introduction to *The Issue is Power: Essays on Women, Jews, Violence and Resistance,*[25] with the following:

> First I learned about rape. I mean, I always knew, cannot remember learning.
>
> First I learned about the Holocaust. I mean, I always knew, cannot remember learning.
>
> (i)

The essays contained in the volume consider anti-Semitism, racism, misogyny, homophobia, and anti-Israel and anti-Palestinian activities. While careful to distinguish between different kinds of oppression and to place it in historical and political perspective, the author asserts that one may learn from comparisons—in particular, one learns to develop resistance to oppression and empathy with the oppressed. Kaye/Kantrowitz sees an analogy between "the Holocaust . . . an exaggerated but logical extension to a pattern" of anti-Semitism in the West, and rape, an extension of pervasive "battering, incest, sexual harassment" that similarly "formed a pattern" (i). Moreover, for Kaye/Kantrowitz, the comparison mitigates against certain facile radical stances. The Nazi genocide has taught Kaye/Kantrowitz that *"it's a contradiction to be a Jew and a pacifist"* (ii). Kaye/Kantrowitz wants to collect and retell stories of women resistors to Nazism "To fortify myself" in contemporary struggles, to "make possible the future," and "to remain human" (ii).

The connections between the struggles of dying Jews in Europe and the very different set of strivings of American women underlie Marge Piercy's novel *Gone to Soldiers.*[26] Linked personally to the Holocaust by her first husband, a French Jew whose family eluded the genocidal net by escaping into neutral Switzerland, Piercy explores the interlocking issues of Jewish, American, and female identity in the novel. Comprised of interlocking stories of European Jews and refugees and Jewish and non-Jewish American soldiers and American women during World War II, Piercy's novel explores the Nazi genocide as well as the effect of the war on American lives. By examining a wide variety of lives, the novel probes the ways in which the war intruded upon and reshaped people's most intimate lives and destinies. In Europe the narrative focuses on one French Jewish family in the Vichy regime, whose destiny comes to represent the fate of the Jews of Europe. Both parents die in the war, while the oldest daughter, Jacqueline, overcomes a measure of Jewish self-hatred to fight in the Resistance. Indeed, Nazism itself—the encounter with radical anti-Semitism—propels her to reclaim and redefine her Jewish identity.

To approach the death camp, the narrative utilizes the device of twinning. Two twin sisters, Naomi and Ruthie, are separated early in the plot. Naomi reaches the safety of America, while Ruthie dies in the gas chamber with her mother. Because they are twins, Naomi dreams what Ruthie experiences. In other words, Naomi experiences death in the gas chambers and lives to testify about it, becoming the impossible, complete witness.[27] The European episodes are well-researched and vivid in detail. The twinning of victim and survivor also allows for the comparison between the European and American experiences. Naomi escapes the Nazi genocide only to discover that other dangers await her as an orphaned female in America. Seduced and raped as a teenager by an older neighbor, she finds herself pregnant.

Just as the encounter with anti-Semitism—whether in Europe or the United States—propels the novel's Jewish characters to reevaluate the terms of their Jewish identity, the encounter with patriarchy and the limitations it places on women propels the women in America—whether Jewish or not—to redefine gender identity. Thus, for example, Bernice reacts against an overbearing and exploitative father to become a bomber pilot, and finally settles down with her gay lover. Louise evolves from a renowned writer of frothy romance fiction to become a foreign correspondent based in Europe during the war. The issues of American, Jewish, and female identities come to a head with the reunion of the surviving French sisters after liberation. Resistance heroine Jacqueline and pregnant Naomi resolve to raise this child in Israel, in remembrance of the dead Ruthie and as a commitment to the future.

The writing of women who imagine themselves into the unimaginable past or who bring that past into the present to understand contemporary experiences interrogates the narratives through which one comes to know history. Their writing challenges readers to formulate new questions about the past—about the experiences and remembrances of women under Nazism—to fill gaps and ultimately to reformulate the master narrative of the Holocaust.

Notes

1. Reprinted in *Accidents of Influence: Writing as a Woman and a Jew in America* (Albany: SUNY Press, 1992), 10.
2. (New York: Harcourt, Brace & World, 1969).
3. (Boston: Houghton Mifflin, 1982).
4. (Boston: Houghton Mifflin, 1953).
5. (Boston: Houghton Mifflin, 1969; reprint, New York: Feminist Press, 1986).
6. See, for example, Ruth Angress, "Afterword," *An Estate of Memory* (New York: Feminist Press, 1986), 445–57; Sidra DeKoven Ezrahi, *By Words Alone: The Holocaust in Literature* (Chicago: University of Chicago Press, 1980), 67–95; and my "Memory and Testimony in Women's Holocaust Memoirs," *Jewish Women in Literary Perspective,* ed. Judith Baskin (Detroit: Wayne State University Press, 1994), and "Ilona Karmel," *Jewish American Women Writers: A Bio-Bibliographical and Critical Sourcebook,* ed. Ann R. Shapiro et al. (Westport, Conn.: Greenwood Press, 1994), 158–64.
7. *The Shawl* (New York: Knopf, 1989), 3–10 and 13–70.
8. (New York: Random House, 1979).
9. Trans. Roslyn Hirsch (Chapel Hill: University of North Carolina Press, 1985).
10. Personal interview, 13 September 1992.
11. To preserve their sanity, they composed poetry together in labor camps, published after the war in Ilona Karmel and Henryka Karmel-Wolfe, *Spiew za Drutami* [Song Behind the Wire] (New York: Polish Jewish Press, 1947).
12. (Philadelphia: Lippincott, 1970).
13. (New York: Dodd, Mead, 1984).
14. (Detroit: Wayne State University Press, 1990; reprint, New York: Harcourt, Brace and World, 1969).
15. (New York: HarperPerennial, 1991),
16. (New York: HarperPerennial, 1993).
17. (New York: New American Library, 1966).
18. *Levitation: Five Fictions* (1982; reprint, New York: E. P. Dutton/Obelisk, 1983), 3–20.
19. (1983; reprint, New York: E. P. Dutton/Obelisk, 1984).
20. *Accidents of Influence,* 47–54.
21. "Notes Toward a Holocaust Fiction," *Accidents of Influence,* 107.
22. Although I have referred to the interviewer and the interviewed as "he," the novel leaves their gender undefined.
23. All poetry references from Irena Klepfisz, *A Few Words in the Mother Tongue: Poems Selected and New (1971–1990)* (Portland, Ore.: Eighth Mountain Press, 1990).

24. See, for example, "*Yom Hashoah, Yom Yerushalayim:* A Meditation," *Dreams of an Insomniac: Jewish Feminist Essays, Speeches and Diatribes* (Portland, Ore.: Eighth Mountain Press, 1990), 115–40.

25. (San Francisco: aunt lute books, 1992).

26. (New York: Fawcett, 1987).

27. For discussion of the impossibility of complete witnessing, see Shoshana Felman and Dori Laub, *Testimony: Crises of Witnessing in Literature, Psychoanalysis, and History* (New York: Routledge, 1992), and my "Rethinking Holocaust Testimony: The Making and Unmaking of the Witness," *Cardozo Studies in Law and Literature,* 4, no. 1 (Spring/Summer 1992): 45–68.

Norma Rosen: An American Literary Response to the Holocaust

S. LILLIAN KREMER

IN the essay "On Living in Two Cultures," Norma Rosen claims to have been "born of an immaculate Jewish conception . . . [of] parents, who were Jews by birth, refrained from intercourse with the Jewish religion and proudly passed me, in an untainted state, into the world."[1] Marriage brought Rosen into intimate contact with Jewish history, which in turn strongly influenced her intellectual and artistic life. As the wife of a Holocaust survivor, a reader of many Holocaust texts, and auditor of the Eichmann trial, Rosen has been powerfully touched by Holocaust evil.[2] Professing, in "The Holocaust and the American-Jewish Novelist," to be a "witness-through-the-imagination," a "documenter of the responses of those who 'had heard the terrible news'" (*AI,* 10), a role she considers appropriate for the American novelist, Rosen has made the Holocaust a recurrent theme of her fiction and essays.

Isaac Rosenfeld spoke of his own and future generations when he perceived that the Holocaust would become the model reality of our time. If one attains Holocaust knowledge, he argued, life cannot go on as before: "it is impossible to live, to think, to create, without bearing witness against the terror."[3] Because Rosen believes the Holocaust is "the central occurrence of the twentieth century . . . the central human occurrence" (*AI,* 9), she explores "what might happen to people who truly took into consciousness the fact of the Holocaust. . . the meaning to human life and aspiration of the knowledge that human beings—in great numbers—could do what had been done" (*AI,* 12). *Heart's Witness,* an early title for *Touching Evil,* and a quotation from Rosenfeld's *An Age of Enormity* as her second epigraph both testify to the importance of Holocaust witness and recognition that assumption of Holocaust knowledge forever forfeits pre-Holocaust normality and innocence. Rosen writes of one protagonist: "Nothing of her life would, after she learned of the existence of the death camps, be as before" (*AI,* 11). She "was to be someone so profoundly affected by the news that she would vow never to live the life that had been lived by people till now" (*AI,* 11).

Like other writers who have undertaken the topic of the Shoah, Rosen grapples with the problematics of writing Holocaust narrative. She asks, How was the Holocaust to be written about? How could the virtues of fiction—indirection, irony, ambivalence—be used to make art out of this unspeakable occurrence?" (*AI,* 9). In "The Second Life of Holocaust Imagery," she writes:

> But the greatest paradox forms about the Holocaust, it seems to me, for novelists, in the tension between writing and not writing about it. If the writer treats the subject, the risk is that it may be falsified, trivialized. Even a "successful" treatment of the subject risks an aestheticizing or a false ordering of it, since whatever is expressed in art conveys the impression that it, too, is subject to the laws of composition. Yet not to write means omitting the central event of the twentieth century. (*AI,* 49)

Writing fiction geographically and temporally removed from the ghetto and concentration camp universe, Rosen engages the Shoah philosophically and morally in fiction that is centered on the sociopsychological impact on survivors and "witnesses through the imagination who allow the Holocaust to penetrate their consciousness. The critically acclaimed novel *Touching Evil* is set in 1961. The place is America; the major characters are gentile women who respond to Jewish history.[4] Jews appear only as journalistic subjects and televised witnesses, ghostly shadows of the documentaries. Past and present collide and merge as the novel alternates between 1944, the year Jean Lamb learned of the death camps through newspaper photographs,[5] and 1961, the year of the Eichmann trial, which is the vehicle for her rediscovery of the central significance of the Holocaust in her life. Juxtaposed to Jean's experience is that of Hattie Mews, a younger woman who watches the trial with her, encountering the Holocaust for the first time. Moments of Holocaust consciousness impinge on one another, varying in intensity from the fleeting to the all-consuming, extending to penetrate the emotions and intellects of the women.

The women are living incarnations of the novel's title and first epigraph, Carl Jung's observation in *Memories, Dreams,*

Reflections that "Touching evil brings with it the grave peril of succumbing to it." Jean and Hattie are touched by the radical evil of Nazism. It is precisely because she wanted to convey both the emotional and intellectual response to Holocaust awareness that Rosen created characters of two generations whose reactions are presented from immediate and distanced perspectives. Hattie's response is governed largely by the emotions of initial encounter with Holocaust evil, whereas Jean acts as a "reflector . . . distanced from her own revelation" (interview). At war's end, as others sought to return to prewar pursuits, Jean elected sacrifice. Because her Holocaust epiphany occurred while making love, her response is sacrifice of marriage and motherhood. By choosing deprivation, she allies herself with her European sisters and testifies to humanity's loss of Jewish progeny.

The Eichmann trial is the catalyst for Jean's reconsideration of the profound effect the Holocaust has had on her life. Reviewing her wartime feelings fifteen years after the primary shock of discovery, Jean assumes that the receding immediacy of the Holocaust will free her from continued immersion in the tragedy. However, despite her temporal distance, and contrary to her expectation of release from Holocaust compulsion, she is reclaimed by history. Once again, her mind and heart are violated: "Up to my ears again in corpses" (9). The horrors reappear, not instantaneously in a unified photographic composition, but piecemeal in daily doses of devastation: "machine guns punching bullet holes," "clubs beating against bone" (209).

Hattie's response to the television coverage of the trial echoes Jean's earlier reaction to newspaper photographs of camp inmates. The younger woman, pregnant—as was Rosen when she watched the Eichmann trial—absorbs the Holocaust experience, takes it thoroughly into her consciousness, claims to feel it in her body; "drinks in the words . . . sucks up the images. . . . Her shoulders watch, her knees watch. Her fetus thrusts forward to watch" (68).[6] As the trial progresses, Hattie is both physical foil and emotional double to the intentionally childless Jean. Even though pregnant, she nevertheless concurs with Jean's judgment that the Nazis so defiled life that propagating the species is a dubious endeavor.

Touching Evil is distinctive in its focus on American reaction and feminine perspective. Because Rosen believes that the Holocaust is not a Jewish problem, but a human problem that non-Jews must absorb, her gentile women are witnesses for Jewish women who endured the devastation. They empathize powerfully with Jewish women who suffered in the camps: Jean with the wounded woman who dug her way from under a mountain of corpses that spouted blood" (221), and Hattie with a very pregnant woman on a forced march and then with another giving birth in typhus and lice-infested straw. The resurrected digger becomes a recurrent presence in Jean's imagination, a shadowy companion overwhelming her spirit, clawing her way into the American consciousness. Hattie proclaims that the failure to watch the trial and listen to the testimony of survivors on behalf of the "gaunt ascetics of the camps" (221)—those "who have passed beyond hunger and terror"—is an act of supreme betrayal. The Holocaust becomes the frame of reference by which the two women measure all else. Holocaust imagery and associations inform their thinking, their speech, even their understanding of postwar urban blight. Contemporary events, people, and conditions are correlated to Holocaust classifications and definitions. A personal betrayal is "like telling the police where Anne Frank is hiding" (60); a person of ignoble behavior is described as "a gold tooth salvager" or "an informer" (60). A skeletal Chinese laundryman is compared to "the near-corpses of last evening's televised trial" (43) and seen, in the mind's eye, stretched out on the freezing shelves with camp inmates whose will to live had been destroyed.

Repudiation of God or at least anger for divine indifference in the face of absolute evil are characteristic responses in literature of the Holocaust. Rosen adds her voice to those of other prominent novelists and poets whose work wrestles with Holocaust-wrought theological crisis. Like protesting Jews in the works of Elie Wiesel and I. B. Singer, Rosen's characters agonize over God's responsibility for the six million. They judge and denounce divine failure. Reminiscent of the young protagonist of *Night* questioning whether he should bless the name of a God who has had thousands of children burned in His pits . . . kept six crematories working night and day . . . created Auschwitz, Birkenaw, Buna"[7] is Jean Lamb's bitter prayer-parody, rebuking the merciless "God of the medical-experiment cell block . . . God of the common lime pit grave . . . God of chopped fingers . . . of blind eyes, God of electrodes attached at one end to a jeep battery and at the other to the genitals of political prisoners" (233). The language of prayer is now grotesquely stained by the Holocaust, grotesquely evocative of torture and death associated with concentration camp reality. Rosen's use of this construction evokes the traditional Jewish response of counter commentary parodying or inverting sacred texts to reveal the subversion of God's principles. Jean's prayer perverts traditional liturgical language as Nazism disrupted the lives of its victims. This prayer-parody anticipates authorial protest of divine failure in "Justice for Jonah" where, nearly two decades later, Rosen writes: "Show me a text that speaks of God's unbounded mercy, and images of the Holocaust appear before my eyes (*AI*, 87). Complementing Jean's prayer is Hattie's Holocaust-wrought transformation to non-believer charted in her progressive reflections: from belief ("There but for the grace of God go I") to skepticism ("what when there is no grace of God?") and finally to disavowal ("there but for the grace of God and there is no grace of God, we see that there is none") (131).

Finally Rosen incorporates the subject of her major critical essays, the problematics of Holocaust transmission, into fictional thematic and structural contexts. Transmission of the astonishing tale leads to Rosen's narrative design of manuscript-within-manuscript-within-manuscript for the characters' subjective responses and incorporation of newspaper accounts and trial testimony to enhance the narrative's historicity. The novel attains its structural unity via a series of letters and diary entries, the letters being written by the self-sacrificial Jean Lamb, describing her Holocaust thoughts and Holocaust-centered friendship with Hattie, the diarist of the novel. Each woman bears witness creatively, Jean in her diary-letters and Hattie in multiple manuscripts for a play, a memoir, a novel. The letters and diary reveal the rite of passage between receiving the news and making it one's own. The distance between listening and telling is traversed as trial testimony sparks Jean's revelatory memory. Hattie formally assumes the task of Holocaust transmission to the next generation through her diary, a form evoking the Holocaust diaries and testimonies of survivors and simultaneously suggesting how personal the Holocaust has become for her. She also bequeaths Holocaust consciousness to her daughter in a play that casts the child as the reincarnation of an infant victim among other young victims. One of the goals Rosen sought to achieve in *Touching Evil* "was to try to find some way that would break through the conventional distancing of the novel that would get at something intense enough and intimate enough, which is how reading about the Holocaust strikes [one]" (interview). Through the fictional texts that simultaneously demonstrate their personal response to Holocaust history and testify to the continuing effect of the Nazi crime against humanity, a crime that will haunt each succeeding generation, Rosen has admirably achieved her objective.

Departing from the emphasis on the novel's gentile "witnesses through the imagination," Rosen turns her attention, in the short fiction, to juxtaposing impressions and reactions of Holocaust survivors and innocent Jewish Americans who have intimate contact with them and strive to understand them. Although she continues to work through indirection, never setting the fiction directly in the concentration camp universe, her Holocaust-haunted characters grow ever more intense as they explore what it means to live with knowledge of the Shoah. Several of these stories incorporate a husband-survivor and an American wife who exhibits various degrees of sensitivity to the implications of her husband's Holocaust background. In other instances, her focus is on postwar encounters of Jews and Germans and the impact of the Holocaust on the second generation.

In "The Cheek of the Trout," Vienna—site of beautiful architecture, exquisite music, and nasty Holocaust history—is the backdrop for the contrapuntal perceptions of a vacationing survivor and his American wife.[8] The husband, whose pleasure in the city is marred by memories of lost family and his own removal in a children's transport, asks his wife to enjoy the city for him. When they venture into the older districts, the survivor identifies the places of his childhood: his family home, the path he took to school, the park bench where the family enjoyed their Sunday outings. The sight of his uncle's confiscated but still prospering shop evokes his speculation about Austrian neighbors benefiting from expropriation of Jewish property.

Tension generated by this trip invades the marital relationship: "From the beginning they knew the trip would be too painful . . . it was too full of silences between them" (400). Despite his wife's empathy, the husband knows "she could never understand" (398). The wife alternates between absorbing her husband's pain and failure to discern. In response to his resentment of nonsurvivors' appropriation of Holocaust memory, she asserts, "I'm not a tourist! How could I know you and not think of what went on here? I would think of it even if I didn't know you!" (404). Despite her desire to share his history, she is also overwhelmed and occasionally wishes to evade it. Reversing the process of entering the Holocaust as "witness through the imagination," this protagonist uses her imagination to meliorate Holocaust reality, albeit briefly. She imagines an alternate identity for herself and her husband, fantasizing that they are younger and that her husband's father is the survivor.

Detachment is temporary. On the second day of the trip, the couple visit a Jewish cemetery in search of a gravestone the husband arranged from America for his father. Gravestone inscriptions provide an ironic and tragic reminder of the diverse experience of Vienna's privileged citizens and its Jews. The couple find elaborate Gothic-lettered stones of gentiles signifying their accomplishments as city administrators and professionals. Modest stones testify to Jewish lives unlived, cut short by persecution: *"Vergast Belsec, Gestorben in Theresienstadt.... Verschleppt nach Auschwitz Umgekommmen in Dachau. Ermordet in Belsen"* (402). Mourner and bystander experience divergent responses at graveside. The survivor wants to believe that they are in the presence of his father's ashes. The American woman remains skeptical of "the bureaucrats of Buchenwald, [ordering] the ashes of individuals to be carefully scooped and labeled and sent home because it was still in the early years of killings" (401).

Progressing from Holocaust encounter through memory in the first half of the narrative, Rosen stages an obligatory dramatic meeting between Jew and German in the latter portion of the tale. Having previously resisted joining the healthy Austrian mountain climbers, who "were all about the right age" (406) to have served the Hitler cause, the Americans finally prepare to join a young German couple for dinner at their hotel. Anticipation is fraught with discomforting speculation as the American wife envisions Heinrich's father counseling his son with homilies from Hamburg:

> "If you meet any Jews, don't hang your head. It's true your grandfather joined the Nazi party for business reasons, and I became an S. S. officer when I was young, but whatever we did, you're another generation—you had nothing to do with it, and you don't owe an apology. (408–9)

Although the Jewish woman exempts the son from the sins of the father in this revery, the remainder of the imagined speech binds the postwar father to his Nazi past. "If you meet a Jew, [he counsels] you can be friendly, offer a glass of wine, if you can stand to be with them, but on no account are you required to apologize" (409). The actual "confrontation" amounts to little. The Americans acknowledge their difficulty in socializing with

Germans and Austrians of an age to have been involved in Hitler's war. Heinrich and Elsa agree that it is a "natural" and "understandable" reaction. The evening and the story conclude with the couples dining on the trout of the story's title, an allusion to Schubert's beautiful composition, *Die Forelle* ("The Trout"), transformed in this context to a stunning symbolic condemnation of Nazism. The musical allusion is a vivid reminder of Holocaust-era Austrian and German appreciation of the arts alongside commission of atrocity. Lest we forget, Rosen reminds us in her note accompanying publication of the story,

> Concentration camp commandants were often men of "culture" who would finish the day's hideous work and then repair to an evening of beautiful German music. In Auschwitz the S.S. commandant kept a quartet of gifted prisoners playing German music day and night as Jews stumbled to the gas chambers. (*AI,* 109)

In "The Inner Light and the Fire," Rosen dramatizes a more compelling confrontation of a Jewish survivor and Germans through the agency of a guileless American gentile who feels they need to be brought together.[9] In the context of cosmopolitan Cambridge, Massachusetts, she arranges a meeting between a recently transplanted German academic and his wife with a Holocaust survivor, Mr. Schneider, in order that the Jew "forever after take [the Traugotts] into account when he thinks of Germans" (5). What the Germans are to take from this meeting is undefined. As in *Touching Evil,* Rosen's focus in this story is on the Holocaust sensibility of the non-Jew, but unlike the sympathetic women of the novel, this woman's response to Holocaust testimony is ambivalent. Although she has wanted to listen to "Man in extremis" (5), convinced that he owes society his legacy, she is impatient with his account and feels assaulted by his tale. Rosen punctuates every line of the survivor's rendition with his auditor's wounded perception:

> "The S. S. put me to work in a storehouse." Thump! "First they send trucks to take out everything from Jewish stores. And if something is missing from the inventory, they shoot the storekeeper!" Thump! "In the ghetto they are starving. They are dropping down." Thump! "Pillows, shoes, suits, blankets, food, whatever is there, is thrown like this in a pile. In a mountain!" Thump! (6)

Repeated use of the word "thump" following each narrated detail conveys and intensifies the auditor's discomfort, an ache that

Rosen differentiates from Jean Lamb's empathetic pain. Similarly, although the American wants the Traugotts to hear the survivor's testimony, she is protective of the cultured Germans. She fears the Jew's testimony will vanquish them: "Brave Gretel, so . . . full of inner light, so vulnerable, has bravely delivered the sword into Mr. Schneider's hands, and must now be brave enough to let it cleave" (6). Responding to Gretel's notice of Kosher butcher shops in Boston and their absence in Germany, Schneider caustically informs her that the lack of these shops in Germany corresponds to the absence of Jews. If Gretel has been sheltered from the truth and magnitude of Germany's Holocaust crimes, her husband has not. He confesses that his family knew what was happening. As he walked with his father in the fields, they saw a hundred ghostlike women brought to work. Lest we think Walter is truly facing up to his nation's villainous past, Rosen characterizes his remark as evidencing "just a trace of residual national pride that pokes, hard as a rock, through the soft snowblanket of general atonement" (7).

Upon their return to Europe, the German couple send a newspaper clipping and their own exuberant commentary hailing the building of a new synagogue in Germany, which "gives the appearance of 'a folded paper construction.' Yet it is the epitome . . . 'of the age of concrete and steel'" (8). The ironic description highlighting the discrepancy between architectural form and function recalls the characteristic duplicity pervading the Nazi administration of the Final Solution, when gas chambers appeared to be ordinary shower rooms. Mr. Schneider ignores the architectural commentary and raises the issue the German newspaper fails to report: "The synagogue that formerly stood on this spot was destroyed by fire" (8) set by the Nazis. Why express glee at the building of German synagogues now that there are no Jews to worship in them? Erection of a synagogue in a Jewless Germany evokes the Nazi plan for a postwar museum of an extinct race.

Neither postwar German synagogue architecture nor the judicial system adequately redresses the criminal past. When Janice speculates that there was probably nothing in the newspaper about the recent trial in which Schneider testified about a sadistic camp commandant, the tailor sardonically observes that as the Nazi defendant is now seventy-nine years old, he will be considered too old to be punished for his crime: "So you see, if you don't allow other people to live to be seventy-nine, and if you escape long enough, then your defense can be that you yourself are now seventy-nine!" (8).

As the reflective mentality is Melville's concern in "Bartleby, the Scrivener," so too is the fictive reflector Rosen's primary interest in this story. The final section returns the reader to the American's consciousness. Having failed to provide an epiphany for Schneider and the German couple, the American—whose false sense of healing, for whom "Memory heals itself the way flesh heals," for whom "'Never forget!' was an idle slogan" (9)—experiences her own epiphany. After listening to Schneider's report of his witness of a group of S. S. men nailing a still-living man into a wooden box and throwing the box down two flights of stairs, Janice dreams of "A figure horribly pierced . . . its clothes drip blood" (9). She dreams of "Mr. Schneider's man [standing] up in the Traugott's box! Pale, dishevelled, his face and body torn" (9). This dream and the crying voice she continues to hear affirm that Holocaust memory cannot, and ought not, be put to rest. A few days later her husband discovers that the large painted wooden box, the German couple's farewell gift, heretofore treasured and prominently displayed, has now been relegated to the basement. Thus, in an ironic reversal, the American who had thought the Holocaust victim needed to be unburdened of the memory by meeting pleasant Germans is herself transformed by the encounter. That she removed the Traugott box from its honored setting implies that she is progressing from unconscious acceptance, manifested in her dream, to conscious recognition of the enormities of Holocaust history and will join those for whom Holocaust knowledge signifies an important transformation.

Protest against God's Holocaust silence and the nature and validity of religious practice in the post-Holocaust era, common themes in the work of Elie Wiesel, I. B. Singer, and Cynthia Ozick, recur in Rosen's Holocaust writing. In an essay on the story of Jonah for *Congregation,* a collection of Jewish writers' responses to the books of the Bible,[10] Rosen invents a scenario of Jonah seeing the future, actually seeing the Holocaust and troubled by God's mercy, which is demonstrated through forgiveness of sinners in ancient times as contrasted with His failure to intervene on behalf of innocents during the Holocaust. In the short story "What Must I Say to You?" she explores rejection and observance of religious ritual as Holocaust response.[11] Husband and wife are in conflict about placing a *mezuzah,* a small case enclosing a roll of parchment on which are transcribed two biblical passages, on the doorframe of their home, as prescribed by Judaic law. The husband, a Holocaust survivor whose family has been annihilated in the Holocaust and who has had a Jewish education, insists on traditional observance. The American-born Jewish wife, uneducated in Judaism, rejects the *mezuzah*, arguing—as Jean Lamb does—that pre-Holocaust and post-Holocaust life styles cannot be similar. To support her contention, the wife who, again like Jean Lamb, has followed the Eichmann trial, quotes the passage about the deported children struggling with their Nazi captors that Hattie had read in the museum scene of the novel. She is astonished that despite Holocaust abominations her husband rejects neither God nor Judaism.

In the symbolic and multilayered short story "Fences," whose title alludes to concentration camp fences and evokes the psychological barriers survivors erect and dismantle between themselves and nonwitnesses, Rosen returns to the theme of religious response to the Shoah, develops the delicate psychological balance of survivors in dialogue and dramatic presentation more thoroughly than before, and introduces the theme of Holocaust impact on the second generation.[12] The chorus of the rescued consists of two primary voices and a minor one. The dominant voices are those of the protagonist Edward, who escaped from Vienna in a children's transport to England, following his father's murder in an early concentration camp, and his antagonist, the family lodger, Frederick, who lost his wife and child. The minor voice is that of Edward's older sister, Bryna, who remained in Austria with their mother. "Coddling the flesh because the heart won't heal" (81), Bryna is more fragile than Edward and Frederick. Aunt Bryna's discovery of a package containing her dead father's prayer shawl is the catalyst for debate regarding transmittal of Holocaust memory and assumption of Judaic religious identity.

The lodger is the quintessential exemplar of clinical psychiatric writings on survivor syndrome and is closest among Rosen's characters to Cynthia Ozick's troubled survivor, Rosa Lublin of *The Shawl*. Frederick, too, remains unmarried, lives in a rented room in an apartment occupied by another survivor, and maintains silence about his lost family. Frederick shares Rosa Lublin's bitterness regarding the Holocaust era's abandonment of the Jews, her contempt for people whose interest in survivors is inauthentic, and her conviction that "No one can enter the Holocaust" (80). Perhaps because Frederick does not have a child to protect, as Edward does, he permits his rage to emerge unbridled while commenting on indifference to the slaughter of European Jewry. Frederick articulates a dilemma that is at the center of Rosen's Holocaust writing: "Between the reality-witnesses and the imaginers there can be no accord. The imaginers . . . wish in subtle ways to extract meanings that the survivors themselves avoid" (80). As choral commentator and author of "a social history of the western world in the Twenties and Thirties" (76), Frederick attests to the difficulties of Holocaust transmission explicitly and evokes a central Holocaust image to articulate the story's theme: "All around there are electrified fences. As the grandparents could not get out, so no one else can get in" (77).

Although Rosen does not explain the family's Holocaust silence, it may be attributed to the parents' effort to shield their ten-year-old son and to Edward's means for coping with contemporary life. Initially Edward fears the sight of the prayer shawl will lead to painful questions from Daniel. Yet it is at his son's urging that Edward's memories take voice. In response to the child's question about when his grandfather stopped wearing the prayer shawl—a query phrased in diction that evades Holocaust reality—the father responds forthrightly, abandoning a protective veneer: "When did my father die, do you mean, Daniel? He was taken to a concentration camp when I was your age. After six months he died" (79). In contrast to this direct approach, Edward later hesitates to answer Daniel's question about his grandmother's history. He seeks, not to spare his son, but to award his mother an extra moment of life, if only metaphorically, as he revels in memory of her nurturing role before disclosing that she was transported "to the East, and shot . . . in a field of snow" (81).

Edward transmits more than Holocaust history to his son. Like the survivor father of "What Must I Say to You?" he passes on the Judaic heritage in the act of sharing the prayer shawl with him.[13] Enacting the ritual associated with donning the *tallis,* kissing the embroidered calligraphic neckpiece, emblematic of embracing the commandments, he covers his head and upper body in the column of black and white stripes and recalls for his son how he had shared a similar religious experience with his father. In Edward's gesture of draping the prayer shawl over his amenable son, Rosen symbolically intimates and then explicitly declares the survival of Jewry and Judaism in the post-Holocaust era. This gesture is confirmed in Rosen's explicit declaration of the prayer shawl's survival through its many migrations in wartime and in peace. Devotion of adherents who cherish and transmit the legacy to future generations prepared to embrace it signifies survival of Judaism and the Jewish people.

Paralleling Frederick's role as nonfamily observer is Daniel's American-born mother, who wavers between engagement and withdrawal. Sensitive to her husband's psychic pain yet protective of her young son's innocence, she observes the conferral scene with some trepidation, mentally urging her son to resist vicarious association with his father's Viennese trial. Aware of the perils of imaginary shifting into other people's places, Rebecca fears that the impressionable boy will be permanently scarred by Holocaust knowledge. Paradoxically, anxiety for the son leads to the mother's epiphany, "with the clarity of sudden electrification" (82). Contradictory responses to the visual stimulus of the prayer shawl's broad black stripes against the white of the bedspread lead the parents to polar perspectives. Edward perceives the black strips as Torahic calligraphy. But Rebecca, religiously unschooled, like the wife in "What Must I Say to You?," can only imagine a Holocaust vision of striped concentration camp uniforms. She construes the *tallis*-clad child symbolically—another generation assuming the burden of Jewish history and oppression. Before Rebecca can remove the *tallis,* she collides with Frederick, whose reaction to the conferral prompts Rebecca's reconsideration. Hitherto secretive about his family, Frederick now shares a photograph that Rebecca presumes to be either his son or the young Frederick himself. The tale concludes with Frederick initiating communication, Rebecca responding to him and refraining from articulating her objection to Holocaust transmittal to her son, and Edward and Daniel commemorating the dead and committing themselves to a Jewish future.

Writing of her own study of the Holocaust in "Notes Toward a Holocaust Fiction,"[14] Rosen claims, "There is no beginning and no end to thinking about the Holocaust. We spend our lives reading witness books, looking at films of testimony, and we know nothing. Behind every degradation, every terror published or recounted, horrors we cannot know lie buried with those who could not survive" (*AI,* 105–6). The moral injunction to remember, central to Jewish thinking, is also at the heart of Rosen's fiction. As she declares in "The Literature of Contempt," "the central question was—and is still—how to write as a Jew after the Holocaust" (*AI,* 42). Her response to this history affirms her place among those writers who will help future generations understand our time, one of the saddest and most bestial episodes in human history. Norma Rosen has made a significant contribution to imaginative literature, which has sought to understand a force hitherto beyond the imagination, not by re-creating the Holocaust universe but by demonstrating that the subject is, and should be, of concern to thinking people, for only when authentic imagination is achieved will lives be changed by an iniquity so absolute that it overpowered earlier concepts of good and evil.

Notes

1. Norma Rosen, *Accidents of Influence: Writing as a Woman and a Jew in America* (Albany: SUNY Press, 1992); hereafter cited in the text as *AI.*

2. Norma Rosen, interview by S. Lillian Kremer, 19 May 1988; hereafter cited as "interview."

3. Isaac Rosenfeld, "The Meaning of Terror," in his *An Age of Enormity: Life and Writing in the Forties and Fifties* (Cleveland: World Publishing Co., 1962), 209.

4. *Touching Evil* (New York: Harcourt, Brace and World, 1969); page numbers will be cited parenthetically in the text.

5. In "Notes Toward a Holocaust Fiction," Rosen writes:

> When I wrote of the devastation in the woman who makes her discovery at the time the camps were opened and photographs were released, I believed it was invention. Later, I read Susan Sontag's *On Photography* and found her description—"a negative epiphany"—of her first sight, at age twelve, of photographs from the camps in 1945. (*AI,* 108)

6. Rosen was pregnant in 1961, "watching the Eichmann trial . . . asking the question "How can we live now?" (*AI,* 107).

7. Elie Wiesel, *Night,* trans. Stella Rodway (New York: Hill and Wang, 1960).

8. Rosen, "The Cheek of the Trout," in *Testimony: Contemporary Writers Make the Holocaust Personal,* ed. David Rosenberg (New York: Times Books, 1989), 398–411.

9. Rosen, "The Inner Light and the Fire," *Forthcoming: Jewish Imaginative Writing* 1, no. 3/4 (Fall 1983): 4–9.

10. "Justice for Jonah, or, A Bible Bartleby," in *Congregation: Contemporary Writers Read the Jewish Bible,* ed. David Rosenberg (New York: Harcourt Brace Jovanovich, 1987); reprinted in *AI,* 87–96.

11. Rosen, "What Must I Say to You?" in *The Woman Who Lost Her Names: Selected Writings by American-Jewish Women,* ed. Julia Wolf Mazow (San Francisco: Harper and Row, 1980), 58–69.

12. Rosen, "Fences," *Orim: A Jewish Journal at Yale* 1 (Spring 1986): 75–83.

13. She notes that her "husband's father's *tallis* was retrieved in the same way" and that, as in "Fences," it was a very moving experience for her to see

that prayer shawl. The conferral of the *tallis* did not occur in her family (interview).

14. "Notes Toward a Holocaust Fiction," in *Testimony: Contemporary Writers Make the Holocaust Personal,* ed. David Rosenberg (New York: Times Books, 1989), 392–98; reprinted in *AI,* 105–11.

Resisting the Melting Pot: The Jewish Back-Story in the Fiction of Lynne Sharon Schwartz

James M. Mellard

Lynne Sharon Schwartz is author of some twenty-eight stories and five novels.[1] While her fiction includes a few stories close to fable and dream-fantasy, it tends toward the conventionally realistic. The subjects of her fiction are urban families beset by marital problems and the difficulties of growing up and growing old. While her characters range from Asian American to middle-class African American to the generically white, middle-class, assimilated European American, they are only occasionally identified expressly as *Jewish* American. Though she gives us surnames and other familiarizing details from which we may infer that many characters in her stories and novels are ethnically Jewish, Schwartz seems on the surface very intent on representing the value and power of the American "melting pot." Except for three stories ("Killing the Bees," "The Melting Pot," and "The Opiate of the People") and one novel *(Leaving Brooklyn),* she seldom makes the specifically Jewish experience or heritage an overt theme. Rather, throughout the vast majority of her fiction she displaces her own inheritance in favor of themes of "ordinary" realism. These include motifs of race or class or gender identity in about a fourth of the stories, male and female relations in about one-third, and life and death in another third. The novels, like most novels, embrace multiple topics, but they too have rather conventional themes. *Rough Strife* focuses on love, marriage, and infidelity. *Balancing Acts* treats the relations of children to parents and the certainty of old age and death. *Disturbances in the Field* embraces love, marriage, and the death of children. *Leaving Brooklyn* emphasizes growing up and leaving the family nest. But in reading through Schwartz's canon, one senses that there is in fact an emotionally charged ethnic or ur-story, a foundational tale about origins that is the invisible bedrock on which Schwartz's fiction rests. This story is like the nine-tenths of the iceberg Hemingway says gives authority to the best fiction. Or, in the metaphor I shall use, it is the "back-story" gifted artists create for their characters in the most powerful of dramatic performances. It is a story both there and not there. While implicit in the details, it is absent in the surfaces. Thus, to understand the virtually hidden back-story of Schwartz's fiction, we must look first at the surfaces presented in the three early novels, then at two stories in which Schwartz's invisible back-story is made visible, and finally at a novel—the fourth—in which surfaces and the depths of the back-story come together quite seamlessly.

Rough Strife is a love story that is also the story of a marriage. Its title comes from Marvell:

> Now let us sport us while we may;
> And now, like am'rous birds of prey,
> . . . .
> . . . tear our pleasures with rough strife
> Through the iron gates of life.

Its story is told from the point of view of the wife, Caroline, a mathematician who specializes in topology. It tabulates the pleasures and afflictions that seem common in marriages of working professionals from about 1960 to 1980. Married to Ivan, an art and architectural critic who works for foundations that aid artists and government, Caroline gets her Ph.D. after marriage and teaches at a couple of small universities before taking a position in New York City. She achieves tenure, a growing reputation as a researcher, and for a time even heads her department at one of the colleges. Amid her professional life she bears two daughters, suffers through Ivan's assumed infidelity, and complacently indulges in her own admittedly selfish affairs, one with a graduate student, one with a French professor, and a third, while on a visiting appointment, with an English professor. Along the way she undergoes an angry feminist awakening, drives herself mercilessly to do and have everything (to be, in short, Superwoman), but eventually moderates her feminist stance, and in her mid forties at the novel's close, seems destined to live happily ever after with Ivan—or as happily as one can in these rough, strife-filled times.

Critics generally liked this novel. In a moderately favorable review of it, Katha Pollitt says, "Lynne Sharon Schwartz registers the fluctuations of marital feeling with the fidelity of a Geiger counter." Pollitt complains, however, that about midway her "admiration for Miss Schwartz's gifts as a reporter of emotional weather turned to irritation at her lack of interest in anything else." She complains of boredom in the novel because "the emotional dynamics of Caroline's marriage are not interesting enough to bear the close inspection Schwartz bestows."[2] But in my view the novel works well. We end up liking both Caroline and Ivan, admiring their willingness to continue to work at their marriage and envying no doubt the sheer physical passion they seem to retain for each other even into their middle years. A more accurate assessment of the novel comes from Dorothy Wickenden, who writes, "The protagonists of *Rough Strife* may seem precious types at first glance but, surprisingly enough, they are a couple whose troubles we can believe in and sympathize with." Wickenden notes that they "inflict casual cruelties on each other and Schwartz invests their marital battles with a viciousness tinged with the ludicrous." Still, says Wickenden, Schwartz "doesn't let Ivan and Caroline wallow in apathy or bitterness or self-pity. They show scars as they grow older and the domestic quarrels continue, but throughout it all they retain their sense of humor. *Rough Strife* is a wise novel, rewarding in its honesty and clarity of vision."[3] Equally to the point, Joyce Carol Oates in a remark quoted on the dust jacket of the novel, calls it "spare but deeply moving and extremely . . . sophisticated." I think Oates is exactly right, for this is a genuinely insightful novel, first or otherwise. But Schwartz's Jewish backstory is almost totally invisible in it.

Schwartz's second novel, however, does not quite reach the quality of her first. Though the Jewish elements are more overt, *Balancing Acts* makes little of them. Worse, it seems not quite to know whether it was written for juveniles or adults. The alternating story of thirteen-year-old Alison Markman and seventy-four-year-old former circus trapeze artist Max Fried, the novel counterpoints the problems of adolescence and health-troubled old age. Cutely and improbably, Alison and Max become buddies who rely on each other to combat the problems each faces, Alison with her somewhat distant family, particularly a mother who is now expecting another child, and Max with his serious heart problems and grief over the loss of his beloved wife. Alison displaces some of her problems onto stories she writes of a heroic teenager much like herself. Max addresses his by becoming a volunteer gym teacher at Alison's public school and by allowing himself to fall in love with a kindly widow named Lettie. Eventually, in the novel's climactic episode, precipitated by Alison's running away to join a circus to be like Max, Max and Lettie join forces with Alison's parents to find the girl and in the course of the search to help the parents better understand their troubled daughter. The novel, though interestingly conceived, is not effective. My reservations are echoed by a reviewer who complains that the "two main characters are too cute and sensitive and wonderful for words, and they converse in such smarmily smug platitudes that it won't be long before you'll be itching to have their funny-bones broken." The critic complains that the novel is "disappointing, derivative, and definitely inferior to the author's demonstrated capabilities."[4]

Disturbances in the Field does not suffer from identity problems. Like Schwartz's first novel, it is a detailed, realistic, capacious novel for mature people. *Disturbances* focuses upon the relationship of a couple who marry, raise a family, separate on occasion, and, amid all the ordinary things, suffer the most devastating blow parents may face—the death of a child; indeed, the deaths of two children in an accident. It is indicative of the capaciousness of the novel that this devastating episode occurs just halfway through, at a moment when Lydia Rowe, the narrator, thinks their lives are "fulfilled and, in a way, over. We had arrived at who we were," she thinks, "and the rest would be simply acting out the roles of ourselves, creating scenes in which our natures and talents could unfurl, the way a playwright writes a part for a specific actress. There would be, "she thinks, "no more great changes."[5] But she learns that a bus accident has killed two of her children and several others as well. Such are the disturbances in the field that make human life. Schwartz's title comes from lines in Alfred North Whitehead's *The Concepts of Nature:* "The object cannot really be separated from the field. The object is in fact nothing else than the systematically adjusted set of modifications of the field." Indeed, we may say that novels in general are virtually nothing but such fields and the succession of objects created in them by "disturbances" called people and events. This is a very Jamasian notion, and James is mentioned everywhere in Schwartz. Carole Cook, in a review of this work, notes the nineteenth-century essence of Schwartz's fine novel. This is, she says, "just such a novel as Henry James would have approved, being not so much a story, moral or otherwise, as the execution of an entire, unique world out of a generous accumulation of detail, character, and incident. In its size and its freedom, it achieves the 'immense and exquisite correspondence with life' that James maintained was the stuff and soul of fiction. It has the total quality of reality, in all its untidiness and muddlement and mulish resistance to logic and formula."[6] *Disturbances* is a throwback to another time, but it brings a sense of truth that is quite timeless. Even so, the truth it bears suggests little of the Jewish back-story that will become more evident in the short fiction that dominates Schwartz's publications between the appearance of her third and fourth novels.

Like the novels, the vast majority of Schwartz's stories focus on themes of love, marriage, families, and life and death. But beneath these themes in the stories is that other theme forming the virtually unconscious bedrock—the necessarily invisible iceberg—on which the surfaces of Schwartz's fictions rest. This theme we might name the Jewish experience of otherness and all that it has brought down upon Jews. In Schwartz, it is linked quite hauntingly to the Holocaust in one story, "Killing the Bees" (*The Melting Pot,* 97–109). But in two other stories the theme is connected to other themes, the assimilation of the first generation within American culture and that generation's well-meant shielding of the second generation from the European background, the Jewish back-story of oppression, ostracism, and death. In Schwartz's fiction, the theme is handled quite directly in one early story and is transformed into a psychoanalytic parable of the child's incorporation of its "parents" in a later one. In the first instance, "The Opiate of the People" (*Acquainted with the Night,* 168–88) seems to offer the truly original version of Schwartz's bedrock story about ethno-religious origins. In "Opiate," the main perspective is that of a young woman. Taking snapshots of Lucy at ages six, eleven, fifteen, in the college years, and finally at twenty-six, the story focuses on the relation between Lucy and her father, David. The bone of contention between Lucy and David is David's origins, his life in Russia—the old country he has "left"—and in the city, Kiev, where he lived the first few years of his life before, mercifully, he was brought to America. At six, watching her father dance as if in celebration of the defeat of Germany after the Second World War, Lucy first asks, "why can't we have a Christmas tree?" (168). At eleven she asks the same question and David answers, "It's not our holiday" (169). But unhappy with that answer, Lucy persists. "It's only a symbol," she says, her precocious use of the word momentarily "charm[ing] away his annoyance" (169). The next morning, still dissatisfied, she asks her mother the same question. "Because," Anna tells Lucy, "they made him wear a yellow arm band when he went to school." But this answer only puzzles Lucy further: "These bizarre facts tossed out at chance intervals made her feel another world, a shadow world, existed at the rim of their own. 'But that was in another country.' 'It makes no difference. The tree is the same'" (169). Schwartz tells us that Lucy "grasped that David was keeping something back from her" and, moreover, that this "something . . . touched herself as well as him" (169–70). But at eleven she cannot quite understand what the real issue is. Thus what David holds back—or that he chooses to hold back—becomes Lucy's preoccupation and the pivot of the story. Clearly the Jewish back-story runs counter to the stories of assimilation and generational shielding.

"The Opiate of the People" is as much the father's as the daughter's story. It gives a very condensed account of David's life in America. With all of his family but one older brother, David had come to New York City probably (the story gives no exact dates) during the Great War or the Bolshevik Revolution in Russia (David is fond of quoting—or misquoting—Marx and Lenin). In the United States, David had done well. While he often thinks he had not made as much money as his father might have expected, still he had made enough to rear Lucy and two sons, all three successful in their professions. But it may well be that David is proudest of having assimilated within the new culture. "Most of the time David was very proud of the way his life had turned out. Considering. He was proud of having married a good-looking American-born girl he fell in love with in high school" (171). He loves his wife for many reasons, but one of them is that the "wholesome, free tone of hers" made her, to him, seem "so American" (171). But more than the wife he marries, the sign of his thorough assimilation is his proficiency in his new language. "He was proud of their children, their house, and their car. He was proud most of all, though he would never have admitted this, of his perfect English, no trace of an accent" (172).

The drive to master the new language comes to David from his father. Told by an uncle who had come to America two years earlier that he should read only the *New York Times,* David's father studied it each night for hours, even after working ten-hour days at his job. This mission becomes as sacred to David's father as once had been the study of his religion. "When David recalled him now it was . . . hunched in the unshaded glare of the kitchen light, studying as he used to, except back there [in Russia] it was the Talmud and here the *Times*" (173). As a child in his new country, David studied just as religiously. To perfect his speech, he imitated his teachers and practiced every spare moment, even giving up time from playing with peers, who ridiculed him for his obsession. But the work pays off for David. "After two years of effort," Schwartz says, "David's speech was flawless, untainted, and he hoped that with the language embedded in his tongue he could do whatever he chose, that no one need ever know how foolish and awkward and alien he had once sounded" (172).

Because she gives no visible sign of her foreign origins, Lucy becomes for David yet another symbol of his successful assimilation in his new country. Therein lies her unspoken conflict with her father. To him, Lucy will do "fine" not only because she can "take care of herself," but also—and to David most important—because "she was good-looking." That is "important for a girl," David thinks. "All in all," he thinks proudly, she is "a fine American girl" (174). David's view of Lucy constructs her in ways that she comes to understand. Lucy knows, for instance, that she dare not confide to David that at college her new roommate—"a blond girl from Virginia whose father was in the foreign service" (176)—asks Lucy where she is from because in fact she takes her to be foreign. The roommate regards her "exotic," though Lucy cannot grasp why, since she has none of the "almost Oriental faces" of some of her aunts, those who sound "foreign" to David. David had warned her of bigotry she might encounter in this "classy" school (176), but in her innocence Lucy is not so sure it is bigotry. Because her roommate regards her as "exotic," she develops a fantasy that directly engages her "foreign" origins. She makes a fetish of appearing Russian. But her desire to impress her professors with a "fine" Russian accent, as Lucy realizes eventually, could never have happened," mainly because she failed to remember her mother's private warning. "Being Russian is one thing," Anna had told her. "Being Jewish, from Russia, is something else" (177). As the child of a Russian Jewish father, Lucy should know things about history that she seems not to know or to understand. On one occasion, David chides her when she asks why he had never corresponded with the brother left behind. They did keep in contact for a time, David tells Lucy, but things changed, got even worse. "How could we write?" he laments. "There were wars and pogroms. . . . There were . . . [*sic*] incidents. Killings. Didn't you learn any history?

didn't you learn about that famous ravine? That was our city" (179). The city is Kiev, near Babi Yar, site of the Russian Nazi regime's brutal mass murder of more than one hundred thousand persons, most of them Jews.

Eventually, however, Lucy learns something more about her father's life in Russia. At twenty-six, she meets Rickoff and Panofsky, two of David's childhood friends, now elderly men, who like David had come to America to escape anti-Semitism and other evils. Their little stories about what it was like to live in Russian winters and summers enthrall Lucy. She "was transported. It was just such privacies she had craved, like something out of a book, alien, exotic, transcendent." Though Panofsky shares some of David's reservations about revealing the darker side of their background and so mocks her romanticism, Lucy nonetheless asks, "Is it so foolish to want to know something about your own history?" (183). Lucy thinks not, and she seizes on these old people as a doorway into an unknown past. "She saw her past as swaddled in secrecy, infused with a vast nostalgia for something she had never known, something which perhaps had never even existed, except as a mystery she herself had created and nourished" (183). However ordinary these friends from the old country might be, Lucy looks upon them "as though they were artifacts, archaeologists' finds" (183). Thus when she sees her father walk away from her and the others, she feels at once "abandoned" by him and yet "finally free to unearth what she wanted."

But the story also gives us David's side. He does not want his children burdened by the history he knows. It is one thing for his generation, these "aging, familiar faces of transplanted people like Panofsky trying desperately, uselessly, to be carefree and self-assured, to be new and free and American" (186). But such people only remind David of the past that he has always hoped to escape, of the reasons he has shielded his children from it. While he means to protect his sons as well, Lucy has special meaning for David. Because he sees his own mother in her, Lucy might represent a way for David even to redeem the past in some measure. When David sees Lucy talking with his old friends, she seems to take on "their old-fashioned expressions and gestures." When she says "something with a swift dramatic flick of her hand," he suddenly sees "his mother brought back to life." But the vision chills him. Rather than seeing the salvation of the mother, it is as if the transformation damns the daughter to hell, "as if he had delivered her over to the very powers he had been shielding her from all these years, and she was all too willingly drawn in, drawn back. For a split second he glimpsed her not in her stylish silky dress but in heavy shapeless skirts and shawls, a dark scarf wrapped around her shaved head, her fine features coarsened by endless childrearing, scrubbing, cooking, and anxiety" (185).

Such a past is by no means what David wants to give Lucy. "For himself he accepted it, it would cling to him no matter what fine words or clothes or houses masked it," Schwartz writes. "But for his children, especially for her—ah, he had wanted them new, untainted, bred without that ancient history" (186). But the story ends with the suggestion that, however well-meant, David's way of dealing with his children—he is no doubt similar to many immigrants—was equally misguided. In response to Lucy's question, "Would it have cost you so much to tell me some of those things? Would it?" David now can feel only a face "hot with shame" and "an unspeakable confusion" (188). The strength of Schwartz's story, however, is that it makes villains of neither father nor daughter. As "Opiate" presents admirable but conflicting ways of approaching the Old World history, Schwartz outlines some sociological implications of the bedrock story that will eventually take on very direct psychoanalytic dimensions in "The Melting Pot."

In suggesting that a story of generational shielding can become a deeply unconscious story of psychological alienation, "The Melting Pot" offers a powerfully evocative variation on the dominant elements of "The Opiate of the People." Where in Lucy "Opiate" focuses on the first American-born generation, "The Melting Pot" concentrates on the second: on Rita, who would in effect be the daughter of one of David's sisters. Rita's father had grown up in New York City, but had moved to San Francisco in adulthood where he had married a Mexican immigrant in 1955. Rita is born in 1957, and in 1959 the tragedy occurs that marks Rita's life, but about which she knows little until 1974, when she is seventeen years old. She knows only that in 1959 she was taken from San Francisco to live in New York with her paternal grandparents, Sonia and Solomon. There she is raised much the same way as Lucy was. But there is a critical difference: it is not the Jewish or Russian origins that are a mystery to Rita, for both Sonia and Solomon speak freely about the old country; rather, it is the mystery of Rita's parentage. Knowledge about her parents and their lives together drives her "quest" (33), which she gives up only reluctantly, after realizing there are mysteries she will never be able to penetrate. Even so, the story turns on a surprising irony. In its psychoanalytic dimensions, "The Melting Pot" subsumes the quest of parentage in the quest of ethnoreligious identity.

The back-story of Rita's grandparents is like that of Lucy's father, uncles, and aunts in "The Opiate of the People." This story is clear in Schwartz's account of Sonia's early life. Sonia was one of a family of three boys and three girls who came to America "in installments" (22). Repeating the gender-related determinations found in "Opiate," "the girls became seamstresses, the boys lawyers." Those gender-related assignments have further consequences. As factory-working dressmakers, the girls find themselves able to "live in small apartments in Jewish ghettos with their husbands, small businessmen like Rita's grandfather" (23). As college-educated professionals, the brothers prefer to live "in modern assimilated suburbs" (23), as David has in "Opiate." Still, though possessing the same back-story as David and his kin, Sonia and Solomon differ radically in their personalities. Indeed, unlike Anna and David, who are rather colorless, Sonia and Solomon have personalities. These prompt Rita to react very differently to them: she is closer to Sonia, but Solomon represents Jewish law.

Perhaps as a faint representation of his biblical namesake, Solomon is an almost obsessive upholder of law. He "loves rules, constrictions," Schwartz tells us, "whatever narrows the broad path of life and disciplines the meandering spirit for its own good. The lust to submit is his ruling passion." But his devotion carries over to others as well. He insists that "others obey" those restrictions too (6). As a child, Rita did obey; she submitted, although not always in her heart. But later Rita resists his view of the world. Whereas he ignores and thereby denies existence to that which "he cannot appropriate, whatever refuses to go down and be assimilated," Rita at fourteen thinks she can "appropriate the world, make it over to fit her vision" (20–21). She understands that not all immigrants assimilate as well as Solomon and his tribe (and David and his); moreover, she feels herself one of the unassimilated. "She feels for those beyond the pillars," says Schwartz. The reason may be that "she is darker than any Jew she knows and has never had a chance to play Queen Esther. With an adolescent's passion to convert, she wants her grandfather to feel for them too, and to agree that breadth of spirit does not mean obeying the most rules but scorning them all, except for the rules of the heart" (20). For her vision, however, Sol calls Rita "a bleeding heart" (21) into her adulthood and continues to judge her and find her wanting. Twenty-eight years old, with a baccalaureate and a law degree from Berkeley and working as an immigration lawyer, Rita according to Solomon lives a life of "disobedience," and so violates her Jewish heritage.

Rita's grandmother is a direct contrast to her grandfather. If Solomon is a theist who speaks only of rules, Sonia is an atheist who speaks of conformity to establish a principle of difference. For example, Sonia "sits in the women's balcony behind a curtain and fasts on the Day of Atonement" (5). She does so not out of obedience, as Rita does, but because she "finds her identity in opposition. She conforms in order to assert her difference in the New World." In the Old World such "obedience" is unnecessary because the principle of difference, of opposition, was established for her and other Jews "in the form of ostracism and pogroms" (5). Still, she does not spend her entire life in conformity. As Sol's health fails, Sonia and Rita both slip out of his control (22), Rita in San Francisco, Sonia in managing the store. But for Sonia these circumstances merely extend a pattern set years before. "For the first three decades of their marriage" (an arranged one that occurred in 1927), she had obeyed the "law." "It was," writes Schwartz in one of her best metaphors, "as if she had sealed up her disobedience the way pioneer women canned fruits and vegetables for a later season, and then she broke it out in abundance, jar after jar releasing its briny fumes" (22). Breaking out, Sonia reverts to the mildly anarchic ways of her family, members of which engage in forms of more or less harmless "civil disobedience" (22). As nonconformists, Sonia and her family seem to Rita totally different from Solomon's. Sonia herself says that Solomon's "are cautious people, supremely timid in the face of life." Worse, they are timid for little reason. While she had experienced the anti-Semitism and other indignities of the Old World, "they came to the New World as infants and know only by hearsay what they escaped" (11). But despite these differences, Sonia recognizes that she can exist because of the law, of lawfulness, of lawful behavior.

The event that transforms Sonia, just as it changes Rita's world when she is two years old, is in Sol's and especially Sonia's view, "truly lawless." It is connected to an earlier violation of the law that Sol more than Sonia had been unable to "appropriate." This earlier event was his son's marriage to the Mexican immigrant.

Had Sol had his way, "according to the rules" he would have declared his son dead. His son would have been interred in absentia and mourned for a week, and neighbors would have visited him and Sonia while they sat on wooden boxes, wearing bedroom slippers, with the mirrors in the house covered by bed sheets. But . . . Sonia refused to do it. It was the beginning of her refusals" (21). Symbolic death is one thing, but real death is another. That constitutes the later, more tragic event. In 1959 their son was stabbed to death in San Francisco by his wife. The lawlessness of this event causes a cataclysm in Sonia's family, those anarchists of the commonplace who, in their grief and mourning, cry, "That is not the kind of lawlessness, the kind of anarchy they intended, no, never, never!" (23). It is, moreover, the kind of lawlessness that drives Sonia for a time to "stop recognizing the world, any world, New, Old, all the same to her" (23). What brings her back into the world and makes Sol a father and her a mother again is Rita, the child who is left.

This, minus the family murder, is the back-story, the story lying behind Rita's life, and the story that seems to lie behind all of Schwartz's fiction. But in the foreground of "The Melting Pot," as in "The Opiate of the People," is the story of a young woman who suffers an existential unease because she does not know who or what she is. For most of her life Rita does not know even the most basic details about her birth parents. It is only at age seventeen that Sonia tells her the full story. Until then Rita feels that "there is something peculiar and mysterious about who she is." It "keeps her silent, open-mouthed like an idiot." When she detects it, it is something that comes to her through "glimmerings of losses below the surface, like sunken jewels that divers plunge and grope for in vain" (p. 12). After Sonia tells Rita about the brief, tragic marriage that had produced her, Rita decides she will find her mother, who by this time is out of prison and presumably back in San Francisco. But Rita never finds her. When Rita turns to her friend Sanjay, she is, as he tells her, "footloose" and does not know where she belongs (p. 27). By that he clearly means that she does not yet know who she is. Who she is, however, is clearer to us perhaps than it is to Rita. For she, like most of us, is manifestly formed by the material facts of her history, by the specular (mirroring) images of her "parental" others, Sol and Sonia. They, moreover, have constructed for her the desire expressed so obviously in Schwartz's representations of Rita's longing for a father.

Rita's desire is plainly, achingly Oedipal, but it is more than that, too. She finds that father in fifty-year-old Sanjay, who was born in India and was therefore an immigrant like her grandfather. Sanjay seems modeled on another fantasy figure from Rita's childhood. Sol forbade her to do many things, but he did not forbid reading. "*A Little Princess* was her favorite story, where the orphaned and hungry heroine is forced to live in a lonely freezing garret, until a kindly Indian gentleman feeds her and lights a fire in her room and finally rescues her altogether, restoring her to a life of abundance" (4–5). Rita believes enough in this fantasy-figure to resurrect it when Sanjay, a widower, beseeches her to marry him, to find a place to belong, and to resolve questions of who she is. But this figure, while fitting well enough the archetype of the sort of father any child might want, seems to be a disguise hiding the real person constituting Rita's desired other. That other is more Oedipal than even Sanjay. Rita thinks herself fatherless, but that does not account for Sol's having played that role since she was two. So it is Sol more than her biological father who is repeated in Sanjay. It is simply that Sanjay, like the later literary fantasy figure, represents a more "maternal" father, the anaclitic father who loves and protects. Schwartz makes the appeal very clear. "It is only natural that Sanjay's fatherliness should appeal to her, a fatherless child—that and his size and bulk, his desire to possess and protect, his willingness . . . to accept the silences during which she tries to extricate herself from her history. His willingness to accept her history itself" (2).

Although Rita does not recognize that Sanjay is constructed for her within her desire, she does recognize the possibility that she can have a relation to Sanjay at all only because he constructs her in a certain way. "Rita has always imagined," we are told, "that she reminds him of his wife, that he wants her because of a resemblance" (3). It may well be, she further imagines, that perhaps Sanjay and his late wife "are communing through her body" (3). Since Rita feels herself as a link between Sol and Sonia and their dead son, she can easily accept such possibilities. But, Sanjay is a link for Rita as well. He connects her to the "parents" who have reared her and who provide her with the images by which she can imagine herself. Sanjay's devotion to law is not far from Sol's—it is merely based on a different system. "He has exchanged the faith in karma for the science of genetics," Schwartz says. "And he wants to help. He wants her to turn around and live facing front." But Rita finds that desire odd, "since he comes from a country imprisoned in history, while she is the young West Coast lawyer. Sometimes it seems they have changed places (8). This motif of role reversal bears out the connection between Rita's Jewish heritage and what she finds in Sanjay. "He's getting to sound like a Jew," Rita decides toward the very end of the story. "They are changing places" (32). In this reversal we begin to see the more than Oedipal theme in Schwartz's story.

Places, indeed, have been exchanged, but the exchanges involve Sanjay and her grandfather. Sanjay wants from Rita what her grandfather had wanted (and as Lucy's father had wanted for her). As the immigrant seeking assimilation, he wants her as the object signifying his success. He wants her as "his entryway to the land of dreams. His bridge. His American girl" (4). Indeed, when Rita and Sanjay first become involved, he tells her, "Well, Rita, I have never courted an American young woman before" (14). Since Rita feels her case is unusual, she tries to explain the truth to Sanjay. "But it's a matter of optics, of the precision of the lens," she realizes. "To a fifty-year-old naturalized Indian widower, she is representative enough. He wants his American girl, . . . the real thing" (26). In "appropriating" Rita, Sanjay shows one more reason why he represents Solomon. Expressing the same desire David projected onto Lucy, Sanjay simply expresses directly Solomon's desire to capture the American dream through an other.

Representing a desire connected to—but to Schwartz more critical than—the Oedipal is another structure, one with multiple positions. It finally becomes clear to Rita that Sanjay not only represents the position of the grandfather-who-was-father, but that he also appears under his aegis, his auspices. At some level of consciousness, Rita grasps this structure. "It is strange, Rita thinks now, that she was with her grandfather when she first saw Sanjay" (10). Equally "strange," no doubt, is that when Rita allows Sanjay to undress her the first time they make love, "she realizes she had wanted him from the moment she saw him from the window three years ago, looking out with her grandfather" (14). But in this structure Rita also has a place, conventionally Oedipal. She wants to be desired by the father and so to stand in place of the mother, in this case Sonia. It is then Sonia who becomes the deepest object of Rita's desire. Rita wants to *be* Sonia, as Schwartz makes clear. Although Rita feels that "appropriation" of the sort enacted by Solomon "is the tactic of the lost and the scared," she nonetheless wishes to appropriate Sonia. The concept she uses, however, is psychoanalytic:

incorporation. "Like a child," Rita "would like to incorporate her grandmother, swallow her, as her grandfather lived by appropriating." Schwartz also uses the conventional oral fantasy, the one underlying ritual gestures such as the Eucharist: "Oh, if only Rita could swallow her whole, if only she would go down, she could have Sonia forever with her. Safe at last." Only in this passage do we learn the deepest truth of Rita's nightmare, with which the story had begun. It is not only the grandfather's death it foretells and defends against, but it is also the grandmother's. Thus, late in the story, Rita feels that if she can incorporate Sonia into her very being, then she can save her from death: "she would never clutch her heart and die as in the nightmare, leaving Rita standing alone, severed" (25).

At story's end, perhaps because Jewish ethnicity is matrilineal, the most crucial identificatory relationship is that of Rita to Sonia. But the identification—and its deepest significance—emerges through transformations within the structure underlying Rita's relation to Sanjay. In this structure, not only does he play the role of the desired father, but Sanjay's wife also plays the role of the desired mother, the figure of identification Rita wants to be. To make these paradoxical desires work, Rita must be what Sanjay wants and what she herself wants to have. Both are visible at a moment when she thinks that she might finally choose to marry Sanjay. There, on the one hand, she invokes her desire for anaclitic safety and what Sanjay desires of her, her representation of the "American girl." "Maybe she should marry him after all," she tells herself. "She is so malleable an American, she could become anyone with ease. And it would be a way to live; it would be safe, safe" (9). On the other hand, she also invokes her own desire to become an other, to take on the habits and styles and raiment of the other represented by Sanjay's wife (already dying at Rita's first sighting of her). Sanjay and his wife become an object of Rita's desire from the first moment she sees them, on the day she graduated from Berkeley. In an ambiguous statement ("That was how Rita first saw them, the Indian gentleman and his wife"), Rita suggests not only how she sees Sanjay, but also how she places herself in the fantasy structure connected to him (9). "In his arms," we are told elsewhere, "Rita forgets who she is. She could almost be his wife" (14). But the unconscious element is yet more complex. In a further structural transformation, Rita finally succeeds in incorporating Sonia by becoming Sanjay's wife. Thus she assimilates the identificatory image of the woman she desires to become within her Jewish heritage. That is why at the end of the story, when Rita identifies with Sanjay's dead wife—"Yes, there is a certain resemblance. The result of nature, history, the migrations of people, love" (34)—and dresses herself in the woman's sari, she finally becomes not the Indian woman, but "Queen Esther, at last" (35). She becomes, therefore, one of the most venerated figures of womanhood in the Jewish tradition. Always before this moment only Vashti, only the rejected beauty, Rita finally becomes the comely queen of her ethnoreligious heritage, becomes, indeed, precisely the figure who in Jewish tradition represents the "hidden" Jew.[7] And in Rita's becoming Esther, we see made visible the symbol of the fundamental back-story operating within Schwartz's fiction. We see the veneration Schwartz devotes, albeit often unconsciously, to her Jewish forebears and so to her Jewish identity.

With its attendant theme of parental shielding, Schwartz's fourth novel, *Leaving Brooklyn,* makes more explicit than any of the previous novels the theme of the Jewish back-story. Early in the novel, the narrator (whose age reflects Schwartz's own) speaks of the World War II years as the ones she first remembers. Because of her extreme youth, she knew little of the war's carnage, but in adolescence and college she picked up details of the Holocaust. She "saw branded on the forearm of a pale girl a many-digited number two and a half inches above the wrist" (7). She tells us that she knows what the number means, but "in Brooklyn we never spoke of those details of the war and I did not read the papers much." Still, she admits that she wishes she could have the girl's knowledge without her pain. But it is, she understands, precisely the protection of the children that has brought her family to America, to Brooklyn and other similar places. The theme of parental shielding is as explicit here as in "The Opiate of the People":

> The immigrants and children of immigrants who settled Brooklyn did so precisely to shield their children from carnage and deprivation and numbers, both the suffering of them and the knowledge: they chose their place and shored it up as a fortress. They were very successful, and it would be naïve to disparage their success out of lethal nostalgia for sufferings never suffered. (7)

But in this novel Schwartz incorporates this aspect of the back-story—resistance to the Jewish past by those demanding assimilation—into the themes of adolescent and, eventually, aesthetic maturation. Ultimately, "leaving Brooklyn" represents the growth of a personal and artistic consciousness that can never, in fact, leave Brooklyn, no more than the Jew can "leave" Europe or Russia or the Holocaust.

Because it melds the back-story with other, more innovative themes found in postmodern fiction, *Leaving Brooklyn* may well be the finest of Schwartz's novels.[8] Much shorter than the Jamesian *Disturbances in the Field,* it shares the compactness of *Rough Strife* and *Balancing Acts,* but it adds a sense of humor, irony, and self-reflexiveness that would be out of place in those novels. Indeed, it is a kind of metafiction, a fiction about fiction, or at least a story about the interrelationship of memory and identity in the profession of the writer. The novel's plot tries to recreate an identity as it interacts with its environment, named metonymically and symbolically "Brooklyn." The plot is taken to be the truth, but truth itself is never taken to be a simple thing. It begins, "This is the story of an eye, and how it came into its own." The novel's narrator, Audrey, has a "bad eye," one with a spot on it and an iris smaller than that of the other. But this eye gives Audrey a unique look at the world. "I had secret vision," she says, "and knowledge of the components of things, of the volatile nature of things before they congeal, of the tenuousness and vulnerability of all things, unknown to those with common binary vision who saw the world of a piece, with a seamless skin like the skin of a sausage holding things together. My right eye removed the skin of the visible world" (4). Nearly sixteen and a precocious high school senior, Audrey ventures from Brooklyn into Manhattan to see a "big" doctor and to get a contact lens that might correct her peculiar vision.

As a first step in her effort to leave "Brooklyn," this episode simply confirms what Audrey's "bad eye" has taught her. When the doctor seduces Audrey (or vice versa), he confirms her notion that there is more in the world than meets the eyes of those with ordinary single vision. Though it might appear that the girl is the victim in a sexual relationship that continues for some months, in the end Audrey turns out to be the tougher of the two lovers; for while the opthamologist becomes obsessed with her, she merely takes the episode as part of growing up, of learning about life outside Brooklyn, outside the carefully fabricated perspectives her parents have given her. Near the end of her affair with the doctor, Audrey experiences a moment of perception that aligns her with the middle-aged writer who is creating—or recreating—her from memories. The fifteen-year-old Audrey "was me," the older writer thinks at this moment. "She already knew what I know. This is so startling to come upon that I have to stop and contemplate it. And her. Oh yes, I see myself plainly, right there, bearing the seeds of all I would come to know" (114). What Schwartz's novel suggests is that one's identity, one's truth, is an impossible Escher construction. The writer-protagonist tells us: "I am not a sheltered child but a grown-up version of a child who never was. And maybe I am this way because she never was, couldn't be. And yet it feels so real. If it wasn't a memory to begin with, it has become one now. . . . No longer a case of double vision, but of two separate eyes whose visions—what happened and what might have happened—come together in what we call the past, which we see with hindsight." Thus, she concludes, "Memory is revision." And so, she says, "I have just destroyed another piece of my past, to tell a story" (146). A novel such as *Leaving Brooklyn* suggests the inevitable complexity of the relation between ordinary fact and artistic truth. Since it seems likely that all Schwartz's fiction emanates from her own memories, it would tell us much about the vocation of the writer—any writer—to be able to untangle the intricate web of relationships between fact and fiction, single vision and double vision, the ordinary vision of the nonwriter and the creative vision of the imaginative writer whose truths always depart from the ordinary. Like us, writers always leave their Brooklyns, but, as Schwartz powerfully suggests here, it is always a leaving that is never completed. Moreover, as Schwartz suggests in other fiction, the departure may inflict scars not only on those who have left, but also on their descendants, particularly when those places left behind are as demonic as the Old Country of Schwartz's Jewish immigrants and their children. Thus, "Brooklyn" becomes a figure like the Euro-Russian sites resurrected in the back-story of her fiction. As Audrey says at the end of her story, "I left Brooklyn. I leave still, every moment. For no matter how much I leave, it doesn't leave me" (145). Brooklyn and the Jewish back-story are what Schwartz can never leave behind.

Notes

1. Born in 1939, Schwartz grew up in Brooklyn, lives in New York City, has taught at Hunter and New York University, and has been a visiting lecturer at the University of Iowa Writers' Workshop (1982–83), a lecturer in the Co-

lumbia University General Studies Writing Program (1983–84), and a visiting assistant professor in the Boston University Creative Writing Program (1984). She worked toward a Ph.D. in comparative literature, but dropped out to fulfill her childhood dream of becoming a creative writer. She has held a Guggenheim fellowship and one from the National Endowment for the Arts. Her novels include *Rough Strife* (New York: Harper, 1980), *Balancing Acts* (New York: Harper, 1981), *Disturbances in the Field* (New York: Harper, 1983), *Leaving Brooklyn* (New York: Houghton Mifflin, 1989; all quotations from the Viking Penguin edition, 1990), and *The Fatigue Artist* (New York: Scribner, 1995), this last published after the completion of this essay and so not treated herein. Her two volumes of short stories are *Acquainted with the Night and Other Stories* (New York: Harper, 1984; all quotations from the Harper Perennial edition, 1985) and *The Melting Pot and Other Subversive Stories* (New York: Harper, 1987; all quotations from the Viking Penguin edition, 1989). She has also published nonfiction such as *We Are Talking about Homes* (New York: Harper, 1985), a narrative account of the problems encountered by her and other tenants of a fire-damaged building owned by Columbia University, and a religious book for young people called *The Four Questions* (New York: Dial, 1989) that explores the meaning of Passover through paintings by Ori Sherman and by explicating the symbolism of the seder and the four questions. *A Lynne Sharon Schwartz Reader: Selected Prose and Poetry* was published in 1992 (Hanover, N.H.: University Press of New England for Middlebury College Press) and includes poetry, essays, and some of her short stories (including "Francesca," not in the two collections).

2. *New York Times Book Review,* 15 June 1980, 14.

3. *New Republic,* 14 June 1980, 38.

4. Paul Stuewe, *Quill & Quire* 47 (September 1981): 67.

5. *Disturbances in the Field,* 176–77.

6. *Commonweal,* 4 November 1983, 590. In one of the few academic treatments of any of Schwartz's fiction, Adelaide Morris discusses ways in which Schwartz elides the first-person "I" in favor of a plural perspective valuing the "we." See "First Person Plural in Contemporary Feminist Fiction," *Tulsa Studies in Women's Literature* 11 (Spring 1992): 11–29. But note that in her catalogue of subjects in the novel, Morris mentions no specifically Jewish themes except Israel, which, no doubt she includes because of its national political provenance.

7. *The Encyclopedia of Religion* (New York: Macmillan, 1987) offers this summation of the significance of Esther:

> In the Middle Ages, the role of Esther took on powerful symbolic dimensions among Jews for at least three reasons. First, Esther came to symbolize the court Jew who risked everything to defend the nation so often slandered, despised, and threatened. Second, Esther, as a "hidden" Jew . . . symbolized in mystical circles the hiddenness of the Shekhinah (divine feminine presence) in the world and in the Jewish exile. And finally, Esther (and the festival of Purim) was a great favorite of the Marranos in Spain and in their far-flung dispersion; they saw in her disguised condition the factual and psychological prototype of their own disguised condition. (166)

8. I exclude *The Fatigue Artist* (1995) from consideration: see note 1.

Adrienne Rich: "Stuck to earth"

KAREN W. KLEIN

> ". . . to track your own desire, in your own language, is not an isolated task. You yourself are marked by family, gender, caste, landscape, the struggle to make a living, or the absence of such a struggle. . . . Poetry is never free of these markings, even when it appears to be. Look into the images."
> —Adrienne Rich, "To Invent What We Desire"

FOR nearly half a century, Adrienne Rich's powerful voice has commanded our attention. Turning hers to "the difficult world," she has ambitiously and generously taken on its various ills, speaking out over and over again against its multiple injustices, believing "poetry and politics aren't mutually exclusive,"[1] seemingly leaving Rilke for Ruykeyser as her model: "Poetry never stood a chance / of standing outside history."[2] She has, therefore, been seen mostly as a polemicist: a feminist spokesperson, a silence-breaking lesbian, even a "moral allegorist."[3] For all this she has been widely read, much praised, severely castigated, and, according to Willard Spiegelman," seldom received the *literary* criticism she most deserves.[4] But there is much of Rilke still in her lyric voice and as much looking inward as looking out: "The core of the strong hill not understood," a probing of identity and allegiance. Central to her work are images of the earth: rocks, roots, growing things, and a pervasive sense of place. From "Natural Resources" to "Sources" to "I am stuck to earth" is not the least profound of her trajectories.

* * *

The title of the poem "Natural Resources," written in 1977,[5] is filled with punning. "Natural resources" sounds like a heading, usually done in bold face, out of an old encyclopedia, the sort a schoolgirl in Baltimore might look into for her report on Ecuador or some exotic country. In the poem it refers to the psychic geography of countless unnamed women, not countries. The imagery of earth—"core of the strong hill"; "the dark lode"; the silver-and-green vein"—is both that of inner strength and of mystery. These mines of strength and mystery underlie women's "routine of life," which "goes on" as women, past and present, go about doing "what an ordinary woman / does in the course of things": nurturing, caring, making the world possible for others. The speaker honors that incessant labor—interrupted, unrewarded, forgotten or reduced to a bargain, a "collectible" at a rural barn sale: "the enormity of the simplest things"; "a universe of humble things." But there is anger too at the waste of women's natural resources, at the pain of their lives, the pain and difficulty of their self-exploration as they mine the "dark lode"; anger too at men, but not their total exclusion. The man sought was the "lost brother . . . a fellow creature / with natural resources equal to our own."

"Transcendental Etude" (1977), the final poem in *The Dream of a Common Language* collection, continues the imagery of deep earth. In closing, the speaker imagines a woman in the "many-lived, unending / forms in which she finds herself," the last of which is "the stone foundation, rockshelf further / forming underneath everything that grows" (77). Like the mine of "Natural Resources," the rockshelf is an image of female strength, permanence, capacity, endurance. But it is more than that since it underlies everything. In *Women Writers and Poetic Identity,* Margaret Homans criticizes these lines as 'poetically terminal." She argues that "Rich's rock is an image of mother as nature, the cthonic feminine object whose existence as the valorized image of womanhood has impeded and continues to impede the ability of women to choose, among other things, the vocation of poet."[6] Not only does this image silence women, but in using it, Rich also is "uncritically accepting what amounts to the male paradigm of the woman who merges with nature."[7]

I believe Homans' reading here reflects a time in feminist criticism when any use of traditional imagery associated with women, especially if the tradition were male, was suspect. It seemed to drag women back into where they were fighting so hard to get out of, that Wordworthian "diurnal round." But lyric poets, whether male or female, must turn to the natural world for their imagery, and Rich does not immure her woman in stone. Instead, she uses earth imagery as one of the many forms woman may find herself in, the others being broken glass that cuts and a soothing leaf that heals. Homans misunderstands this earth image of strength as one of silencing, of passive merging. Rather, it is an active image of female foundational endurance that solidly underlies our common life. It may also reflect our need for and dependence on that endurance.

In both poems, these images of the "core of the strong hill" and the "stone foundation, rockshelf" are positive, approbationary for the speaker who in "Natural Resources" "casts [her] lot" with those who, like the women who were miners, "with no extraordinary power, reconstitute the world." And in "Transcendental Etude," her vision of the woman implies that the speaker commits herself to the kind of life in which such a vision can happen. These images, however, have other resonances that are more problematic, but not in the way Homans believes they are. The core of a hill and a rockshelf are literally penetrable only with extraordinary difficulty, if at all. What can the psychological ramifications of these images be? "The core of the strong hill" is, after all, "not understood." What courage is needed to access that kind of difficulty, to begin to understand? These inner explorations take Rich's poetics beyond the lyric speaker to the place where the voice in the poem must be her own. The poet merges with the speaker and the details of Rich's biography and her life struggles with identity and allegiance become the substance of poems.

* * *

Moving from "Natural Resources" to "Sources" (1981–82) is not merely a play on words. In a 1987 interview by David Montenegro, in response to a question about which poems since 1971 are "landmarks of your development," Rich lists certain "poems that reflect to me some kind of watershed, perhaps."[8] "Watershed"—the line dividing two drainage areas or the drainage area itself—is consistent with her earth imagery. Among the poems that she lists as marking this division between phases are "Natural Resources" and "Sources."[9]

"Sources" begins on a road, "Route 5 / south of Willoughby," in rural Vermont, "the northeast kingdom." Time is specifically located as well: "Sixteen years" since the poet had been in this spot "in nineteen sixty-five." She sees "Shapes of things": "so much the same / they feel like eternal forms." These forms, however, are not Platonic ideas, but the simple and specific forms of house and barn situated in the earth's "granite, brookwater, pine . . . needles, queen anne's lace, bladder-campion, multifoliate heal-all." The poem does not spell out why the poet is here, but there is an ominous sense in the omen of the surviving vixen leading her cubs, glimpsed those years ago—a sense too that the poet will need all her strength to deal with what must be dealt with, to write this poem.

She recognizes "Everything that has ever / helped me has come through what already / lay stored in me." The phrase "stored in me" echoes the "Rockshelf" of "Transcendental Etude," "the privacy of the mines" of "Natural Resources." Like the miners of that poem, she is on a digging expedition, an inner exploration to find that strength.

> Old things, diffuse, unnamed, lie strong
> across my heart.
> This is from where
> my strength comes, even when I miss my strength
> even when my strength turns on me
> like a violent master.
>
> (2.4)

Touching that strength, then, is no reassuring task of resourcefulness or a feel-good activity, but dangerous; it is lodged in old and threatening things that have not yet received their poetic names.

In section 3, another of her voices repeatedly interrogates the poet. In an incremental series of repetitions, she asks; "From where? . . . From where does your strength come? . . . From where does your strength come, you Southern Jew? split at the root, raised in a castle of air?" Each of these phrases has meaning and occurs in other poems, in other contexts, but this section of the poem does not answer the question. Instead, the poet names where it cannot come from: "Protestant separatists, Jew-baiters, nightriders." With the fourth repetition, as abbreviated as the first *"From where?,"* the poet turns to describe the natural world, as if she were turning away from the pain and inability to name that the question brings. But it is not a turning away; it is a turning inward. The objects of her gaze metaphorize her inner state in relation to the question: "the mountains stand in an extraordinary / point of no return." The question, as impenetrable as ever, as impenetrable as those mountains of "Natural Resources," must be confronted now. But the reluctance remains; even the ground cover is "Touch-me-not," although "fiery with tiny tongues," with the urgency to utterance.

The question, though, does not take this self-described "Southern Jew, split at the root" by surprise: "I expected this. I have known for years / the question was coming." In section 4, Rich repeats the question, pairs it with another question, indicates the intensity of their importance and their significant distinction; her life work can be organized around these lines:

> With whom do you believe your lot is cast?
> From where does your strength come?
>
> I think somehow, somewhere
> every poem of mine must repeat those questions
>
> which are not the same.
>
> (4.6)

In the ending of "Natural Resources," her lot was cast with women "who . . . reconstitute the world"; in "Sources," Rich tries to understand to what degree and in what way her lot is cast with the Jews. That these questions are not the same is part of her struggle to understand the difference between what is given and what is chosen, when and how the two come together in her, what happens when they do not. If her strength comes from the Jewish side of her, need her lot be cast with them? only with them? If Jewish is only one side of her, can it be cast with them?

The problems of source, of heritage being worked through in this poem, are made explicit in her 1982 essay "Split at the Root," the title of which echoes the earth imagery of "sources." In the Montenegro interview Rich explains:

> . . . a lot of my . . . essays have points of intersection with poems, probably none so much as "Split at the Root" with "Sources"—which I was writing at about the same time. I was having a lot of difficulty with the poem, and then I wrote the essay, and came back to the poem feeling very freed because I'd worked out a great deal in the essay, and then didn't have to spell it out in the poem at all.[10]

The essay, subtitled "An Essay on Jewish Identity," presents details of her life as the southern, white child of Protestant mother, a "fine pianist" and frustrated composer, and a Jewish father, an academic pathologist at Johns Hopkins, whose "silence" and "taboos" and contradictory and complex ways of relating to Jews and his own Jewishness are at the core of what she is trying to understand about herself.

> Because what isn't named is often more permeating than what is, I believe that my father's Jewishness profoundly shaped my own iden-

> tity and our family existence. They were shaped both by external anti-Semitism and my father's self-hatred, and by his Jewish pride [which he called] something else: achievement, aspiration, genius, idealism. Whatever was unacceptable got left back under the rubric of Jewishness or the "wrong kind" of Jews: uneducated, aggressive, loud. The message I got was that we were really superior.[11]

Can her lot be cast with the Jews when her primary connection to them, her Jewish father, did not want to be Jewish? "It's not important to me. I am a scientist," he had said.[12]

Complicating Rich's attempt to deconstruct her father's attitudes toward Jewishness and how these shaped her is their intense intellectual involvement; he is her mentor. It is he who watches over her homework, critiques her early poems, gives her books on rhyme and meter. While she assesses his investment in her "intellect and talent" as "egotistical . . . and terribly wearing," she acknowledges the gifts he gave her. "He taught me, nevertheless, to believe in hard work, to mistrust easy inspiration, to write and rewrite, to feel that I *was* a person of the book, even though a woman; to take ideas seriously. He made me feel, at a very young age, the power of language and that I could share in it."[13] No wonder she feels "like a betrayer of [her] father"; his gifts are so central to who she is that this exposure of him engenders feelings of "fear and shame." Writing about these "sources" is "dangerous," not only because it involves silence about religion, but also because it is deeply implicated in racist and classist attitudes. Yet for one who herself has taken stands against race and class hierarchies, working honestly through her "sources" is also "necessary."

Doing so, she has to confront her inherited "ambivalence as a Jew," the betrayals wherein she denied her Jewishness. But why take on this allegiance? As a lesbian/feminist, she affirms Virginia Woolf's belief that "We think back through our mothers if we are women," and therefore need not consider herself a Jew. The social Christianity of her mother, however, is implicated in the silencing, the racial injustices, the class privilege, the "heterosexual fantasy." Although "at different times in [her] life [she has] wanted to push away one or the other burdens of inheritance,"[14] she cannot escape her "outsiderhood," either lesbian or Jew. In a letter to a friend included in *What Is Found There: Notes on Poetry and Politics* (1993), she says, "I've been a problem within a problem: 'the Jewish Question,' 'the Woman Question'—who the questioner? who is supposed to answer?"[15]

In her attempts to answer in "Split at the Root," she acknowledges that, although under Nazi law she would not be exempt from the Final Solution, Jewish law does not regard her as a Jew. While she does not explicitly say so, it seems obvious that emotional law is at variance with Jewish law here. We are all part of each of our parents; what they are lives in us psychologically as well as genetically.

In closing, she acknowledges that the essay has no conclusion. She has "seen too long from too many disconnected angles: white, Jewish, anti-Semite, racist, anti-racist, once-married, lesbian, middle-class, feminist, exmatriate southerner, *split at the root*—that [she] will never bring them whole."[16] Her desire to "bring them whole" is unexamined, as is its desirability. She does not see herself as that unique wholeness, but rather as a collection of parts, of identities, of attitudes. Her image, the split root, is negative; it seems to call for repair, to be put together, to be healed. Literally, gardeners split the roots of certain plants to make them grow better, but Rich's split-root image is not one of growth; it is, like her mountains, one of inner exploration and tension.

When she explicitly brings her father into "Sources," Rich's image of split root becomes her "father building / his rootless ideology his private castle in air" (6.8). The imagery surrounding her father is not substantial, like that of earth, but unsituated: "the floating world of the assimilated who know and deny they will always be aliens." When she speaks of him in the poem, there are few images and many conceptualizations: "overthrow the father," "face of patriarchy," "principle you embodied," "ideology" (7.9). Addressing him, she uses prose. While expressing her struggles with him, her anger at him, and hate for the system he represented, "the kingdom of the fathers," she now sees what she could not see before: "the suffering of the Jew, the alien stamp you bore, because you had deliberately arranged that it should be invisible to me. It is only now, under a powerful, womanly lens, that I can decipher your suffering and deny no part of my own" (7.9).

Denying no part of her own means, in part, incorporating the central image of Jewish communal suffering, the Holocaust. This image has multiple resonances for her. It refers not only to what she was spared, but suggests also that her being spared must mean some sort of "special destiny"; but what? "there had to be a reason / I was growing up safe, American" (5.7). That "special destiny" links up later in the poem with Rich as a child whose "penmanship, hard work, style will win her prizes" (20.23). That child

> becomes the woman with a mission, not to win prizes
> but to change the laws of history.
> How she gets this mission
> is not clear
>
> (20.23)

Nor does the poem make it clear, but she is "dragged by the roots of her own will" towards this overwhelmingness. Here roots are explicitly an image of an inner state, somehow complexly expressive of both inherited and chosen tendencies.

These tendencies link her, the spared one, to the victims: "The Jews I've felt rooted among / are those who were turned to smoke" (16.18). This image presents the impossible contradiction that she is—an earth image where there is no ground, roots in smoke, substance in the insubstantial. In this section of the poem, the Holocaust provides familiar imagery: "chimneys"; "fog," "railroad tracks," "the place where all tracks end." Ironically, she and her father are united in this imagery, in fact, riveted by it, which he had once prohibited her:

> You told me not to look there
>
> to become
> a citizen of the world
>
> bound by no tribe or clan
>
> (16.18)

It is their mutual concern for the fate of this tribe that unites them: dying, he follows the progress of the Six Day War; worrying about the Middle East in 1981 and 1982, she wears the traditional star of David around her neck (16.18).

There is a certain impoverishment in her use of traditional, communal imagery around Jewishness; an impersonal and flat quality, categorizing rather than specifying, which makes me wonder what the effect of all that silencing was on her fund of personal imagery, her "wordhoard," around these unspoken, interdicted issues. In an earlier poem, "Granddaughter" (1980), she asks, "what were the lessons to be learned?" and answers her question, "If I believe / the daughter of one of you—Amnesia was the answer."[17] Her mother, then, is also implicated in bequeathing her the daunting task of excavating imagery from amnesia. The price for the child is so high. In "Distance between Language and Violence," an essay from the *What Is Found There* collection, she writes about herself: "She develops facial tics, eczema in the creases of her elbows and knees, hay fever. She is prohibited confusion: her lessons, accomplishments, must follow a clear trajectory" (184). As she says in "Sources," "that dangerous place / the family home" (13.15).

Rich left that family home for a succession of chosen ones in the Northeast. "Sources" interrogates her relation to that place of "endless rocks in the soil," to people "who are not my people by any definition" (9.11; 11.13). She seeks to understand "the passion [she connects] with in this air; is it trace of the original / existence that knew this place / is the region still trying to speak with them" (12.14)? Poetically, Rich is always attentive to the significance of place as if to know the place is to know her place in it. When she describes her forebears, she specifies locations: "the Jews of Vicksburg or Birmingham" (5.7); "white gentile roots in Virginia, North Carolina."[18] Place names with their meaningful resonances and the many and varied landscapes in which she has dwelled are among the strongest of her sources, especially of her imagery.

A precursor poem, included in *A Wild Patience Has Taken Me This Far,* which foreshadows some of the language and explorations of "Sources," is titled "The Spirit of Place" (1980). Here the place is central/western Massachusetts; place names are of its towns. Here too the crucial question "With whom do you believe your lot is cast?" is asked. "If there's a conscience in these hills / it hurls that question" (1.41). This image of the hills, like that of the mountains of "Natural Resources," is one that evokes inner exploration, but in this poem a psychological/moral term is explicitly included and placed in the hills. "Conscience" belongs both to the poet and to the place; the challenge to the poet to deal with these issues of belonging and allegiance comes from within and from without. Integrity is demanded "by the spirits / of place who understand travel but not amnesia" (5.45). But here she can "trust roots," or urges herself to do so, and here the imagery of the natural world is alive and can sustain the necessary psychological resonances:

> here in the north where winter has a meaning
> where the heaped colors suddenly go ashen
> where nothing is promised

learn what an underground journey
has been, might have to be; speak in a winter code
let fog, sleet, translate; wind, carry them

(4.44)

"Sources" is, in part, that "underground journey" and what must be confronted is not only the father, but also "the other Jew," the wrong kind, the one she left her father for, the one who "tried to move in the floating world of the assimilated who know and deny they will always be aliens. Who drove to Vermont in a rented car at dawn and shot himself" (17.19). She has written tangentially of that marriage and the trauma her choice of husband caused her father in "For Ethel Rosenberg" (1980), whose execution in 1953 preceded Rich's wedding by a week. Each, in her own way, is a "bad daughter," is condemned as such.[19] When, in "Sources," she speaks to her father about her husband, she says, "For so many years I had thought you and he were in opposition. I needed your unlikeness then; now it's your likeness that stares me in the face" (17.19).

It is that "likeness," theirs and hers, that constitutes much of the urgency of the section in which she directly addresses her dead husband; she wants to speak "to you, not simply of you" (22.25). As when she speaks to her father, it is in prose—direct, honest, loving. All three have wrestled in different ways with the issue of identity, specifically Jewish identity, but they did not share the struggle, its confusion or pain. In anger and in love, the poet says: *"no person, trying to take responsibility for her or his identity, should have to be so alone"* (22.25). She speaks to her husband, but could be speaking of herself, or of her father who, like her husband, "ended isolate" (17.19). She seeks a community, but it is not described in the language of a traditional community, or even a Jewish one: "There must be those among whom we can sit down and weep, and still be counted as warriors. . . . I think you thought there was no such place for you, and perhaps there was none then, and perhaps there is none now; but we will have to make it, we who want an end to suffering . . ." (22.25).

What is this place? For whom will it be? In the quotation above, the pronouns shift. "I" is the speaker, "you" presumably her husband whom she addresses, but who is the "we"—the speaker? the husband? the father? all who are caught in issues of identity and allegiance? And who are the "we" who will make the new place for which the poem provides no imagery? Defining the "we" as those "who want an end to suffering" widens the category way beyond the subject at hand. Who does not want an end to suffering? And there are so many kinds of suffering: how is the reader to understand how this place that must be made answers the suffering around issues of Jewish identity?

Further, Rich's own issues of Jewish identity differ from those of the assimilated Jews, her husband and father who both, nevertheless, understood that "there was more left than food and humor" (22.25). She is not an assimilated Jew, but that socially constructed creature, part Jew/part gentile. I say socially constructed, for that is how the world names and thinks of such persons. From the inside such persons cannot think of themselves that way because persons cannot be parts; discussions like these descend into idiocy—which part is which: intelligence, sexuality, and so on. Such persons are simultaneously both their parts and neither; Rich understands this when she describes herself as "neither gentile nor Jew" (5.7). Or they are wholly Jewish and wholly non-Jewish simultaneously, a logically impossible position. This concept is very difficult to grasp and probably must be lived in to be felt and understood; persons whose backgrounds are not radically mixed often don't understand what it means. My own background is similar to Rich's, and my colleague, Luis Yglesias, is Anglo Cuban. We speak often about our sense of identity, and it is he who first expressed his as complexly, wholly both.

Or, to put it another way, persons whose backgrounds cross strongly opposite religious and racial lines are new creatures, outside linguistic categories. No language exists to describe us accurately. The language that serves for description—part this, part that—is the language of the old, the language of the categories of tribe, ethnicity, nationality; it describes where we came from, not who we are. Rich is right; we will have to make a place for such persons. But the place cannot be made until new words or new images are found or invented to name both persons and place. And that is a poet's task. But as long as Rich remains committed to ethnicities, or appears to be so, she will continue to use the old language, the old names, and, as a result, be bound by the old concepts.

* * *

The final section of "Sources" returns to earth imagery. The poet laments: "I can never know this land I walk upon" and follows with a list of what inhabits it: "rockledge soil insect bird weed tree" (23.26). Here the rockledge functions literally, part of the landscape, not of the poet's psyche. She understands why she cannot experience a sense of place as, say, an English priest and writer experienced his Selbourne. She has "chosen / something else: to know other things" and "Because [she] grew up in a castle of air / disjunctured" (23.26). The "other things" she has chosen follow from her aware acceptance of the meanings of the "air / disjunctured" imagery, which is in opposition to the imagery of earth. That imagery has served her well metaphorically as inner exploration and source of knowledge, and, in later poems, will do so again. But here she is now somehow cut off or cutting off from it, although not completely. Her desire is to "rest among the beautiful and common weeds [she] can name," the phrase here linking the earth image of weeds with the naming power of poetry. However, she rejects desire, affirming "there is no finite knowing, no such rest" (23.27).

Alice Templeton sees this as a "feminist hermeneutics . . . a way of being that is never completed or static."[20] I see it less as an issue of a general or feminist way of being and more as an issue about being a poet. The responsibility of that, of wanting "an end to suffering" and "knowing the world and [her] place in it," means making other choices and other images. The poem closes in the tension between desire and responsibility; Albert Gelpi sees the ending as "not a conclusion but a renewed commitment to the difficult process of definition.[21] In David Montenegro's interview he asks if what she was working out in "Split at the Root" was, in this poem, "in a sense, resolved." Rich replies, "If such things ever are."[22]

* * *

The poem "Yom Kippur, 1984"[23] continues some of the complexities of belonging raised in "Sources"; in it, Rich expresses the paradox of her desire for community, including Jewish community, and her simultaneous need for solitude, a paradox that she deems "a nightmare" (76). "[T]o be with my people is my dearest wish / but that I also love strangers / that I crave separateness" is her Yom Kippur confession. She also wonders whether loving solitude and strangers is "a privilege we can't afford in the world that is" (77). That world hates and persecutes Jews, blacks, and homosexuals, the "we" among whom she is counted. Although she does not name it as such, her "drifting from the center, drawn to edges," can be seen as another betrayal. As she notes in "The Genesis of 'Yom Kippur 1984,'" the day of atonement is

"A time when we attempt to make reconciliation first with our community because it is said you cannot look to forgiveness from God before you have been forgiven by your people."[24] So she asks: "but do my people forgive me? If a cloud knew loneliness and fear, I would be that cloud."[25]

In this context Rich seems fully identified with her Jewishness, naming Jews as "my people." Although she explains the source of the cloud image as Wordsworth and her inclusion of it as her attempt to negate his "bliss of solitude,"[26] for me, the cloud lines up with her other insubstantial images around Jewishness such as castles in air, and so forth. Her Jewish imagery, it seems, is either communal, as in the poem's title or her earlier star of David, or unconvincing, not full or personal. Only in "Sources," when she speaks of typical Jewish foods, does the imagery pour out in a Whitmanesque cascade, ending in a personal observation about the challah "which turned stale so fast but looked so beautiful" (22.25).

In part, the answer to her old question in "Sources"—"From where does your strength come"—is, poetically at least, from her earth imagery, and in "Living Memory" (1988) in the *Time's Power* collection[27] she places Jewish images and earth images in proximity. In this poem, landscape and place are once again stimuli to personal stocktaking. She muses on graveyards in Vermont, Birmingham, Alabama, Washington, D.C., and wonders where she will end. Among the places she imagines is "wherever the Jewish dead / have to be sought in the wild grass overwhelming / the cracked stones. Hebrew spelled in wilderness."[28] In these lines, the stones commemorating the dead have been incorporated into the earth landscape of wild grasses. Rather than the earlier poems' uninspired use of the imagery of Jewish communal symbols, the last sentence is wonderfully original and not only captures the literal tombstones and their surround, but also resonates with the history of a nomadic people whose formative myth involved wilderness years. Her Jewishness begins to receive its poetic names.

* * *

The tension expressed at the end of "Sources" between her love as a poet for the earth and the poetry that names it and her responsibility as a poet to speak to the suffering of our times seemed to make the two mutually exclusive. But subsequent poetry refuses this disjuncture; Rich can express what Vendler recognizes as her "poet's deep attachment to the beautiful,"[29] without ignoring or evading the ills that must be confronted:

> I don't want to know
> wreckage, dreck, and waste, but these are the materials
> and so are the slow lift of the moon's belly
> over wreckage, dreck, and waste, wild treefrogs calling in
> another season, light and music still pouring over
> our fissured, cracked terrain.

These lines, from "An Atlas of the Difficult World,"[30] find her in a new "terrain," that of the West coast. There, too, she admits "as always / I fix on the land. I am stuck to earth" (5). This admission is followed by an intense description, in a fullness of line and imagery, of what she loves and sees there in this new place, "[w]ithin two miles of the Pacific." This description is not a "finite knowing" or "a rest," which "Sources" repudiated, but a torrent of grounding herself, an immersion and a preparation for understanding. This earth, however "fissured, cracked," remains her source and resource.

Notes

1. *What Is Found There: Notebooks on Poetry and Politics* (New York: Norton, 1993), 23.
2. "North American Time," *Your Native Land, Your Life* (New York: Norton, 1986), 33.
3. Helen Vendler, *Soul Says* (Cambridge: Harvard University Press, 1995), 216.
4. "Driving to the Limits of the City of Words," in *Adrienne Rich's Poetry and Prose*, ed. B. C. Gelpi and A. Gelpi (New York: Norton, 1993), 369.
5. *The Dream of a Common Language: Poems 1974–1977* (New York: Norton, 1978), 60.
6. Margaret Homans, *Women Writers and Poetic Identity* (Princeton: Princeton University Press, 1980), 229.
7. Ibid., 234–35.
8. David Montenegro, ed., "Adrienne Rich," in *Points of Departure: International Writers on Writing and Politics* (Ann Arbor: University of Michigan Press, 1991), 17.
9. *Your Native Land, Your Life,* 3–27.
10. Montenegro, "Adrienne Rich," 16.
11. Adrienne Rich, "Split at the Root (1982)," in *Blood, Bread & Poetry: Selected Prose, 1979–1985* (New York: Norton, 1985), 112–13.
12. Ibid., 110.
13. Ibid., 113.
14. Ibid., 114.
15. "Dearest Arturo," *What Is Found There,* 23.

16. Rich, "Split at the Root," 122.

17. Adrienne Rich, *A Wild Patience Has Taken Me This Far: Poems, 1978–1981* (New York: Norton, 1981), 39.

18. "Dearest Arturo," 23.

19. *Wild Patience,* 28.

20. Alice Templeton, *The Dream and the Dialogue: Adrienne Rich's Feminist Poetics* (Knoxville: University of Tennessee Press, 1994), 122–23.

21. Albert Gelpi, "The Poetics of Recovery: A Reading of Adrienne Rich's *Sources*," in *Adrienne Rich's Poetry and Prose,* ed. Gelpi and Gelpi, 401.

22. Montenegro, "Adrienne Rich," 16.

23. 1985; in *Your Native Land, Your Life.*

24. Rich, "The Genesis of 'Yom Kippur 1984,'" in *Adrienne Rich's Poetry and Prose,* ed. Gelpi and Gelpi, 254.

25. *Your Native Land, Your Life,* 77.

26. Rich, "Genesis," 256.

27. Adrienne Rich, *Time's Power: Poems, 1985–1988* (New York: Norton, 1989).

28. *Time's Power,* 49.

29. In *Soul Says,* 218.

30. Adrienne Rich, *An Atlas of the Difficult World: Poems, 1988–1991* (New York: Norton, 1991), 4.

Kael and Farewell

Steven G. Kellman

> To prove my out-of-it-ness once again, in my pantheon Pauline Kael never came close to replacing Edmund Wilson.
>
> —Joseph Epstein

THE force of Epstein's quip[1] derives from the fact that, following Edmund Wilson's death in 1972, Pauline Kael was for many the preeminent public intellectual in the United States. Untenured and untethered, she addressed the educated nonspecialist in a way that was accessible but rarely facile or banal. For most of her long tenure reviewing film at *The New Yorker*, from 1968 to 1991, she was probably the most respected working critic, on any beat, in North America. Kael's manifest zest for the task—which, three years after Parkinson's disease compelled her retirement from *The New Yorker*, she called "the best job in the world"[2]—and her airy erudition engaged readers and commanded admiration. "You must use everything you are and everything you know that is relevant," insisted Kael,[3] the compleat critic for whom reviewing became a total expression of self.

She defined herself as a writer whose subject happened to be movies, and what is most memorable about her work—in thirteen volumes that have been honored with the National Book Award and other tributes—is, first, the vivacity and clarity of the prose. Kael was an enthusiast and champion of the American vernacular, even the vulgar, and she emerged, along with Robert Altman, Francis Ford Coppola, Brian De Palma, Arthur Penn, Martin Scorsese, and Steven Spielberg, when American cinema was experiencing a renaissance. "A few decades hence," she wrote in 1976, "these years may appear to be the closest our movies have come to the tangled, bitter flowering of American letters in the early 1850s."[4] In part because of Kael, film became central to educated culture, and she helped to shape the terms and texture of the national conversation about the medium and our lives.

An autodidactic polymath, a man of scattered letters who was equally illuminating on the Civil War, Proust, commercials, and the Dead Sea Scrolls, Wilson remains a paragon of literary freelancers. But Norman Mailer, the nonfiction stylist for whom prose is performance, provides a closer analogy to Kael's own writing.[5] In contrast to Wilson, both are also unmistakably, uneasily, Jews. Reviewing Mailer's 1973 biography of Marilyn Monroe, Kael might as well be discussing herself: "His writing is close to the pleasures of movies; his immediacy makes him more accessible to those brought up with the media than, say, Bellow. You read him with a heightened consciousness because his performance has zing. It's the star system in literature; you can feel him bucking for the big time, and when he starts flying it's so exhilarating you want to applaud" (*R,* 218). With the casual intimacy of its second-person pronoun, its tarting up of learned terms like "immediacy," "accessible," and "consciousness" with demotic neologisms such as "zing" and "buck," its valorization of exhilaration, and its tacit assumption that movies are the model of human pleasure, the passage is vintage Kael. And the assessment it offers is as applicable to Kael's flamboyant style as to Mailer's.

Kael, who never grew above five feet ("I think that the disjunction between my strong voice as a writer and my five-foot frame somehow got to people"),[6] grew up, far from Manhattan, as the youngest of five children. "One nice Jewish boy from Brooklyn on another" (*R,* 219) is the way she describes Mailer's treatment of Arthur Miller in *Marilyn,* but Kael herself must be understood in part as a nice Jewish girl from Petaluma. Of course, nice Jewish boys and girls often go out of their way to deny that they are either nice or especially Jewish. Much of Kael's work must be read as a midcentury ordeal of civility, the record of cultural anxieties felt by a California Jewish woman avid for immersion in America and by an American wary of the residual authority of Europe.

Born in 1919 to Isaac Paul and Judith (Friedman) Kael, who had immigrated from urban Poland to rural northern California during the previous decade, she spent the first eight years of her life—before stock market losses forced the family to move to San Francisco—on a Sonoma County farm. In telephone conversations with this author, Kael noted that her alien family name was tamed and abbreviated by immigration officials but that she could not recall its original form. She also emphasized that her parents, who came from Warsaw, were "not shtetl Jews" and that English, certainly not Yiddish, was the language of their California household. Kael belongs to the cohort of assertive American Jews born during or shortly after World War I that includes not only Mailer, Miller, Bernard Malamud, and Leonard Bernstein, but also Diane Arbus, Betty Friedan, Lee Krasner, Grace Paley, and Beverly Sills. Created and dominated by European greenhorns, including Samuel Goldwyn, Carl Laemmle, Louis B. Mayer, Harry and Jack Warner, and Adolph Zukor, motion pictures during Kael's childhood were the most conspicuously Jewish of American industries. Kael's own career as apologist and antagonist of the business can be seen as an arduous attempt by a second-generation Jew to negotiate a place for herself within American popular culture. Almost fifty when invited by William Shawn to join *The New Yorker,* Kael ultimately managed, in fertile middle age, to become one of the foremost foes of Old World stuffiness, a champion of the youthful American vernacular. It is a compelling but not bewildering paradox that, just as Jewish immigrants created the celluloid images of middle America that most forcefully defined the nation to itself and others, Pauline Kael became the Huck Finn of American critics. She launched her career as movie maven with a review of Chaplin's *Limelight* in an issue of San Francisco's *City Lights* for 1953, the same year that Saul Bellow reinvented Twain's Great American Novel as the adventures of a Chicago Jew named Augie March.

A Kael review often begins in synecdoche, in a canny closeup on a small but telling detail, such as the moment in *Shampoo* that Warren Beatty asks Julie Christie: "Want me to do your hair?" After a defiantly preposterous hyperbole ("*Jaws* may be the most cheerfully perverse scare movie ever made"),[7] Kael teases out an ample exegesis through liberal use of archly epic similes. "Seeing it," she writes of *The Thomas Crown Affair,* "is like lying in the sun flicking through fashion magazines and, as we used to say, feeling rich and beautiful beyond your wildest dreams."[8] A merry reader along for the ride may well respond with "Cheers!"—a reaction that Mailer, following a similar exhibition of verbal dexterity, sometimes inscribes within his own texts. Kael's pieces frequently conclude in sly bathos; following a cataract of—largely negative—comments on *Raging Bull,* her boisterous voice trails off with the savorless sentence: "An end title supplies a handy Biblical quote."[9]

Pauline Kael is perhaps the most exuberantly ludic figure in the history of American criticism. Whether or not that claim is valid, it is itself a kind of Kaelian superlative—the tentative assertion of a very odd distinction. She thus characterizes *Mon Oncle Antoine* as "probably the most plangent movie ever made in and about Canada" (*T*, 421), as if the category admitted of subtle gradations and numerous contestants. The contention that *Altered States* is "probably the most aggressively silly picture since *The Exorcist*" (*T*, 128) admits the possibility of another as well as of passively silly pictures before *The Exorcist*. With just a soupçon of hesitation, she pronounces *An Englishman Abroad* "probably the best hour of television I've ever seen,"[10] the early frames of *Iceman* "perhaps the greatest opening shot I've ever seen" (*S*, 160), and an exchange between Ed Harris and Mary Jo Deschanel in *The Right Stuff* as "perhaps the wittiest and most deeply romantic confirmation of a marriage ever filmed" (*S*, 65). When she declares that *The Trial of Billy Jack* "probably represents the most extraordinary display of sanctimonious self-aggrandizement the screen has ever known" (*R*, 504), that *Godfather II* "may be the most passionately felt epic ever made in this country" (*R*, 529), that *The Last Tango in Paris* "may turn out to be the most liberating film ever made" (*R*, 53), that Carol Burnett "is probably the most gifted comedienne this country has ever produced" (*R*, 126), that *The Iceman Cometh* is "perhaps the greatest thesis play of the American theater" (*R*, 271), and that *Days and Nights in the Forest* "is perhaps the subtlest, most plangent study of the cultural tragedy of imperialism the screen has ever had" (*R*, 200), Kael keeps her eyes wide but her options open, barely. The critic who proclaims that a dinner party in *My Left Foot* "may be the most emotionally wrenching scene I've ever experienced at the movies,"[11] that Jeff Bridges "may be the most natural and least self-conscious screen actor who ever lived" (*R*, 233), and that *Padre Padrone* "may be the only fully conscious animistic movie ever made" (*W*, 299) may be the most hyperbolic of eminent authors since Dickens. So persistent is she in devising a radical epithet for almost every movie and moviemaker that Kael might be the most fervent enforcer of the law of the excluded middle. If not a conscious mockery of puffery in an industry in which every new release is either a blockbuster or an award-winner, her extravagant rhetoric does call attention to itself and to criticism as performance. Kael speculated that her best talent may be "a real gift for effrontery,"[12] and that gift finds its most gaudy wrapping in the audacious hyperboles that she repeatedly conceives.

Borrowing her own testy trope for the plethora of closeups in *Downhill Racer,* one could claim that the superlatives in Kael's prose "keep hitting one like the Yo-Yos in 3-D movies."[13] That is a veritably baroque comparison, and, if there is any stylistic device in Kael's prose with more resilience than her hyperboles, it is the mock-epic simile. "*The Pope of Greenwich Village* is like a doughy plum cake with wonderful plums sticking out of it," she declares and then, like a bard ecstatic over extending an analogy, adds: "The plums are the performers" (*S,* 201). Kael characterizes *One, Two, Three* as "a comedy that pulls out laughs the way a catheter draws urine" (*L,* 150), *Risky Business* as "a George Bernard Shaw play rewritten for a cast of ducks and geese" (*S,* 40), and *Star Wars* as "like getting a box of Cracker Jack which is all prizes" (*W,* 291). Sometimes she applies her gymnastic comparisons not to movies but to how to talk about movies, as when she declares that lambasting "a Ross Hunter production is like flogging a sponge" (*R,* 194), when she concedes that warning connoisseurs away from *How to Save a Marriage—and Ruin Your Life* is "as superfluous as warning a gourmet against canned spaghetti" (*G,* 21), or when she complains that "A critic with a single theory is like a gardener who uses a lawn mower on everything that grows" (*L,* 309). As handy with a manure spreader as a lawn mower, Kael does not confine herself to a single theory. She celebrates her nimbleness by concocting comparisons between wildly divergent terms. The similes are often so manifestly far-fetched that the reader shares the thrill of giddy ingenuity.

Kael's bravura style is a creature of her guerrilla campaign against gentility. As staff reviewer for that most urbane of glossy weeklies, *The New Yorker,* she aroused fierce and continuing resistance from the magazine's decorous older guard, who resented both her raffish subject, movies, and her congruent, breezy style. Precipitating the most notorious of several rows that Kael has had in print with other critics, Renata Adler, a Knickerbocker loyalist, assailed Kael's flamboyant verbal art as "a form of prose hypochondria, palpating herself all over to see if she has a thought, and publishing every word of the process by which she checks to see whether or not she has one; it is also equally true that she can hardly resist any form of hyperbole, superlative, exaggeration."[14] Adler's account of Kael's histrionics is largely valid, though not necessarily damning, for all its evident animosity. It has had no demonstrable effect on Kael's work, though it might have confirmed the California woman in her outsider's determination to stun and wow proper New Yorkers. Her praise during a 1989 interview for exorbitance in 1930s movies also justifies her own verbal campiness: "Part of the fun for many of us—you see it now if you look at old movies of the '30s—is that extravagance of gesture, doing things to excess. Every emotion is made bright. And it helps us satirize ourselves, helps put our own emotions in perspective, because they are so overdramatized."[15]

Kael's first book, *I Lost It at the Movies,* a collection of pieces written before she moved East to join *The New Yorker* and when she still could mock its occasional reviewer John McCarten, announces Kael's insurgency against the canons of critical respectability. She is as contemptuous of the entire tribe of movie reviewers—"a destructive bunch of solidly, stupidly respectable mummies—and it works either way, maternal or Egyptian" (*I,* 72)—as of Hollywood malarkey. She offers herself as a lively alternative to Bosley Crowther and Andrew Sarris and flaunts her mischievous manner as a weapon of rebellion. Edward Murray has analyzed the "Huck Finn complex" that he finds in Kael's writing,[16] as if her brazen hyperboles and similes were the whoppers of a wayward frontier child.

Despite her explicit admiration for the works of many foreign directors, notably Bernardo Bertolucci, Jean-Luc Godard, Jean Renoir, and Satyajit Ray, Kael devotes most of her attention to domestic releases and writes with a nativist mistrust of cinematic imports. Like Emerson in "The Poet," she demands a declaration of independence from the tyranny of the European Muse. Offering herself as a champion of local genius, Kael denies that American culture is an oxymoron and indeed argues for the superior vitality of New World art, as long as it remains true to its autochthonous inspirations. She reveres and attempts to personify Yankee irreverence. Rejecting Europe as the gauge of artistic achievement, particularly for something as quintessentially American as comedy, she notes that: "It's a bad joke on our good jokes that film enthusiasts here often take their cues on the American movie past from Europe, and so they ignore the tradition of comic irreverence."[17] Kael dared refuse to worship at the Swedish shrine of Ingmar Bergman. And she famously dismissed three fashionably ponderous new European films, *La Notte, Last Year at Marienbad,* and *La Dolce Vita,* as "The Come-Dressed-As-the-Sick-Soul-of-Europe Parties" (*L,* 179). She concluded her extended act of deflation by imagining a zestful American alternative to Antonioni, Resnais, and Fellini: "All we need to undermine and ridicule this aimless, high-style moral turpitude passing itself off as the universal human condition is one character at the parties—like, say, Martha Raye in *Monsieur Verdoux*—who enjoys every minute of it, who really has a ball, and we have the innocent American exploding this European mythology of depleted modern man who can no longer love because he has lost contact with life" (*L,* 196). Kael presents herself as a lively Raye among the mummies of Momus—no less American for her European lineage, no less indigenous for her Jewishness, and no less sophisticated for her girlhood on a West Coast farm.

In 1953, when Kael began to publish and broadcast her thoughts about movies, the industry, like the culture at large, was tyrannized by narrow definitions of nationality; blacklists and congressional committees were ostracizing studio employees judged insufficiently "American." In contrast to earnest native patriots, however, Kael—a Jewish woman one generation removed from the Iron Curtain—dared to equate Americanness with irreverence and to celebrate the impudence of American popular culture impudently. "We want the subversive gesture carried to the domain of discovery" (*G,* 120), she proclaimed, to explain the kind of movies that she craved. But the recipe applies as well to her own seditious style of commentary. Kael's fractious form of (Groucho) Marxism threatened the Margaret Dumont primness that dominated discussions of "culture." Diagnosing solemnity as "a crippling disease" (*R,* 324), she went to battle against snobs, prudes, and censors to restore American culture to robust health. During the era that the august *New Yorker* carried Kael's essays—for several years in six-month cycles alternating with Penelope Gilliatt's—she carried the subversive gestures of provocative prose into the domain of discovery. Her final review appeared on 11 February 1991, barely a year after the fall of the Berlin Wall. For almost four decades, her vigorous celebrations of American pluck and cheek were as palpable a response to the Cold War as were J. Edgar Hoover's xenophobia and Richard Nixon's jingoism. While her fans were as numerous and devoted as those of many move stars, Kael also provoked hostile letters—some scrawled anonymously and ominously on their authors' own *New Yorker* letterhead.

"Our movies are the best proof that Americans are liveliest and freest when we don't take ourselves too seriously," she declares, as though thumbing her nose at a HUAC inquisitor, early in her first book (*L,* 82). If Europe is the stern arbiter of manners, Kael finds greater strength in the social gaucheries to which untutored but affable Americans are prone: "We are bumpkins, haunted by the bottle of ketchup on the dining table at San Simeon. We garble our foreign words and phrases and hope that at least we've used them right. Our heroes pick up the wrong fork, and the basic figure of fun in the American theatre and American movies is the man who puts on airs."[18] Kael exults in deflating the air from pretentious productions, particularly if they are from Europe. "There is more energy, more originality, more excitement, more art," she insists, "in American kitsch like *Gunga Din, Easy Living,* the Rogers and Astaire pictures like *Swingtime* and *Top Hat,* in *Strangers on a Train, His Girl Friday, The Crimson Pirate, African Queen, Singin' in the Rain, Sweet Smell of Success,* or, more recently, *The Hustler, Lolita, The Manchurian Candidate, Hud, Charade,* than in the presumed 'High Culture' of *Hiroshima Mon Amour, Marienbad, La Notte, The Eclipse,* and the Torre Nilsson pictures" (*L,* 24). Her favorite way of dismissing a movie is to pronounce the experience "logy." Writing about a Japanese import, Kaneto Shindo's *The Island,* she lambastes both the work and the pervasive premise that bombastic tedium is lofty art: "This work has been widely acclaimed as a masterpiece, largely I suspect because it is so ponderously, pretentiously simple. A lot of serious-minded people will think it must be art because it sure as hell isn't entertainment" (*K,* 357).

America at its best, she suggests, is sassy, not stuffy, and its arts are characterized by audacity devoid of pomposity. In her vocabulary, *pulp* and *trash* ceased to be terms of abuse. Because gentrification has betrayed its feral native roots, she attacks the choreography in *West Side Story*: "What is lost is not merely the rhythm, the feel, the unpretentious movements of American dancing at its best—but its basic emotion, which, as in jazz music, is the contempt for respectability" (*L,* 147). For Kael, *Moby-Dick* is the great American novel precisely because its author was a barbarian: "Melville is not a civilized, European writer; he is our greatest writer because he is the American primitive struggling to say more than he knows how to say, struggling to say more than he knows" (*L,* 238). Because she takes delight in disorder, Kael opposes prigs and pedants—real and imaginary—in defense of both American culture and the movies. In *The Citizen Kane Book,* Kael champions the rumpled, flippant Herman J. Mankiewicz over grandiloquent Orson Welles as true *auteur* of the upstart movie on which both worked. She rejects the exquisitely sophisticated John Simon as a patrician critic constitutionally unsuited to appreciate the commoners' art: "Movies are for everybody—except people with arctic temperaments."[19]

Kael cooks her own prose enough to melt a polar cap. Rejecting the pretense of objectivity, she denies by statement and example the possibility of detachment from an art for which she feels such enthusiasm and of writing anything of value without enthusiasm. Convinced that pleasure is the motive for both movies and movie criticism, she exults in her own exuberance. At a time when books by D. H. Lawrence, Henry Miller, and Vladimir Nabokov were still banned because of erotic content, she celebrated the sensuality of movies. The notoriously sexual innuendoes in the titles to many of her books—*I Lost It at the Movies, Kiss Kiss Bang Bang, Deeper into Movies, When the Lights Go Down*—prepare the reader to encounter an unabashedly passionate critic.

When Kael began writing, cinema had not yet become an academic discipline or a canonized art. The United States, in contrast to its devastated wartime enemies and allies, felt itself a parvenu of nations, newly rich and powerful, but more than a bit uncouth. Kael exulted in the crude vitality that she identified with both movies and America. "Vulgarity is not as destructive to an artist as snobbery," she wrote in the pages of *The New Yorker*, an illustrious institution whose luminaries continued to snub her, "and in the world of movies vulgar strength has been a great redemptive force, cancelling out niggling questions of taste" (*D*, 412–13). Kael's commitment to vulgarity—*vulgus,* the people—extended to her preference for viewing movies with the general public rather than during private critics' screenings and to her tendency to incorporate audience reactions into her reviews. Like theater, moviegoing is for her a supremely social experience in which collective reactions and later conversations are crucial elements.

Because the sharing of impressions is so integral to her experience at the Bijou, Kael has admitted that she would find it hard to maintain a close friendship with someone whose reactions differed fundamentally and frequently from her own.[19] Many of her reviews begin with the comment a companion made while watching the movie or with what was said afterward at a party or a meal. In *Hooked,*[20] she begins her analysis of a film performance by recounting a "late-night-overdrinks conversation" in which she and a friend concluded that Morgan Freeman is the greatest living American actor. Her disappointment over the relationship between Robert De Niro and Meryl Streep in *Falling in Love*—"They don't share any tastes; they don't enthuse over anything; they don't argue over a book, a movie, a painting, a building, or even TV" (*S,* 279)—suggests that to her mind the clash of passions is essential to both moviegoing and love, if not mere friendship. "Being able to talk about movies with someone—to share the giddy high excitement you feel—is enough for a friendship" (*M,* xii), she claims, implying that such sharing is also crucial to the full experience of a movie.

Kael did most of her reviewing before the advent of the video cassette recorder, which made every viewer a projectionist and further atomized audiences. But because of continuous shows and seating, moviegoing was never the discrete communal event that live drama is, whose audiences arrive and depart in unison. What is gloriously gregarious for Kael, though, is the fact that memories of movies have the power to shape conversations and connections among large numbers of people. "Who wants to be a crazy alone?" ask Kael during a parenthetical aside about Woody Allen. "That leads to melancholy" (*R,* 329). In Kael's pharmacology, movies are an antidote to melancholy. And movie reviewing is a way to avoid being crazy alone, especially if you implicate your reader in almost every clause you write, as Kael does with her persistent use of "you" and "we." Reviewing *A Cry in the Dark,* Kael pretends to have seen each of us emerge from the dark theater: "You come out moved—even shaken—yet not quite certain what you've been watching" (*M,* 33). She has lamented that the demands of writing to a deadline enjoined a solitary regime: "What began for me as a gregarious activity—talking about movies—became, at last, a monastic pursuit."[21] By peppering her prose with the second-person pronoun, however, she invents an interlocutor and avoids being crazy alone.

To Simone Weil, "The intelligence is defeated as soon as the expression of one's thoughts is preceded, explicitly or implicitly, by the little word 'we.'"[22] The first-person plural both assumes and asserts complicity between writer and reader—an agreement, complain her detractors, that Kael does not earn. Like the reflexive "you," "we" is indeed a way of camouflaging idiosyncrasy as collective norm. When Kael asserts, "When you were a kid, you wondered if your crayons would kill you if you ate them" (*M,* 25), many of us will balk at the rum biographical assumption. We are not amused, as we are by most of her other acts of ventriloquism, her talent for projecting a manic voice that presumes to speak for all.

In 1953, when Kael began broadcasting movie commentaries on Berkeley's noncommercial Pacifica radio station, KPFA, the doctrine of impersonality still held sway in analyses of modern art, and the New Criticism's dismissal from aesthetic consideration of everything but the text itself still dominated academic studies. From the first page of her first book, a caustic account of a visit to Hollywood, Kael nevertheless dared to intrude into her discussions of movies. As though the stance of Mandarin detachment were itself the dreary enemy against whom she fashions an answerable style, Kael sometimes proffers autobiography disguised as movie criticism. "I'm frequently asked why I don't write my memoirs," wrote Kael in a coda to her years at *The New Yorker*.[23] Her terse response, "I think I have," suggests not only that writing about movies has been her life, that who touches those thirteen books touches the woman, but it also acknowledges that personal information is scattered throughout her prose. Over the years, readers have learned about her student days as a philosophy major at the University of California, about the time she caught a glimpse of William Randolph Hearst, about the five-month sabbatical she took in 1979 to work for Paramount, about her experience managing the Berkeley Cinema Guild and Studio, about her fondness for dance, jazz, and opera, about her daughter, and about her dog. Her three failed marriages are not discussed. During a review of *Hud* (*L*, 78–94), Kael recalls her childhood on a Petaluma chicken farm and describes her father who, she confides, was generous, kind, and Republican, and frequented brothels. More tantalizing than anything she has to say about a particular epic of range wars or cattle drives is the improbable claim—reaffirmed during a telephone conversation I had with her—that "My father went to a Western just about every night of his life that I remember" (*K*, 54). More intriguing than any of Kael's insights into *The Paper Chase* is her parenthetical recollection of having vomited after seeing a play directed by John Houseman (*R*, 263). What is most memorable about her piece on *Shoeshine* (*L*, 114) is the way it evokes a memory of the lovers' quarrel she had just before seeing the film. Kael informs us that she cannot remember the name of the prizefighter she once dated (*K*, 278), but she does note that the man who accompanied her to the theater in 1938 when she laughed so hard she fell out of her seat is now a judge (*H*, 438).

Kael denies herself the privilege of Olympian judgment. Though she wears her erudition—in literature, music, art, dance, and, of course, movies, among other subjects—lightly, she frequently unveils the process of how she arrives at impressions. Readers get to witness the critic on deadline making sausage out of sweat. She also concedes, even boasts of, her derelictions. "There are people who can sit through any movie, but I'm a walker-outer," she wrote, early in a career in which she has probably deserted more movies than most have sat through.[24] Thirty minutes seems to be the threshold of Kael's impatience. "I walked out after a half hour of my first Schlesinger film" (*D,* 369), she declares, and apropos of *Tora! Tora! Tora!,* virtually boasts that "After a half hour I fell into a comatose state . . . then sneaked away" (*D,* 186). What makes her assessment of Mailer's *Wild 90* as "the worst movie that I've stayed to see all the way through" (*G,* 10) such an ambiguous reproach is our awareness of how often Kael does not stay to see a movie all the way through. To explain why she did not review *Betrayal,* she confesses: "Because I couldn't sit through it. My body wouldn't let me" (*S,* 14).

Kael also concedes trouble sitting at the typewriter. She explains her absence from the 16 January 1971 issue of *The New Yorker* as justifiable hooky: "The new movies defeated me—I couldn't think of anything worth saying about them" (*D,* 292). Kael is nothing if not conscientious about her professional delinquency. She flaunts her negligence in viewing and writing as though waywardness were further proof of vivacity. In contrast to steadfast drudges who also test the patience of their readers, Kael presents herself as the Huck Finn of reviewers, ready to light out for the territory ahead when civilization seems too tedious. She identifies going to the movies with childhood spontaneity, and when a visit to the theater becomes a grownup duty, she is out of there. "Who the hell goes to movies for mature, adult, sober art, anyway?" (*K,* 42), she asks, and her own slightly naughty use of "hell" echoes Huck Finn's defiant "All right, then, I'll *go* to hell!" that both damns the boy and saves him.

Kael's theology appears to be cinematic, inspired by the varied visions that appear on giant movie screens. In 1976, long before *Schindler's List* and *The Last Temptation of Christ* expose a strain of latent piety in their directors, Kael chided Steven Spielberg, Martin Scorsese, and other young filmmakers as amoral aesthetes for whom technique is its own value. "Film is their common religion," she complained (*W,* 203), though the same might be said of Kael herself, who finds a kind of sacramental beatitude in the rituals of sharing flickering images with other avid viewers. But if virtue is its own reward, it is not what Kael seeks out in darkened movie houses: "If there is any test that can be applied to movies," she claims, as though endorsing a Blakean/Nietzschean élan vital that transcends pious categories of good and evil, "it's that the good ones never make you feel virtuous" (*H,* 197). The worst thing that Kael can find to say about James Agee, her most distinguished American predecessor as a movie reviewer, is that "his excessive virtue may have been his worst critical vice" (*G,* 60).

Anyone who brushes off virtue as an important value is likely to lose patience with the 613 commandments of the Jewish bible. The religion of Kael the reviewer hardly seems to be the Judaism of her ancestors. She is not the only modern Jew who prefers to spend her Friday evenings in a movie house rather than a synagogue. Examining Joan Micklin Silver's immigration drama *Hester Street,* she states that Jake, the protagonist, is trying to escape from "that oppressive messianic Jewish tradition, with its stress on worthwhile activities" (*W,* 80). The casual, derisive remark confounds several threads of Jewish tradition, not all of which shared a stress on messianism or on worthwhile activities. Despite its faith in the imminent advent of Messiah, Hasidism, for example, is a populist movement whose emphasis on personal fervor and disregard for the pedantic niceties of the Law resemble Kael's own rebellion against the orthodoxies of secular high culture. She also confounds Jewish tradition with Anglo-American Puritanism and Victorianism, the genteel, gentile culture of "virtue" against which so much of Kael's prose is in open rebellion. Kael's references to Jewishness are either rare or anxious, in part because she, the critic as liberator, seems to identify the ancient religion with oppression.

Kael sees Woody Allen (né Allen Konigsberg), not Eddie Cantor, Morris Carnovsky, Paul Muni, or Zero Mostel, not Molly Picon, Shelley Winters, or Barbra Streisand, as the most overtly Jewish of movie performers. "No movie star (not even Mel Brooks) can ever have been more explicit on the screen about his Jewishness than Woody Allen," she declares, despite the fact that Allen's third-generation Jewishness is distinctive and comic for how very attenuated and vexed it is. If to be Jewish is to be ill at ease either in or out of Zion, then it might be asserted that no movie critic (not even Manny Farber) can ever have been more explicit in print about his Jewishness than Pauline Kael.

"For Woody Allen, being Jewish is like being a fish on a hook" (*T,* 91), observes Kael, who does not acknowledge other, freer fish. She dubs *Interiors,* Allen's austere, Bergmanesque study of an emotionally constipated family of uncertain ethnicity, "the ultimate Jewish movie" (*W,* 428). Ultimately, *Interiors,* whose characters could pass for patrician Protestants, can be said to be Jewish only in its scrupulous avoidance of identifiably Jewish characteristics.

Despite Kael's (unfavorable) assessment of *Interiors* as the quintessential Jewish film, she elsewhere faults another somber Allen drama, *Another Woman,* for being purged of precisely that "Jewishness" that she claims gives life to Allen's comedies. "You can see in his comedies that he associates messy emotions with Jewishness and foolishness and laughter" (*M,* 15), observes the naughty Jewish girl from Petaluma, who usually champions messy emotions, foolishness, and laughter but does not herself associate them with Jewishness. The critic who dubs *Intolerance* "the greatest film ever made in this country" (*D,* 403) is hardly an advocate of ethnic or religious tribalism. It comes almost as a noble repudiation of Jewish American sectarianism when Kael claims that "Casey at the Bat" is better poetry than anything by Paul Simon (*D,* 28) or when she distances herself from fugitives of the Holocaust. Kael disparages the new Jewish immigrants she encountered in the 1930s for attempting to perpetuate precisely those elitist European attitudes against which her own demotic, Capraesque Americanism would rebel: "As a schoolgirl, my suspiciousness about those who attack American 'materialism' was first aroused by the refugees from Hitler who often contrasted their 'culture' with our 'vulgar materialism' when I discovered that the 'culture' consisted of their having had servants in Europe, and a swooning acquaintance with the poems of Rilke, the novels of Stefan Zweig and Lion Feuchtwanger, the music of Mahler and Bruckner" (*L,* 78). Kael's nonmaterialistic alternative to Rilke, Zweig, Feuchtwanger, Mahler, and Bruckner would not be Rashi, the *Zohar,* Yehudah Ha-Levi, and Agnon but rather *Citizen Kane, Godfather II, Mean Streets, Nashville,* and *The Last Tango in Paris.*

"I regard criticism as an art," Kael declared, defensively but proudly. For almost four decades, the kind of criticism she practiced was brilliant performance art. To correspondents who belittled criticism, she replied: "If you think it so easy to be a critic, so difficult to be a painter or film experimenter, may I suggest you try both? You may discover why there are so few critics, so many poets" (*L*, 234). The answer is a bit disingenuous. Without an institutional base, who bothers to write movie criticism? By contrast, the country is filled with uncommissioned, and even unpublished, poets. It is also true, however, that film, the people's medium, is the one art about which everyone has an opinion. Americans who would not presume to comment intelligently on a chamber concert, an exhibition of paintings, or even a novel feel no compunction about expressing their reactions to any movie shown in the local shopping mall. The number of professional reviewers has multiplied epidemically since Kael began more than forty years ago; virtually every general-interest newspaper and magazine and radio and television station now runs movie commentary, and regular commentators have included Edward Koch, Yogi Berra, and sundry schoolchildren. The artistry in all this prose is not always apparent, even as it accentuates Kael's distinctive merits. Choosing to align herself more with the impassioned American vernacular of Mark Twain, Will Rogers, and H. L. Mencken than with the Mandarin stance of T. S. Eliot, Kenneth Burke, and Cleanth Brooks, she provokes strong reactions to the movies on which she reports and to her reports on those movies. You antagonize more readers more easily if you write about *The Song of Norway* than about a recital by a visiting Norwegian contralto. Many remember Kael as a cranky contrarian, the critic with particularly harsh remarks about popular or critical favorites, including *Awakenings, The Big Chill, A Clockwork Orange, Gandhi, Rain Man, Shoah, The Sting,* and *West Side Story.* A stint at *McCall's* came to an abrupt end when she was fired for panning one of Hollywood's greatest hits, *The Sound of Music.* She dared call it "*The Sound of Money.*"

However, Kael's books are the archives of an unusually receptive sensibility. She was an early, lonely enthusiast for many important figures, including Robert Altman, Bernardo Bertolucci, Jonathan Demme, Brian De Palma, Jean-Luc Godard, and Satyajit Ray. Her ardent prose can be credited with saving *McCabe and Mrs. Miller* and *The Last Tango in Paris* from oblivion and with at least doing valiant battle on behalf of *Hour of the Star, Melvin and Howard,* and *Shoot the Moon.* In her later years on the job, Kael railed increasingly against the soullessness of contemporary corporate productions, but it is remarkable how much she still could find to praise. Even in *Movie Love,* which covers eighty-five movies from 1988 to early 1991—not, a preface warns us, "a time of great moviemaking fervor" (xi)—one reader counted thirty-three favorable reviews.[25] She completes her final weekly contribution to *The New Yorker* with a word of affirmation. On 11 February 1991 Kael's parting review concludes with a comment on Sarah Jessica Parker in *L.A. Story* "She's the spirit of L.A.: she keeps saying yes" (*M,* 328). Yes, like Molly Bloom's closing words, is a fitting valediction for the American critic who did most to spread the democratic creed of movie love.

Notes

1. Joseph Esptein (Aristides), "Nicely Out of It," *American Scholar* 62 (Autumn 1993): 488.
2. Pauline Kael, "The Movie Lover," *New Yorker,* 21 March 1994, 133.
3. Pauline Kael, *I Lost It at the Movies* (Boston: Little, Brown, 1954), 309; subsequent citations appear parenthetically in the text as *L.*
4. Pauline Kael, *Reeling* (New York: Warner, 1976), 17; subsequent citations appear as *R.*
5. Norman Mailer advertises himself by reiterating in *The Armies of the Night: History as a Novel, The Novel of History* (New York: New American Library, 1968), 70: "Norman Mailer was as fond of his style as an Italian tenor is of his vocal cords."
6. Kael, "The Movie Lover," 134.
7. Pauline Kael, *When the Lights Go Down* (New York: Holt, Rinehart and Winston, 1980), 195; subsequent citations appear as *W.*
8. Pauline Kael, *Going Steady* (New York: Bantam, 1971), 136; subsequent citations appear as *G.*
9. Pauline Kael, *Taking It All In* (New York: Holt, Rinehart and Winston, 1984), 112; subsequent citations appear as *T.*
10. Pauline Kael, *State of the Art* (New York: E. P. Dutton, 1985), 311; subsequent citations appear as *S.*
11. Pauline Kael, *Movie Love* (New York: Plume, 1991), 178; subsequent citations appear as *M.*
12. Hal Espen, "Kael Talks," *New Yorker,* 21 March, 1994, 135.
13. Pauline Kael, *Deeper into Movies* (New York: Bantam, 1974), 57; subsequent citations appear as *D.*
14. Renata Adler, "The Perils of Pauline," *New York Review of Books,* 14 August 1980, 34.
15. Ray Sawhill and Polly Frost, "Kaleidoscope," *Interview* 19 (April 1989): 101.
16. Edward Murray, *Nine American Film Critics* (New York: Ungar, 1975), 131.
17. Pauline Kael, *The Citizen Kane Book: Raising Kane* (Boston: Little, Brown, 1971), 15.
18. Pauline Kael, *Kiss, Kiss, Bang, Bang* (New York: Bantam, 1969), 67.
19. Sawhill and Frost, "Kaleidoscope," 101.
20. Pauline Kael, *Hooked* (New York: Dutton, 1989), 292; subsequent citations appear as *H.*
21. Kael, "The Movie Lover," 134.

22. Simone Weil, *The Need for Roots: Prelude to a Declaration of Duties Toward Mankind,* trans. Arthur Wills (New York: Octagon, 1979), 27–28.

23. Kael, "The Movie Lover," 134.

24. Pauline Kael, "The Function of a Critic," *McCall's,* February 1966, 38.

25. Marc Smirnoff, "Pauline Kael: The Critic Wore Cowboy Boots," *Oxford American* 1 (Spring 1992): 42.

Wendy Wasserstein and the Crisis of (Jewish) Identity

Stephen J. Whitfield

Born in Brooklyn on 18 October 1950, Wendy Wasserstein has drawn on features of her family life to inspire all four of her major plays. She was the youngest of four children, including two other daughters—one of whom became a high executive at Citicorp, while another married a doctor and raised three children. "She did the best," the "bachelor girl" playwright once sardonically announced,[1] in comparing the siblings whose lives would be transmuted into *The Sisters Rosensweig* (1992). The Wassersteins themselves were very solidly and successfully middle class—"a sort of traditional family, eccentric but traditional," the playwright later recalled. Morris was a successful textile manufacturer; and among the fabrics that he patented was velveteen, which Holly Kaplan's father has invented, according to *Uncommon Women and Others* (177). In *Isn't It Romantic* (1983), Janie Blumberg's father manufactures stationery. Wendy Wasserstein's bohemian and liberated mother, Lola, was a devotee of theater and of dance classes, which Tasha Blumberg, the aerobically inclined mother in *Isn't It Romantic,* continues to take.[2]

When Wendy was twelve, the family moved to the Upper East Side of Manhattan, reinforcing the expectations of high academic and professional achievement with the presumptions of a future combining maternity and domesticity. Beginning at the Yeshivah of Flatbush, she hit the ground running, and already by the second grade, she realized that she was funny: "I was good company . . . an elementary school Falstaff." She graduated from the Calhoun School and went on to major in history, class of 1971, at Mount Holyoke College. (The eponymous protagonist of *The Heidi Chronicles* [1988] becomes an art historian.) Wasserstein got a master's degree in creative writing at City University of New York in 1973 (studying with playwright Israel

Horovitz and novelist Joseph Heller) and then studied at the Yale School of Drama, from which she received a Master of Fine Arts in 1976. Drawing on her undergraduate experience, she had submitted a thesis play at Yale, a one-act acorn that would grow into the Obie-winning oak entitled *Uncommon Women and Others*.[3] Moving back to New York City, which is where the two young women in *Isn't It Romantic* inaugurate a similar stage in their lives, Wasserstein was soon recognized as among the most sparkling playwrights of her generation.

Luck did not hurt: when *Uncommon Women* was elevated to the Public Broadcasting System's Great Performances series a year after opening at the Marymount Manhattan Theatre, her Yale classmate Meryl Streep played Leilah, replacing another soon-to-be legendary actress, Glenn Close. Talent mattered too: Wasserstein's first play won the *Village Voice* Off-Broadway Award;[4] her third to be staged won the Pulitzer Prize for drama and the Antoinette Perry (or Tony) Award, plus honors from the New York Drama Critics' Circle, the Outer Critics Circle and the Drama Desk—just about everything but the Heisman Trophy. *The Heidi Chronicles* was also her first to prove Broadway-bound. And when *The Sisters Rosensweig* opened there, the character of Sara Goode was played by Jane Alexander, whom President Clinton soon appointed to head the National Endowment for the Arts. Though Wasserstein's total output has not been huge (and has inspired little extensive scholarly criticism), she merits attention for another reason besides the recognition and acclaim that her gifts have elicited. Perhaps more than in the work of any major American dramatist of this century (even including Clifford Odets, for example), the vicissitudes of Jewish identity should be included among the primary themes of Wendy Wasserstein's work.

Its ethnicity is not emphatic. The author herself has not advanced a communal agenda, nor does she insist that her dramaturgy be used for Jewish purposes. She has not assigned herself the responsibility of speaking for the Jewish people—or even necessarily *to* it. The first noteworthy Jewish American leader, Mordecai Manuel Noah, also happened to be a playwright, yet his melodramas were not overtly placed in the service of Jewish interests and were even barren of Jewish characters.[5] Although Wasserstein may not have Jewish audiences (or critics) primarily in mind and does not wish to be judged primarily as a Jewish playwright, neither is she Lillian Hellman, whose plays betray no obvious signs of Jewish origins, idiom, or purposes. Wasserstein is also a product of the *Zeitgeist.* Born five years after Bess Myerson of the Sholom Aleichem Cooperatives Houses of the Bronx had become Miss America, Wasserstein is heir to the legitimation of ethnicity—including Jewish ethnicity. Born five years before Will Herberg's *Protestant Catholic Jew* (1955) inflated his own Judaism to tripartite status as one of the nation's three presumptive if unofficial faiths, she grew up in an era of frictionless integration into American society, in which its Jews did not feel in *galut.*

Unlike the bleak desperation that animates the Berger family during the Great Depression in Odets' *Awake and Sing!* (1935), unlike the rapacity that motivates the Hubbards in the ruined, post-Reconstruction South of Hellman's *The Little Foxes* (1939), Wasserstein's Jews need not worry where the next meal is coming from or how best to stay ahead in an ambience haunted by the experience and the fear of poverty. In the Group Theatre of the 1930s, the edgy characters played by Jules Garfinkle (a.k.a. John Garfield) faced the problem of how to make money. For Larry "the Liquidator" Garfinkle (called Larry Garfield in the movie version of Jerry Sterner's 1989 play, *Other People's Money*), the problem was how to make his money make money. The trajectory is thus sharply upward, from the working-class Bergers to the lower-middle-class Lomans in *Death of a Salesman* (1949) to the sisters Rosensweig, whose roles in life range from an international banker based in London to an international travel writer living in exotic Asia to a leader of the Temple Beth El women's auxiliary. Its Sisterhood may not be powerful, but at least it is based in posh Newton, Massachusetts. Theatrical history thus reflects the gravity-defying upward mobility of American Jewry. It is almost too good to be true that the only brother to the sisters Wasserstein became a Master of the Universe, using other people's money to specialize in leveraged buyouts. In 1988 Bruce Wasserstein was an architect of the $25 billion RJR-Nabisco merger that capped the buccaneering, let's-make-a-deal capitalism of the Reagan era.[6] No wonder his sister's characters, who have attended the best schools and have inherited the comforts of young urban professionals, come out ahead of the progeny of the Bergers and the Lomans.

The accident of birth also made Wasserstein the beneficiary of enhanced sensitivity to the female condition and to the injustices of gender. "I can't understand not being a feminist," she admits,[7] having turned thirteen when Betty Friedan's *The Feminine Mystique* was published and "the problem with no name" specified. If the perplexities of peoplehood do not spring to mind when considering the thrust of Wasserstein's work, that is because, though multifarious identities need not be incompatible, she writes far more directly as a woman than as a Jew. The perspective that her plays offer is feminist (and not Judaic); and in them feminist speeches are given even to men like the faux furrier Mervyn Kant, who punctures the cliché that Jews Do Not Drink: "I think it's a myth made up by our mothers to persuade innocent women that Jewish men make superior husbands. In other words, it's worth it to put up with my crankiness, my hypochondria, my opinions on world problems, because I don't drink."[8] Some evidence suggests that Heidi Holland herself is not Jewish, and the contemporary challenge that she faces would be familiar to virtually any young professional American woman thrown off balance when the rules of engagement keep shifting.

Though the social problem that *Isn't It Romantic* addresses is defined with a New York Jewish accent, Janie is not exactly looking (in theater critic Carolyn Clay's pun) for Mr. Good Bar Mitzvah. The protagonist is deft at playing back the mixed messages that Tasha Blumberg, who has already inhaled the air of emancipation even as she was raising Janie, has communicated to her daughter. "Mother, think about it," Janie announces. "Did you teach me to marry a nice Jewish doctor and make chicken for him? You order up breakfast from a Greek coffee shop every morning. Did you teach me to go to law school and wear gray suits at a job that I sort of like every day from nine to eight? You run out of here in leg warmers and tank tops to dancing school. Did you teach me to compromise and lie to the man I live with and say I love you when I wasn't sure? You live with your partner; you walk Dad to work every morning."[9] It is hard not to detect here a note of envy for an earlier generation that at its luckiest managed to combine intimacy with security and to reconcile expanded vocational and avocational possibilities with conventional middle-class comforts.

The plays of Wendy Wasserstein are populated with Jews but are even more frequently filled with women. Her oeuvre has constituted, according to one critic, "comedies of feminine survival that explore the ambiguous effectiveness of the women's movement during the past quarter of a century. Using the pattern of her own life as a paradigm, she has dramatized with a sharply satiric wit the problematic intersection of the individual experience and the collective feminist ideology that would explain and transform it."[10] Though the special burden of expectation for women to marry is a recurrent theme in Wasserstein's work, an even more special burden that is placed upon Jewish women privileges marriage within the faith. World Jewry is not even a blip on the demographic screen, no bigger than the margin of statistical error in the Chinese census;[11] and continuity requires philoprogenitiveness and endogamy, values that are not quintessential either to the ideology of feminism or to the pleasures of romantic love. The pressure comes from parents who do not want their own child to be *aharon ha-aharonim* (the last of the last), a terminal Jew; and that anxiety is erratically conveyed, with mixed and uncertain results.

Thus Holly Kaplan phones (or pretends to phone) a young Jewish physician in Minneapolis, but fears to establish such a connection even as she seeks it. Thus Janie Blumberg is comically fixed up with a Russian cab driver. And isn't it romantic that Heidi Holland, though probably not Jewish (but not specified as a gentile either), cannot escape from the clutches of Scoop Rosenbaum, even at the raucous Jewish wedding that ratifies his compromising decision to marry someone else. In the controversial climax to the play, Heidi has adopted a daughter and become a single mother. Thus Gorgeous Teitelbaum wishes that her sister's loneliness might be cured, and tells Tess Goode, her niece: "I always said to mother, if only Sara would meet a furrier or a dentist." The fifty-four year-old Sara is permitted to wonder whether her one-night-stand gentleman caller merits a longer commitment. "You're just like all the other men I went to high school with," she tells Merv Kant. "You're smart, you're a good provider, you read *The Times* every day, you started running at fifty to recapture your youth, you worry a little too much about your health, you thought about having affairs, but you never actually did it, and now that she's departed, your late wife, Roslyn, is a saint."[12] Men like him and Scoop Rosenbaum and perhaps even the unseen and unheard Doctor Mark Silverstein have the right business and professional credentials to embody success and security. But they also threaten the autonomy and egalitarianism that a feminist vision encourages and an expanding economy sanctions.

The ideology of the women's movement can collide with the dictates of patriarchal Judaism. Though Wasserstein's writing betrays no awareness of such tension, not even her most militant sisters would confuse a conclave of the Union for Traditional Conservative Judaism with the boys-will-be-boys raunchiness of a Tailhook convention. Religious faith and ritual have nevertheless become diminished in the observably Jewish but unobservant families that are dissected in Wasserstein's satire. Few can be classified among the "good ga davened," whom Holly Kaplan, the lone Jew among the *femmes savantes* at Mount Holyoke, defines as "those who davened or prayed right. Girls who good ga davened did well. They marry doctors and go to Bermuda for Memorial Day weekends. These girls are also doctors but they only work part-time because of their three musically inclined children, and weekly brownstone restorations." It is akin to "a 'did well' list published annually, in New York, Winnetka, and Beverly Hills, and distributed on High Holy Days. . . ."[13] Upward mobility and a securely middle-class status have become so central to the ethos of American Jewry that even a far less savvy undergraduate than Holly cannot fail to notice.

Of course anti-Semitism has not entirely evaporated; when the uncommon women play conjugal games with one another, Samantha Stewart realizes that she cannot "marry" Holly because back home "there would be a problem at the club." But secularism has narrowed the gap between Jew and gentile. Holly would never concur with an earlier Jew, a Venetian who declines an invitation to dine with Bassanio: "I will buy with you, sell with you, talk with you, walk with you . . . but I will not eat with you, drink with you, nor pray with you" (*The Merchant of Venice* 1.3). Secularism is also powered by the sexual revolution. Filling a diaphragm with Orthocreme, Holly announces: "Now . . . whenever I see a boy with a yarmulke, I think he has a diaphragm on his head. I shouldn't have said that. I'll be struck down by a burning bush."[14]

Wanting to connect (by telephone) with Dr. Mark Silverstein, whom she had met at the Fogg Museum the previous summer, Holly reveals through her monologue her insecurity, her smarts, her uncertainties, her taste in culture, and her yearning for both interdependence and intimacy, as well as her need to forge her own future. In 1978, six years after graduating, Holly is unmarried, her life in limbo. "I haven't made any specific choices," she tells her college friends. "My parents used to call me three times a week at seven A.M. to ask me, 'Are you thin, are you married to a root-canal man, are *you* a root-canal man?' And I'd hang up and wonder how much longer I was going to be in 'transition.'" She may still be unattached because of the historical factors beyond her control. To find the right (Jewish) man has become dicey. Jet planes had already made Miami no harder to visit than the Catskills, narrowing the distinctive sites for dating and mating, as Kutsher's came to be considered a last resort.[15] Reluctant to compromise, Holly may have to remain single. Refusing to compromise, her creator forfeited a chance to bring *Uncommon Women and Others* to Broadway. One producer considered the play "too wistful" and proposed a revised ending: "When everyone asks Holly, 'What's new with you?' she should pull out a diamond ring and say, 'Guess what? I'm going to marry Dr. Mark Silverstein.'" The playwright herself thought: "Well, she'd have to have a lobotomy, and I'd have to have a lobotomy too."[16]

The focus of Wasserstein's next play is the third of the inalienable rights that Jefferson had enumerated: the pursuit of happiness. Its possible incompatibility with Jewish continuity is a variation on the major theme of *Isn't It Romantic*—the only one of Wasserstein's four major plays in which parents appear. Janie Blumberg knows she can please them by making them grandparents. But she cannot tell them, "Here are your *naches*"—at least not yet. How Simon Blumberg and especially his wife scheme to *kvell* and seek to ensure bliss for (and through) the children (especially the daughter, who has moved from Brookline to Manhattan) gives their relationship the tone of an adversary proceeding, a family feud *l'dor vador* (from generation to generation). Tasha Blumberg advises Janie to "always look nice when you throw out the garbage: you never know who you might meet,"[17] and serenades her with a prenuptial "Sunrise, Sunset" (from *Fiddler on the Roof*). But on the common ground of cultural pluralism and status seeking, religion is no barrier to friendship or romance. Contemporary mores even encourage a certain philo-Semitism, as when Janie's friend Harriet (Hattie) Cornwall studies the *Oxford Companion to Jewish Life* and her mother, Lillian, tells Tasha that both of them "deserve a little *naches*." Intermarriage has ceased to be a fear and has become a fact. (Guess who's coming to the *seder?*) The Blumbergs' son, Ben, has married a Nebraskan named Chris (whom the parents call "Christ"). Cynthia Peterson, known to the audience only as a voice (Meryl Streep's in the Broadway production) on Janie's answering machine, feels so lonely that she wonders—intertextually—whether she "should have married Mark Silverstein in college."[18]

The task of reconciling the ideal of female independence with a yearning for intimacy and maternity is borne by the twenty-eight-year-old protagonist. Here is how Janie ponders her options: "I resent having to pay the phone bill, be nice to the super, find meaningful work, fall in love, get hurt. . . . [But] I could marry the pervert who's staring at us. No. That's not a solution. I could always move back to Brookline. Get another master's in something useful like Women's Pottery. Do a little free-lance writing. Oh, God, it's exhausting." One option is Dr. (again!) Marty Sterline, né Murray Schlimovitz, a kidney specialist with a love of Jewish cuisine. His restaurateur father has prospered in part by hustling popovers in television commercials. The "toastmaster general for the United Jewish Appeal," Sterling *père* risks losing that status because the commercials promote free shrimp at the salad bar. Although such lapses and foibles make the Jewish community a tempting target for satire, the playwright does not mock the comfort that Marty himself derives from *ahavat yisrael,* or solidarity with the Jewish people. "I worked on a kibbutz the second time I dropped out of medical school," he tells Janie. "Israel's very important to me. In fact, I have to decide next month if I want to open my practice here in New York or in Tel Aviv." He worries about assimilation (of which the indices are "intermarriage, Ivy League colleges, the *New York Review of Books*"); and he believes "Jewish families should have at least three children."[19]

But does Janie want what Marty offers? Does she *love* him? He is nice enough to be appealing. But his very attractiveness also seems to foreclose the future, to narrow her options, to block her freedom of choice. As with some of the uncommon graduating seniors, Janie sees tracking as a threat to be avoided, a conventionally bourgeois life as something to be dreaded. "He's decided to open his practice here next month," she tells Hattie, "and he's invited me to his parents' house for Chanukah. . . . [Maybe] I'll marry Marty. Whatever happened to Janie Blumberg? She did so well; she married Marty the doctor. They're giving away popovers in Paramus." Marty upholds traditional ways, preferring to live in the parts of Brooklyn "where people have real values. My father never sees those people anymore, the alta kakas in Brooklyn. . . . I miss them. . . . My father thought my brother was crazy when he named his son Shlomo. . . . And my father will think I'm crazy when we move to Brooklyn." Janie, who admires the true grit of Israelis, is not sure about leaving Manhattan but characteristically deflects (or defers) conflict with a quip: "I like the alta kakas in Brooklyn too. I always thought Herman Wouk should write a novel, *Young Kaka.* I don't know."[20]

She still resists facing a destiny that is signed, sealed, and delivered, the sort of finality that can be predicted in the headline with which the Sunday *Times* will certify their wedding: "Daughter of Pioneer in Interpretive Dance Marries Popover Boy." That destiny entails too many expectations to fulfill; and, using a joke to escape a yoke, she telephones her mother: "This morning I got married, lost twenty pounds, and became a lawyer." Yet the dramatist plays fair and allows Marty the dignity of decent ambitions. He too wants "a home, a family, something my father had so easily and I can't seem to get started on." He has also "wanted something special [as well]. Just a little. Maybe not as special as you turned out to be, but just a little. Janie, I don't want to marry anyone like my sister-in-law." Though Janie can imagine a wedding at the Plaza Hotel, where "baby Shlomo could carry the ring in one of my father's gold-seal envelopes," it wouldn't be right. As for her own "settling down," "there's nothing wrong with that life, but it just isn't mine right now."[21]

A sympathetic and sprightly romantic comedy about young people just starting out in Manhattan, combined with the daughter's mother very much on the scene and a possibly amorous foreigner, sounds a little like *Barefoot in the Park* (1963). *Isn't It Romantic* is indeed indebted to Neil Simon. Attorney Paul Bratter's announcement that he had won his first case, but that—because the court awarded his client only six cents—his law firm would henceforth give him "all the cases that come in for a dime or under," is akin to Janie's pride in getting to write the letter *B* on *Sesame Street*: "If they like this, they'll hire me full-time. In charge of consonants." The troubling part of Wasserstein's dialogue is not that it is unamusing but that it is, which is how Janie ends a confrontation with presumably feminist Harriet about the importance of autonomy, even if it means the pursuit of loneliness ("I'm not going to turn someone into the answer for me"). Janie and her creator deflate rising dramatic tension into the denouement of self-deprecating humor to ward off an invasion of privacy. Humor for the playwright herself has "always been just a way to get by," she has confessed, "a way to be likable yet to remain removed."[22] After a while, however, serious audiences have the right to expect more and harsher truths to be uncovered.

Even Neil Simon slowed down the pace of his wit and revealed unsuspected depths of pathos and loss in his autobiographical trilogy of the 1980s (*Brighton Beach Memoirs, Biloxi Blues,* and *Broadway Bound*). Wasserstein's most recent play lightly mocks such artistic growth when Geoffrey Duncan, the British director, boasts to Pfeni Rosensweig: "If not for me, you'd still think that

Uncle Vanya was a Neil Simon play about his pathetic uncle in the Bronx."[23] Witticisms are ultimately no substitute for wisdom; they are no more than a local anesthetic, as Wasserstein herself is the first to acknowledge. "Although I am proud of the last scene in *Isn't It Romantic*" and its declaration of independence from parents and men, she told an interviewer that "the play doesn't deal with the pain of that subject. The real reason for comedy is to hide the pain. It is a way to cope with it." The perky wit of the protagonist "gives her the ability to distance herself from situations,"[24] a locale that is the opposite of the vortex of the tragic hero. But to keep creating such characters is to remain with the junior varsity.

A considerable segment of Wasserstein's audience nevertheless expects her to entertain and implicitly keeps issuing gag orders, imperatives that ought to be resisted for the sake of her own growth as an artist. She did become more serious in her next and most ambitious work, *The Heidi Chronicles,* without forsaking her flair for snap-crackle-and-pop dialogue and satiric observation. The quarter of a century that the play spans ends in desolation, with the loss of friends, the stretching of bonds to the breaking point, and the plague of AIDS raging outside. Above all the play is a chronicle of abandonment. Sisterhood is powerful—but not enough to resist infection by the culture of narcissism—and the conclusion that the plucky and sensitive protagonist draws from this failure is justly famous: "I feel stranded. And I thought the whole point was that we wouldn't feel stranded. I thought the point was that we were all in this together."[25] To be sure, Heidi Holland would not have concurred with the 1853 claim of Henry James, Sr., that "the 'Woman's Movement,' as it is called, does not . . . presage any directly valuable results," nor with his reasons (since the second sex is the male's "inferior in passion, his inferior in intellect and his inferior in physical strength").[26] But Heidi is at least vaguely aware that no meaningful substitute has been found for the cohesiveness of earlier generations of families, and until she adopts the infant Judy, her isolation may reflect the almost 25 percent of U.S. households now consisting of one person (up from only 8 percent in 1940).[27]

Nuclear families remain standard, however. They persist, get reconstituted and—when given up for dead—play possum. Even the extended family has become reconstituted in a way with the invention of joint custody, "in which two formerly married people share in raising their children. Your basic extended family today," Delia Ephron adds, "includes your ex-husband or -wife, your ex's new mate, your new mate, possibly your new mate's ex, and any new mate that your new mate's ex has acquired. It consists entirely of people who are not related by blood, many of whom can't stand each other."[28] Families divide too, and other loyalties are articulated. The first edition of Betty Friedan's classic was dedicated to her husband "and to our children—Daniel, Jonathan, and Emily." After a divorce, a new 1974 edition of *The Feminine Mystique* was dedicated to "all the new women, and the new men." Some of those men were indeed new: by 1986 even Superman was becoming "more vulnerable" and "more open about his feelings," according to a vice president of DC Comics.[29] But a gendered community like the company of women envisioned in Charlotte Perkins Gilman's *Herland* (1915) is an unrealized utopia. Nor does Heidi have the option of recreating the "loveless intimacy" of the Brownsville neighborhood that in 1951 Alfred Kazin could at least summon from his memory: "We had always to be together: believers and nonbelievers, we were a people; I was of that people. . . . We had all of us lived together so long that we would not have known how to separate even if we had wanted to. The most terrible word was *aleyn,* alone."[30] He could still recall the ethics of the fathers, still savor the cooking of the mothers. But "Brunzvil" had its obvious limitations, only one of which was its diminution of women.

The corrective that feminism was designed to represent is scrutinized in *The Heidi Chronicles,* which shows how that ideology can clash with the feminine mystique. Such tension had earlier surfaced in *Uncommon Women and Others.* "I suppose this isn't a very impressive sentiment," Muffet Di Nicola asserts shortly before her graduation, "but I would really like to meet my prince. Even a few princes. And I wouldn't give up being a person. I'd still remember all the Art History dates. I just don't know why suddenly I'm supposed to know what I want to do." In *The Heidi Chronicles* Scoop Rosenbaum is no prince. Having played lacrosse at Exeter before entering Princeton, he is a cad and an attorney, a trendy leftish journalist in the 1960s, a trendy publisher of the fluffy *Boomer* in the 1980s, a Jew and "a charismatic creep" with no redeeming value. Heidi is irresistibly drawn to him. As in Wasserstein's earlier plays, the female protagonist anticipates a future that she needs to elude. At thirty-five, Scoop predicts, Heidi will be "picking your daughter up from Ethical Culture School to escort her to cello class before dinner with

Dad, the noted psychiatrist and Miró poster collector."[31] Evasive action will prove successful; her daughter will presumably be raised without Dad.

Although praiseworthy as Wasserstein's most important critique of the effects and limitations of feminism, *The Heidi Chronicles* is the least illuminating on the topic of the Jewish condition in the United States—largely because the central character is almost certainly not Jewish. (Wasserstein spurned an offer to make the Hollywood film version a vehicle for Goldie Hawn, who *is* Jewish, but hardly stereotypically so.[32]) When Scoop weds Lisa Friedlander of Memphis, he conjectures that his friend Heidi and *her* friend Dr. Peter Patrone are romantically involved: "Makes sense. Lisa marries a nice Jewish lawyer, Heidi marries a warm Italian pediatrician. It's all interchangeable, isn't it?" Yet Scoop's preference for Lisa over Heidi is not, he insists, because "she's Jewish" but because, Heidi counters, "she's blandish." Peter's homosexuality torpedoes not only Scoop's speculation, however; the model future that (Jewish) parental expectation has formed is also made risible. Told that Peter is living with an anesthesiologist and gardens with him during the summers in Bucks County, Scoop replies: "A handsome doctor and a country house. Peter's living my mother's dream come true!"[33]

The centrality of Jewish identity to her fourth play, however, comes out when the bisexual Geoffrey Duncan tells Pfeni Rosensweig: "You really don't understand what it is to have absolutely no idea who you are!"[34] An identity crisis can be tiring, but as a theme in American Jewish drama, identity was not yet tiresome. In the plays of Elmer Rice or Sidney Kingsley or Lillian Hellman, it rarely if ever came up. Wasserstein makes the faulty transmission of *Yiddishkeit* central, however, while hugging the shore of gender that she finds most congenial. The five uncommon women have been reduced to three and have become middle-aged as well. Two of them are single, but all are Jewish.By making them not just a trio of white chicks sittin' around talkin' but actual sisters, the playwright has injected Anton Chekhov into the Jewish family constellation.

If Wasserstein's previous work consisted mostly of episodes, of sketches woven together as much by chronological order as by action, with her fourth play emerged the formal satisfactions of structure, honoring the "unities of time, place, and action."[35] Perhaps as directly from Chekhov as from any other influence, Wasserstein learned to mix detachment with sympathy, objectification with wry feeling. The distinction between the cosmic and the comic is, after all, a matter of spacing—and, at least on stage, of pacing. (Or consider the virtuosity of film star Amy Irving, who had played Masha in *The Three Sisters* in Williamstown in 1987, and then played Heidi Holland in Los Angeles three year later.) In *The Sisters Rosensweig* the author's nimble wit is intact; her particular version of Moscow does not believe in tears. One might even be tempted to report that in this work Chekhov meets Neil Simon—except that they had already been formally introduced: Simon had already paid homage on Broadway to the Russian master in *The Good Doctor* in (1973), and Chekhov himself was no slouch in extracting mellow laughter from the stupendous folly of human behavior. (If the reputation that his plays enjoy is of unsparing gloom, the performances and the translations may be accountable.[36]) The three American Jewish sisters may not pine away and suffer unbearably from ennui. Indeed, from Newton to Nepal, their lives throb with excitement. But the sisters are not exactly fulfilled either, and feelings of disappointment and frustration are among the promises that the structure of human existence never fails to keep. Moscow is not mecca (and Mecca certainly is not), but disenchantment and misplaced dreams are familiar to the sisters Rosensweig.

They are, in the playwright's categorization, "a practicing Jew, a wandering Jew, and a self-loathing Jew."[37] They are also a gloss on the poet Randall Jarrell's line: "The ways we miss our lives are life."[38] In the closing scene of the play, seventeen-year-old Tess Goode asks Sara: "Mother, if I've never really been Jewish, and I'm not actually American anymore, and I'm not English or European, then who am I?" It is a question that goes beyond the special status of the expatriate adolescent, that taps into the peculiar history of the modern Jew—the "rootless cosmopolitan," the extraterritorial, "the wandering Jew" (as Pfeni calls herself).[39] Identity can be altered in a nation that spawned such protean Midwesterners as Jay Gatsby, Bob Dylan, Malcolm X, and Judy Chicago; by bestowing new patronymics upon themselves, they tested the possibilities of self-invention. But Jewish identity itself is too impalpable and too demanding to be easily transmitted, and the institutions that have been built to foster and sustain it *The Sisters Rosensweig* treats ambivalently, as objects of respect as well as of satire. Merv Kant, for example, has been monitoring Eastern European anti-Semitism on behalf of the American Jewish Congress; his allegiances are taken seriously. At least they are not undercut by any of the other characters. But what should audiences make of Gorgeous Teitelbaum? Endowed with the silliest given name, she matches a stereotype so completely that even Merv falls for it: "So you're the sister who did everything right. You married the attorney, you had the children, you moved to the suburbs."[40] Yet she is not to be scorned: members of synagogues like Beth El—and its organizations like the Sisterhood—have kept Judaism alive for yet another generation.

That responsibility is hardly shared by thoroughly modern Sara, who wonders: why light Sabbath candles when there is electricity? Disdaining the Fourth Commandment ("Remember the Sabbath Day to keep it holy"), she orders Pfeni to "blow out the god-damned candle" that Gorgeous has lit and sanctified with the Hebrew blessing.[41] Yet Sara offers no substitute, no alternative gesture that might convey the beauty of Judaism to her own daughter. The international banker whose birthday has drawn the sisters from America and from Asia is deracinated. In London she herself may have rubbed against some genteel bigotry, embodied in Nicholas Pym. Jews in Britain, as the South African writer Dan Jacobson once put it, felt as though a room in the house had been given to them; but they were treated like boarders rather than members of the family.[42] Sara is even more adrift. She is alienated from her country, her family, and her faith: "I'm an old and bitter woman." Though she has twice appeared on the cover of *Fortune,* "I'm a cold, bitter woman who's turned her back on her family, her religion, and her country! And I held so much in. . . . Isn't that the way the old assimilated story goes?"[43] The play offers no clues, however, to account for the psychic sources of such utter self-denial.[44] Her sensibility is hardly exceptional. But for well over a generation, American society was in some ways moving in the opposite direction—exalting ethnic diversity and the rediscovery of roots, and harboring the most pious Christians (other than the Irish) in the Western World.

Sara has propelled herself furiously away from the parochialism of the Jews and the rituals of their faith. Twice divorced and homeless, she cannot return home. Her ties to her people are very tenuous. But they are not completely forfeited. Significantly, they reach only backwards into the past, as when Sara and Merv discover common ground—the spa resort named Ciechocinek, "the Palm Beach of Poland." There she had gone to provide financial expertise; there his own grandparents had vacationed. And now, "fifty years after the lucky few had escaped with false passports, Esther Malchah's granddaughter Sara was deciding how to put bread on the tables of those who had so blithely driven them all away."[45] (Aharon Appelfeld's 1980 allegory of doomed, assimilated Middle European Jews, *Badenheim 1939,* has them coming to a resort town.) Sandra Meyer, to whom the play is dedicated, told an interviewer: "That Polish resort town in *The Sisters Rosensweig* is really where my grandparents had their villa, with tennis courts and their own pastry chef. They were very sophisticated and had a lot of money." Lola Wasserstein's father—and Wendy's grandfather—had escaped from Poland. While serving as a high school principal in Paterson, New Jersey, Simon Schleifer wrote some Yiddish plays. But it would be both reductive and idle to speculate that the sisters Rosensweig represent the playwright herself in triplicate, or that she has created Pfeni as a surrogate, though she is the youngest of the three sisters and the only writer among them. That is also true of Wendy Wasserstein. But the peripatetic Pfeni is an invention.[46]

With her charming but gentile companion, she is also unaffiliated with institutions that might keep her (or indeed her generation) from being terminal Jews. When Geoffrey, flushed with excitement, imagines their future kids as so dynamic "they'll be running Metro-Goldwyn-Mayer before age seven," Pfeni asks: "But will they be Jewish children?" Geoffrey rebuts with an eccentric case for remaining within the fold: "They'll have to be if they're going to run M.G.M." Forty-year-old Pfeni's biological clock is ticking away like Captain Hook's crocodile (the playwright herself was named for *Peter Pan*'s Wendy), but the British theater director is probably not going to succeed as a "closet heterosexual."[47]

Pfenie is an advocacy journalist, endowed with a passion for social justice, a champion of the rights of women in Tajikistan. Yet she realizes that such concerns may preempt other forms of self-expression: "Somewhere I need the hardship of the Afghan women and the Kurdish suffering to fill up my life for me."[48] Devoid of any interest in the welfare of her own people, Pfeni is a paler version of the Marxist revolutionary Rosa Luxemburg, who wrote to a fellow Jew from a prison cell in 1917: "What do you want with the special Jewish sorrows? To me, the poor victims of rubber plantations of Putumayo, [and] the negroes in Africa . . . in the Kalahari desert . . . are equally near. . . . I have no special corner in my heart for the ghetto: I feel at home in the whole world."[49] Such generous feelings the world did not reciprocate. Having ignored a wake-up call like the Kishinev pogrom of 1903, Luxemburg would be murdered by right-wing thugs in 1919, and could scarcely have foreseen that, little more than two decades later, genocidal killers would not spare her own Jewish community of Zamosc.[50] In Pfeni's capacity to empathize with other groups (but not with her fellow Jews), she is a descendant of Rosa Luxemburg.

Compared to Sara and Pfeni, the defense can therefore make out a pretty good case for Gorgeous. It is not an airtight case: she is flaky, garrulous, and materialistic. Nor are her ambitions noble: *The Dr. Gorgeous Show* might expand from a radio call-in into a cable-TV talk show ("talking has always come easily to me"). Challenged to reveal the provenance of that professional prefix of "Dr.," she replies with another question: "You've heard of Dr. Pepper?" With her "funsy" vocabulary, Filene's shopping bag, and thrill at wearing a Chanel suit instead of a knockoff, she does invite ridicule—as well as the urge to shut her up with a "Say goodnight, Gracie." But Gorgeous does get briefly beneath her shallowness, even if—rather implausibly—she voices the Chekhovian hope "that each of us can say at some point that we had a moment of pure, unadulterated happiness! Do you think that's possible, Sara?" Gorgeous also gets to deliver one of the play's very few searing lines: "How did our nice Jewish mother do such a lousy job on us?"[51] None of the Rosensweigs has an answer or a comeback, nor is it obvious that their mother did muck up their lives. And to whom, in any case, should Rita Rosensweig be compared? To Tennessee Williams' Amanda Wingfield or Eugene O'Neill's Mary Tyrone or, for that matter, Mother Courage?

More than an ethnic caricature, less than a full-scale figure of pathos, Gorgeous exemplifies and complicates Wasserstein's difficulty in finding the right tone for "my most serious work." Exploring such phenomena as "identity, self-loathing, and possibility for intimacy and love when it seems no longer possible or, sadder yet, no longer necessary," she and her director were startled when the first preview audience soon became "convulsed with laughter."[52] Yet she is not the first Jewish writer to have trouble knowing which characters are cockamamie and which are not, what comes across as funny and what does not, what tastes as sweet as *haroset* or as bitter as *maror*. When Kafka read aloud to a few friends the first chapter of *The Trial,* they laughed; and the presumably mordant author himself "laughed so much," his first biographer reports, "there were moments when he couldn't read any further."[53] While writing *Death of a Salesman,* Arthur Miller claimed that he "laughed more . . . than I have ever done, when alone, in my life." When he read one scene to his (first) wife, she wept; the playwright considered it "hilarious."[54] Joseph Heller professed to have been unaware that "*Catch-22* was a *funny* book until I heard someone laugh while reading it."[55] Such short-circuited artistic aims may stem from the condition of post-Emancipation Jewry in the Diaspora, which has been so fraught with uncertainty and absurdity. "A kingdom of priests and a holy people" had to make room for the sisters' father, Maury Rosensweig (a manufacturer of "Kiddie Togs"), and for a leader in the field of "synthetic animal protective covering" like Mervyn Kant. Marginality has encouraged the exercise of irony and a sense of the ridiculous as well as anguish, and wit became, like the violin, mostly a Jewish instrument. Satire was a way of getting even, as well as a protective device.

Wassertstein's flair for wisecracks is so dazzling that it has raised doubts about her significance for the American theater. "I had hoped, after *The Heidi Chronicles,* that my very gifted former student was shaking her witticism habit," Robert Brustein wrote. "*The Sisters Rosensweig* has a lot of charm, but it is a regression. . . . By its own internal measure, which is to be likable, *The Sisters Rosensweig* is a success. People will be entertained and will leave the theatre feeling warm and wise, which are the requisites of a commercial hit."[56] Yet an earlier Jewish female playwright like Lillian Hellman had also produced Broadway hits and has elicited considerably more scholarly attention and critical accolades. The U.S. Geological Survey even named a crater on Venus for her. What Hellman lacked in the power to amuse she compensated for with political commitment, of which Wasserstein seems bereft.[57] (In the spring of 1995, however, she did accompany Joanne Woodward and Melanie Griffith on a Literary Network-sponsored lobbying visit to Capitol Hill. In an effort to save the National Endowment for the Arts, they met with dozens of legislators.[58] Perhaps the charm and ebullience that Wasserstein's plays exude make them seem frivolous; too much brio can spike critical interest. She has declined to set herself up as a maven in a heartless world. Because her deftness at comedy dwarfs her other gifts, scholars are compelled to seat her below the salt, next to others who entertain more than they enlighten.

Here a useful comparison might be with David Mamet, who

paid his own tribute to Chekhov with a version of *Uncle Vanya* (1989) and whose high-testosterone dramas often depict Jews and other shell-shocked veterans of the wars between the sexes. (He is undoubtedly the only dues-paying member of both the Dramatists Guild and the United Steelworkers of America.) Though Mamet has also recently attempted to record the costs that assimilation has imposed, his style is, of course, quite different from Wasserstein's. Staccato and elliptical, his dialogue can be obscene enough to make even the Wife of Bath blush. The usually male characters have trouble stating precisely what they mean—and these corrupt, cynical low-lifes *are* mean. By contrast, Wasserstein's mostly female characters tend to be articulate, brilliant, classy, vulnerable, gentle and genteel,[59] as they try to approximate the ideal of "gracious living" that her play shows Mount Holyoke to have fostered. Her characters are warm, while Mamet's perspective—and language—are scalding. In contrast to the savagery that he exposes beneath the veneer of civilized life, Wasserstein portrays "very nice girls" who, according to Tasha Blumberg, "deserve a little *naches*."[60] What is missing in Wasserstein's work, and keeps it too close to merely clever entertainment, is menace—the spooky, subterranean impulses that threaten to tear apart the skein of everyday existence. Sophisticated audiences need to ruminate over more than lively repartee, tossed back and forth by characters fearful of the truth-telling that comes from introspection and confrontation. Serious audiences need to hear more often a little night music.

To Wasserstein's four major plays to date, attention must nevertheless be paid. She cannot be expected to rip apart the barbarism of selling Chicago real estate (or the ambiguities of leveraged buyouts), but she has drawn astutely on what she does know. Indeed, the distantly autobiographical aspects of her work constitute its strength and give its details verisimilitude: she knows that Gorgeous would not buy a gift for her sister at Filene's Basement.[61] Wasserstein knows how her characters behave and—since repartee enables them to skirt the truth—how her characters talk. (Contrast the guffaws that should punctuate a reading of Herman Wouk's use of a hokum hillbilly accent in *Youngblood Hawke*: "Ah should be hung fo' mah cramm against the English language in rahtin' that book. . . . An can raht better than that. Ah'm rahtin' betta raht now."[62]) Wasserstein's satiric powers have been cultivated enough to fulfill the promise that Rita Altabel makes in *Uncommon Women*: "When we're forty, we'll be incredible."[63] And however inadvertently, her plays also constitute an entree into the subculture of American Jewry. Barely a teenager when Thomas B. Morgan's reverberant article, "The Vanishing American Jew" (1964), was published in *Look* Magazine, she has lived through a period of even more accelerating assimilation.[64] The signs are unmistakable: low birth rates, ever-higher intermarriage rates, declining affiliations with institutions that have served Diaspora communities for centuries. It is not easy to be sanguine about a viable future for this most ancient and adaptable of peoples. Yet the American Jew has not vanished (though *Look* Magazine itself did), and his—and her—fate can be traced in the dramaturgy of Wendy Wasserstein.

Notes

1. Quoted in Leslie Bennetts, "An Uncommon Dramatist Prepares Her New Work," *New York Times,* 24 May 1981, 2.5.

2. Quoted in Iska Alter, "Wendy Wasserstein (1950–)," in *Jewish American Women Writers: A Bio-Bibliographical and Critical Sourcebook,* ed. Ann R. Shapiro et al. (Westport, Conn.: Greenwood Press, 1994), 449; Wendy Wasserstein, "My Mother, Then and NOW," in her *Bachelor Girls* (New York: Knopf, 1990), 15–22.

3. Wasserstein, "Jean Harlow's Wedding Night," in *Bachelor Girls,* 184; "Wendy Wasserstein," in *Interviews with Contemporary Women Playwrights,* ed. Kathleen Betsko and Rachel Koenig (New York: William Morrow, 1987), 425, 429.

4. Anita Gates, "Today Most Are in Their 40's, and Pretty Amazing," *New York Times,* 16 October 1994, 2.5; Nancy Backes, "Wasserstein, Wendy," in *Notable Women in the American Theatre: A Biographical Dictionary,* ed. Alice M. Robinson, Vera Mowry Roberts, and Milly S. Barranger (Westport, Conn.: Greenwood Press, 1989), 902.

5. Jonathan D. Sarna, *Jacksonian Jew: The Two Worlds of Mordecai Noah* (New York: Holmes and Meier, 1981), 6–7, 12, 47–50.

6. Stephen J. Whitfield, "Stages of Capitalism: The Business of American Jewish Dramatists," *Jewish History* 8, nos. 1–2 (1994): 312, 315, 316–18; Wasserstein, "Big Brother," in *Bachelor Girls,* 83–84.

7. Quoted in Bennetts, "An Uncommon Dramatist," 1.

8. Wendy Wasserstein, *The Sisters Rosensweig* (San Diego: Harcourt Brace, 1993), 27.

9. Wendy Wasserstein, "Isn't It Romantic," in *The Heidi Chronicles and Other Plays* (New York: Vintage Books, 1991), 149–50.

10. Alter, "Wendy Wasserstein," 449.

11. Milton Himmelfarb, *The Jews of Modernity* (New York: Basic Books, 1973), 135.

12. Wasserstein, *Sisters Rosensweig,* 53, 74.

13. Wasserstein, "Uncommon Women and Others," in *Heidi Chronicles and Other Plays,* 62.

14. Ibid., 33, 39.

15. Ibid., 61–63, 71; William Novak, "Are Good Jewish Men a Vanishing

Breed", in *Jewish Possibilities: The Best of Moment Magazine,* ed. Leonard Fein (Northvale, N.J.: Jason Aronson, 1987), 60–66; Edward S. Shapiro, *A Time for Healing: American Jewry since World War II* (Baltimore: Johns Hopkins University Press, 1992), 139–43.

16. Quoted in "Wendy Wasserstein," *Interviews with Contemporary Women Playwrights,* 426.

17. Wasserstein, *Heidi Chronicles and Other Plays,* 85, 148.

18. Ibid., 143, 152.

19. Ibid., 82, 97.

20. Ibid., 103–4, 110.

21. Ibid., 120, 124, 138–39, 148.

22. Neil Simon, "Barefoot in the Park," in *The Comedy of Neil Simon* (New York: Equinox, 1973), 147; Wasserstein, *Heidi Chronicles and Other Plays,* 143–45, and "Jean Harlow's Wedding Night," in *Bachelor Girls,* 184.

23. Wasserstein, *Sisters Rosensweig,* 17.

24. Quoted in *Interviews with Contemporary Women Playwrights,* 420, 425.

25. Wasserstein, "The Heidi Chronicles," in *Heidi Chronicles and Other Plays,* 232.

26. Quoted in Alfred Habegger, *The Father: A Life of Henry James, Sr.* (New York: Farrar, Straus & Giroux, 1994), 339–40.

27. Robert Wright, "The Evolution of Despair," *Time* Magazine, 28 August 1995, 53.

28. Delia Ephron, *Funny Sauce* (New York: Viking, 1986), ix.

29. "But Can He Cook?" *New York Times,* 15 June 1986, 4.9.

30. Alfred Kazin, *A Walker in the City* (New York: Grove Press, 1958), 44, 60.

31. Wasserstein, *Heidi Chronicles and Other Plays,* 25, 170, 181, 174.

32. Carolyn Clay, "The Wendy Chronicles," *Boston Phoenix,* 1 March 1991, 3.11.

33. Wasserstein, *Heidi Chronicles and Other Plays,* 196, 202, 245.

34. Wasserstein, *Sisters Rosensweig,* 88.

35. Wasserstein, Preface to ibid., ix.

36. John Bush Jones, "'You Are What You Are': Jewish Identity in Recent American Drama," syllabus of Brandeis University National Women's Committee (Waltham, Mass. [1994]), 41–42.

37. Quoted in "Wasserstein's World," *Reform Judaism* 21 (Summer 1993): 45.

38. Randall Jarrell, "A Girl in a Library" (1951), in *The Complete Poems* (New York: Farrar, Straus and Giroux, 1969), 18.

39. Wasserstein, *Sisters Rosensweig,* 103, 106.

40. Wasserstein, *Sisters Rosensweig,* 30.

41. Ibid., 12, 36–38.

42. Cited in Calvin Trillin, "Drawing the Line," *New Yorker,* 12 December 1994, 56.

43. Wasserstein, *Sisters Rosensweig,* 81.

44. Jones, "'You Are What You Are,'" 44.

45. Wasserstein, *Sisters Rosensweig,* 79–80; see Howard Kissel, "The Banker, the Writer, and the Yenta," *Reform Judaism* 21 (Summer 1993): 44–45.

46. Phoebe Hoban, "The Family Wasserstein," *New York,* 4 January 1993,

35; Judith Miller, "The Secret Wendy Wasserstein," *New York Times,* 18 October 1992, 2.8.

47. Backes, "Wasserstein, Wendy," 901; Wasserstein, *Sisters Rosensweig,* 65, 68.

48. Wasserstein, *Sisters Rosensweig,* 77.

49. Quoted in J. L. Talmon, *The Myth of the Nation and the Vision of Revolution* (Berkeley and Los Angeles: University of California Press, 1981), 217.

50. Ibid.

51. Wasserstein, *Sisters Rosensweig,* 30, 31, 94, 96.

52. Ibid., ix, x.

53. Max Brod, *Franz Kafka: A Biography* (New York: Schocken, 1963), 50, 76–77, 133, 178.

54. Arthur Miller, "The 'Salesman' Has a Birthday" (1950), in *Death of a Salesman,* ed. Gerald Weales (New York: Viking, 1967), 148.

55. "Playboy Interview: Joseph Heller," *Playboy* 20 (June 1975): 73.

56. Robert Brustein, *Dumbocracy in America: Studies in the Theatre of Guilt, 1987–1994* (Chicago: Ivan R. Dee, 1994), 162.

57. David Richards, "Wendy Wasserstein's School of Life," *New York Times,* 1 November 1992, 2.5.

58. "LitNet's Advocacy Highlights," *Literary Network News,* August 1995, 2.

59. Backes, "Wasserstein, Wendy," 903.

60. Wasserstein, *Heidi Chronicles and Other Plays,* 119.

61. Joan Kron, "All-Consuming Art," *New York Times,* 6 December 1992, 2.12.

62. Herman Wouk, *Youngblood Hawke* (Garden City, N.Y.: Doubleday, 1962), 203, 270.

63. Wasserstein, *Heidi Chronicles and Other Plays,* 12.

64. Thomas B. Morgan, "The Vanishing American Jew," *Look* 28 (5 May 1964): 42–46.

Immersions in the Postmodern: The Fiction of Allegra Goodman

Gloria L. Cronin

> There is this whole spiritual existence out there and I can't get there. What do I need to do? How many books? How many journeys? What are the words and what kind of food? Macro, micro, do roots feed the soul? carrots, turnips, potatoes? or the ancient songs? I lift up my voice in the wilderness, eyes to the hills, my timbrel and lyre to the mouth of the sea whence cometh my aid and dance on the sand a song of praise with words I don't understand.
>
> —"Onionskin," 35

Introduction

In these elegant words reminiscent of the Davidic psalms, one of Allegra Goodman's far from elegant religious questers laments her inability to escape the quotidian experience and make that old leap into a transcendental beyond. Yet in Goodman, a post-assimilationist writer, this perennial theme takes on a different set of nuances—specifically the ethical and philosophical concerns of the late-twentieth-century academy with its endless debates about gender, class, race, otherness, power, difference, dialogue, world peace, ecology, absolute truth, transcendental pretense, and the whole postmodern reckoning of the authority of the text. What impact do all these immersions have on the life of orthodox and other less orthodox seekers after spiritual life, asks Goodman. What are the current conditions of the contemporary American spiritual pilgrimage? And toward what *fin de siècle* Canterbury are these mostly Jewish Americans making their way?

Within the contemporary American tradition of religious fiction, however, Goodman is most naturally compared with Flannery O'Connor, whose religious seekers operate within the

Protestant Bible Belt and Roman Catholic Christian traditions of the Agrarian South. Goodman, however, operates within the combined traditions of university-educated discourse communities, Yiddish comedy, and urbane *New Yorker* social satire. Unlike O'Connor, Goodman is less concerned with the visible or invisible manifestations of grace than she is with its comic human obstacles. Instead of looking for epiphanic moments and obvious transformations, Goodman focuses on the parochialism of the individual characters who must journey through the tangled byways of their own family psychology, kitchens, synagogues, universities, family weddings, life passages, think tanks, interfaith dialogues, conferences, and wailing walls as they face the perennial intransigence of ordinary consciousness, the apparent absence of omniscience, and the stubborn fleshliness of the ordinary.

Goodman, unlike many American Jewish writers, willingly accepts the label *Jewish American writer* and indicates that she resides somewhere between a Conservative and an Orthodox viewpoint. She writes out of the richness of historical Jewishness, her community, and her literary, scriptural, and Jewish theological traditions. Her work resonates with psalms and liturgical phrases, Jewish family relationships, and a general Jewish presence. In her 1994 MLA address, "Writing Jewish Fiction In and Out of the Multicultural Context" (included in this volume), she states, "my most intimate and immediate audience comes from the American Jewish community." Being called a Jewish writer is for her also a "symbol of an essential resource; a community of passionate readers in an increasingly difficult world for serious fiction." Her expressed desire is to be part of a Jewish literature that in the postassimilationist era can recapture the spiritual and religious dimension of Judaism. In her conclusion she comments that Jewish American writers are

> confronting an old problem—the problem of every artist. Ultimately . . . all writing is ethnic writing, and . . . all writers are ethnic writers grappling with great ambitions and a particular language and culture. . . . Each strives to make a specific cultural experience an asset instead of a liability. I look at this as an old problem, and I turn to old resources—the deep Jewish tradition beneath the self-deprecating Jewish jokes, the biblical language and the poetry welling up beneath layers of satire.

She creates a fiction uniquely her own whose locus is the familiar parochial territory of the Jewish American family and its community's political concerns. Onto a crowded and noisy canvas she projects Jewish familial disputes, temple politics, orthodoxy fights, academic disputes, family scandals, scams, crosscultural misunderstandings, and postmodern philosophical and gender conundrums. Antic and myopic personalities all, their colliding ideologies, neuroses, obsessions, and self-contradictions make them seem amusingly familiar to us in this disjointed postmodern age.

In a letter to Sanford Pinsker, Goodman comments:

> I grew up in an interesting place, [the Jewish community of Honolulu] but I think all places are interesting. One of the themes I explored in *Total Immersion* is that what we imagine as exotic is actually familiar, and what we think is familiar is really exotic. . . . I am interested in the universality of parochialism—the fact that all over the world communities look into themselves/at themselves. I am interested in getting readers to recognize other places, people, experiences, as real, true and their own. Why not get people to imagine other places? See themselves in other people? Enter into other worlds. Fiction does that.[1]

In two distinct sets of stories, *Total Immersion* (1989) and *The Family Markowitz* (1996),[2] she presents without rancor or apology hypochondriacal Jewish grandmothers, escapist sons, rambunctious teenagers, senile oldsters, schizophrenics, Hasidim, politically inept academics, culture Jews, radicalized graduate students, con artists, young marrieds, Yemenites, rabbis, and self-deceivers. In this typically postmodern "charade," the characters all experience the thwarting gravitational tug of self, family, and community. Stuck in a human space that prohibits the transcendental leap beyond, Goodman's characters are engulfed in the hilarious great earthbound suck of the mortal self—the predicament of "total immersion."

Total Immersion

In Goodman's first short story, "Variant Text" (1986; published in *Commentary* when she was just seventeen), Cecil, an orthodox observant Jew who reads deconstructionist criticism and espouses feminist notions, produces old-fashioned textual criticism.[3] While fascinated with Derrida and Paul De Man, he enters a seemingly contradictory redemptive project: he wants simultaneously to fix in place and to modify the Jewish cultural traditions in which he is living. "Cecil has always enjoyed his contradictions" (72), we read, and so does the Piaget educator who grafts Piaget and Torah because he wants every child to be at Kohlberg stage three by the end of the term. "We're trying to develop a Torah life-style" (79), he announces proudly. Cecil's feminism is presented in equally ironic terms, for he gives no real thought to the gender roles his daughter, Attalia, is learning as he dresses her in unisex clothing and then leaves her in the cloakroom to play with the other girls while he goes into the men's section of the *shul* to pray. The postmodern contradictions in Cecil's immersions of the contemporary deepen. He wants to do variant textual studies despite his postmodern belief in the loss of authority in the text: "when he studies sacred texts, he feels even more powerfully that the words themselves are enough for him; that they need no author or interpreter. The strict beauty of the law is complete in itself, needing no stalk for support or external scaffold for restoration" (88). Cecil insists on the immutability of sacred law but at the same time he savors the fluidity of secular texts. He loves one as explicit and complete, the other as open and ambiguous. Goodman invites all of us to recognize ourselves in Cecil's postmodern condition.

"Wish List" (1986) contains similar ironies.[4] The Wantage Center is a much "wanting" think tank located in an Elizabethan boarding house in Oxford. It is the place where international scholars of Middle Eastern studies dedicate their scholarship to the spiritual enterprise of world peace. The Wantage Center is a parody of the contradictions that characterize contemporary secular and academic "redemptive projects." Ed Markowitz is an American Jew who admits he has no firsthand knowledge of the Middle East and deplores field work. Nevertheless he wants to convince his colleagues of the perspectives of terrorists who construe themselves as freedom fighters and see the West as the principal agent of terror and colonization. He attempts to apply what are obviously postcolonial, Levinasian, and postmodern ethical perspectives while challenging the moral turpitude of his own culture. Not surprisingly, Ed fails to arouse the sympathy of his less openly hostile audience.

The spirit who broods over the old house from her imprisoned space in the attic is a ghostly suicide who once loved a Moor and was locked up by her family. It is a fable of Western culture that does not augur well for Ed's or anyone else's ability to cross the divide confronting Protestant English tradition and American and Muslim customs, not to mention Arab-Israeli politics. When

Mujahid Rashaf explodes Ed's unpopular thesis by violently declaring that the Israelis will be driven into the sea, Ed argues naively that terrorism is "a dynamic process involving elements of anarchic creativity . . . [with] four terroristic elements [of] secrecy, surprise, team or theistic loyalty, and escape" (104). This sounds entirely too ridiculous to Gavriel, a recent victim of terrorism; he angrily tells Ed of the other victims of terrorism he tried to help while they lay dying on landing strips, waiting to be rescued. It is a story that brings us to the heart of issues of otherness as they impact the human processes of intercultural understanding.

In "The Succession" (1987),[5] the egocentric Rabbi Siegel and his congregants exemplify the collisions and differences that prevent the spiritual functioning of a small Jewish community in Hawaii. Here in miniature are all the contemporary issues of diversity that threaten community. Framing the issues of intergenerational and factional diversity within the temple community is the wildly diverse interdenominational landscape without. The Jewish temple itself is located in the midst of a Christianized and Easternized Polynesia. Next door to the Jewish temple is the Kwan Yin Temple and seminary. Both are located on Old Pali Road, where the colonial mansions of the 1930s are now occupied by numerous consulates, churches, and shrines; these include the Japanese Consulate and that of the Kingdom of Tonga, along with the "Methodist, Greek, Orthodox, Episcopalian, and Shinto" (27).

This highly visible multicultural atmosphere functions as a comic metaphor for the petty diversities and political divisions within the MBT. For many years Rabbi Siegel has intoned sonorously from the MBT like "Gauguin among strange blessed people, holy in their exotic rituals" (29). Now he must share space with two younger rabbis, Steve Gottlieb and Barry Leibowitz, sermonizers of a very different kind. Here Jewish congregants in flowered tropical clothes cannot agree on child-rearing or how to teach sex education in the MBT religious school. The story is a parody of differences without and within the community of the chosen.

"Total Immersion" (1987)[6] continues the comedy of difference and otherness, of social surfaces that do not quite meet. The Jewish Sandra Lefkowitz is beginning her first teaching job at the very organized and controlled congregationalist missionary school, Oahu Prep, Hawaii, where she is to teach French entirely in French. The social chaos at the home of Ephraim Tawil, to which Sandra and her husband, Alan, have been invited, is a marked contrast. Ephraim has grown up with nine brothers in Rechovot, Israel, apparently in a kibbutz, and he continually tries to recreate this communal experience by inviting everyone he meets home for a meal, usually without telling his wife. His children are described as barely socialized monkeys who do not know how to eat with guests. Sandra and her husband are bewildered and disappointed. Meeting another couple, the Gluecks, at Bet Knesset later is just as frustrating and confusing, as Terrence Glueck waxes intellectual on an assortment of subjects that Alan is sure he is not qualified to speak. Inevitably the argument begins about the nature of the services at Bet Knesset, whether they are orthodox enough, and how or if women should be included in the service.

At another social gathering of the Jewish community, the conversation soon centers on a certain Barbara Ruth who left the Jewish community in Hawaii, went to Miami University, married a Sikh, had a miscarriage, entered therapy, and ended her marriage. She then became a dental hygienist in Hawaii and met an Hawaiian named Brian Akimoto, who converted to Judaism. They have ended up living a totally orthodox life in Me'ah She'arim, where they have lots of babies. Ironically, such complete immersion in Hasidic orthodoxy is horrifying to Sandra's old Hawaiian friends, who had begun the conversation complaining about the laxness of their own temple.

This discussion about Barbara Ruth parallels Sandra's experience in trying to teach French in a manner that does not seem orthodox enough to the bossy Hilda, her formidable supervisor. The central irony is that while some of Sandra's students do not seem to be able to learn French as well as students in the other classes, the one girl, Ginnie, who usually does not even come to class, wins third place in a national championship. It is a telling social comment on the egocentrism of social location, the random effects of orthodoxy, the judging of others, and the prediction of winners. It is also a commentary on the magical processes by which outsiders and the seemingly handicapped (like Barbara Ruth and Ginnie) go from margin to center in dazzling moves that seem to defy prior immersions or nonimmersions, one system of learning or another, or none at all.

In "Oral History" (1989),[7] a much simpler exemplum of social comedy, the focus is once again on the ironic gender obstacles and bourgeois immersions that seem to preclude the elderly Rose and the younger Alma from communicating. Neither is able to escape the illusions of bourgeois identity with which she has grown up—Rose in Europe at the beginning of the century and Alma in California at the end of the century. Rose Markowitz is an egocentric old Jewish lady who has created for herself the caste identity of the European bourgeois intellectual elite. However, it is highly likely she came from a less-than-illustrious Yiddish-speaking family. Rose's account, says Alma, the frustrated oral history interviewer, is a wildly concocted and contradictory tale of her family and childhood. The wily Rose seems to be enacting an upward-mobility project in remembering her family in a "rose"-colored light. Alma is just as busily masking her own origins, however. She comes from a wealthy family but enacts a downward move by wearing expensive catalogue-purchased grunge and scrap-metal earrings. She has just enough race, class, and gender consciousness to apply her awareness to others, but not to herself. Alma, who ought to understand women's nonlinear self-narrative as performance, does not. "I said I would help you, but some things should be forgotten. . . we'll make something up, dear. The university will never know" (3), says the ingenuous Rose. Ron, Alma's Jewish boyfriend, complains of her interview methods: "Every other question is about class struggle. . . . Use your head. These women don't know what you're talking about. First of all, stop trying to indoctrinate them. What does Eileen Meeker know about patriarchal power structures?" (7). Rose's tricky self-narrative and denials are matched only by Alma's equally self-deceptive Marxist-feminist revisionist self-narrative as performance. Goodman seems to tell us that Alma will have to examine her own female bourgeois revisionism and ideological blinders before she can understand Rose's.

"Fait" (1989)[8] also examines issues of difference and orthodoxy. At the metaphorical core of the story is Ginnie's endless acquisition of multiple languages and their respective literatures. A student at Berkeley, she is totally absorbed in *Mein Kampf* and her comparative literature course. Yet Ginnie is intolerant of nearly everyone in the family. She hates the Christian evangelical notes her mother leaves on the refrigerator door and wonders if she consults "with animists under poisonous trees" (51). She looks down on her sister Terri, whose wedding she has come home to attend, because Terri is immersed in visions of bridesmaids, orchids, and the honeymoon on Maui. We read with amusement that whereas she favors such coloring books as *Great Civil Rights Leaders, World Feminists from Lesbos to*

NOW, Politburo Paperdolls, Whales of the World, and *The Jumbo Book of Protest Leaders,* Ginnie cannot accept the sister who is playing the traditional noncollege-bound woman to her elitist, liberated Berkeley undergraduate intellectual.

Goodman's "And Also Much Cattle" (1989)[9] takes its title from the biblical reference in Jonah about blessings given to the Patriarchs who, in addition to being promised numerous progeny, are also assured many cattle. Goodman's underlying question is, how did they distinguish the two? Chosen people and cattle. Here, more than in any other story, Goodman illustrates the intransigence of ordinary consciousness, the stubborn fleshliness of that ordinary life which surrounds all attempts at communion with the holy.

The occasion is the fast day of *Yom Kippur,* the Day of Atonement. The Schicks, having broken away from an unsatisfactory synagogue, are attempting to establish an ultraorthodox synagogue in their own home in Hawaii. Their house is grubby and only half-unpacked, reminiscent of the tents of the early patriarchs. Likewise, their "caravan" includes all manner of lost-tribes people: visiting young Hasidic rabbis, teenagers, neighbors, strangers, and old boyfriends. The diversity of this group would seem to defeat any attempt to bring them together, even or especially at the heart of the moment of sacred *Yom Kippur* worship. We hear the senile grandmother scream out through the prayers of the black-coated and black-hatted nineteen-year-old Hasidic rabbis. Whiskey, the dog, races in and out of the *shul* while the women gossip loudly. Teenage boys talk about national baseball and the nightlife of Oahu. Greg wanders around in a tee-shirt and cutoffs, while Avi, the professional beach bum, appears in a grass hat. Through it all, Dovidl, the young Hasidic rabbi, comments ironically. He does so by telling an old Eastern European tale about a boy who, not knowing the words for prayer, went to the altar and said the only Hebrew he knew, the *aleph bes.* It is at this very sacred moment, in true biblical fashion, that two brothers quarrel. "Fuck off, Elliott," screams Greg (154). Dovidl, however, is unperturbed. To those who would angrily declare the whole feast day a "charade" rather than a religious experience, Dovidl patiently explains the lovely irony: "This is a charade. That is a very good word, because truthfully, in this whole world there is nothing here except *Hashem.* Just *Hashem*" (162). The reader wonders if this is a profound religious insight, if Dovidl has been deaf to the previous hullabaloo, or if he has merely found a clever way to con people back to reform the *minyan* so they can finish the lengthy prayers.

In "Retrospective" (1989),[10] the fiercely respectable Henny Pressman has taken serious social-climbing as her life's redemptive project. But now all is revealed. Lillian, her supposedly reformed bohemian sister, even as cancer eats away at her aged body, still poses secretly as an artist's nude model for the art department at the University of Hawaii. Henny is even more horrified when she discovers that Lillian has given the department permission to hold a retrospective of her pictures. All Henny's efforts at respectability will be undone if the naughty Lillian goes up on the wall in all ages and stages of nudity.

The deeper irony of the story, however, hinges on whether Lillian has been erased by others' representations of her, or whether she has escaped them all by offering herself as a "blank sign" for all to write on. As Henny's conversation with Mohanty (the organizer of the retrospective art exhibit) reveals, it is evident Lillian won't really be there:

> Lillian was the perfect illustration of the mind at rest. It was her gift to stand or sit for hours, relaxed and yet centered in her pose. Her face became so impassive, so clear, you would hardly notice that she, a person, was there at all. She was like those horoscopes in the newspaper—for each artist she could mean a different thing. . . . Her gift was she was so unexpressive. . . . She was a blank sign, open for interpretation. (129–30)

Is Lillian merely passive and stupid? Have Mohanty the artist and Henny the Jewish bourgeois matron erased her with their various appropriations? Or has Lillian, by offering herself as a blank sign, invited such an erasure as a fine act of subversion? It seems that Lillian has miraculously found her way from margin to social center despite them all.

In "Further Ceremony" (1989),[11] Goodman reflects on the fragmented surfaces of contemporary family life and centers on a "pseudo" wedding ceremony for a couple, one of whom is still married to someone else. In a sense it is a nonevent involving a disunited family that consists of grandmother, daughter, sister, and the dysfunctional granddaughters. The grandmother furiously chides her daughter, Margaret, that there is no need for further ceremony since this man is married to someone else. The broken surfaces of this modern family's existence are mirrored in Margaret McCrae's ill health. She has suffered decades' worth of junk collecting, broken marriages, and her children's inability to cook or even carry out the normal "ceremonies" of life. Nevertheless, at the heart of this nonceremony, the little Yemenite caterers, Ruti (very pregnant) and Natan, bring their small children with them, and despite a shortage of authentic ingredients, produce a miraculous feast to grace the strange occasion. In their love and simplicity, they offer a telling comparison with the disunited members of the McCrae family, as does the extended Polynesian family that Emily, Margaret's sister, has been living with for two years. Behind the chaotic social surfaces of the story there is a yearning by all of the characters for the orderly ceremonies of a more traditional and cohesive family life. Perhaps it is even a spiritual hunger for those rituals and foodways that are generally associated with traditional Jewish holidays.

Goodman plays again on the device of bringing together five individuals locked helplessly inside their own realities while conducting a strange surface relationship with each other in "Clare" (1989).[12] Henry is a gourmet cook, collector of silver and draperies, manager of Laura Ashley's of Oxford, and a publisher of obscure poets. He is happily preparing a party to celebrate the publication of Clare's second book of poetry. The neighbor, Sid Bergland, is a physicist and another seemingly lost soul. He appears to partake of the celebration and to ask Clare to the animal-rights demonstration at Wantage the next day. In the midst of all this appears an outraged Israeli writer who has apparently paid Clare for a translation that has not been done, and now he wants to sue her. As a certified schizophrenic, Clare is a literal embodiment of the comic fragmentation and isolation of contemporary social life. The extremes of encapsulation or imprisonment in one's own reality are reflected in Clare and become a powerful metaphor for emotional immersion. Yet Clare is, after all, a poet, translator, and recorder of reality, and she does not seem much crazier than Henry, Sid, Cecil, or Yaffa.

In "Onionskin" (1989),[13] Sharon, a woman in search of God, complains that she is involved in unproductive masculine and postmodern forms of religious life: theology, religious biography, synagogues, creeds, universities, and even pop religious culture. Her impassioned letter to her "Religious Thinkers" professor, Dr. Friedell, reveals both the truth of this insight and her own myopias and intellectual immaturities:

> This is to apologize if I offended you in class a few weeks ago, though I realize you have probably forgotten the whole thing by now. I was

> the one who stood up and said Fuck Augustine. What I meant was I didn't take the class to read to him [Augustine], I took it to learn about religion—God, prayer, ritual, the Madonna mother-goddess figure, forgiveness, miracles, sin, abortion, death, the big moral concepts. (29)

She has had the naiveté to believe that the university, the pilgrimage site of latest resort, might actually lead her to religious experience. In a fascinating act of subversion, she replaces Friedell's formal term-paper assignment (and Augustine himself) with a female narrative of her own spiritual pilgrimage. This has taken her through the folk music and dance movement of the late 1950s, the civil rights movement, the women's movement of the 1960s, the granola and back-to-nature experience of the early 1970s, the inevitable trip to Israel, "Save the Whales," New Age, and the back-to-school trend for re-entry women in the 1980s. Hence she announces proudly that she will not act like a grateful outcast, a member of "the lowly unwashed" newly arrived at the gates of the university to be "blessed by the big phallus" (29).

Sharon sits outside by the sausage trees near Moore Hall on the University of Hawaii Campus and expresses disappointment that "the universe part of the university . . . all about Life and Time and God, and Freedom . . . was just so male and linear and that there wasn't any religion in the religion classes" (29). As currently taught in this postmodern age, "religion was all a construct—angels were symbols and the miracles were just things in nature" (29). Within the hour she has sold her postmodern texts back to the bookstore.

Sharon's refusal to write a formal term paper replete with footnotes or to get "all uptight about plagiarism" (29) is her way of writing herself into the Western canon of spiritual autobiography. In her definition, plagiarism is merely the university teaching process with its endless recirculation of dead, mostly male ideas. Hence she uses a typically feminine form—a letter written by hand, on onionskin no less.

Goodman illuminates Sharon's intellectual and spiritual innocence as she applauds her spirit. Like the ancient Jews of the Babylonian Captivity and those of the continuing Diaspora, Sharon has strayed far from home. She explains how she dropped out of college in her early twenties, went to Hawaii, taught Israeli folk-dancing, and finally rejected the patronizing Rabbi Siegel for "the chosen-people crap" (30), which for her is a merely historicized, aestheticized version of Judaism. Years later she rejects Friedell for his parallel betrayal:

> All that stuff about us living on the last mushroom of the dunghill of Romanticism and the pygmies on elephants and all you can do when you go back to school is learn how to use the library and document everything. . . . Not that I think you are actually reading this, since it's written on onionskin in ball point when you only accept typed stuff. (29)

He too is a Pharisee obsessed with "classical shit" (32).

Sharon's earlier attempts to penetrate the veil have failed, as has her journey into nature. Hawaii is already ruined with its deceptive greenness and profusion of "colonialist hotel moguls," "chrome and glass," "penned-in dolphins," "chlorinated pool bars," "Day-Glo golf courses," and "raked hotel beaches" (30). She has, unsuccessfully, tried to go "to professors and rabbis and missionaries and lovers, and to myself—sober, high, clean, dirty, unemployed, working, etc. in other words, 'the empirical method'" (32). After a disappointing pilgrimage to the bankrupt Torah Light Institute in Jerusalem, she finally explodes: "What is God, Where is s/he? and What should I do? and what is the earth here for?" (33). Jerusalem, with its crazy Wailing Wall "wishing well"—stuffed with dead messages—turns out to be just another place:

> I thought it was going to be so much more—I mean not like I thought I was actually going to see the valley of the shadow of death, but I did keep seeing plain hills and valleys and that's it. Which has got to be me, right? I know it's what you bring, I realize that. It makes me cry because I don't have it in me. I just don't understand and I want to. (35)

Like King David and the Jews of old, she dances in faith before the Lord a song of praise whose words she does not understand. Yet she has inserted herself into the velum-bound male tradition of original spiritual autobiography.

The Family Markowitz

Goodman continues to examine the obstacles to human communication in her cycle of stories about the Markowitz family. "Young People" (1989),[14] the first in this cycle, is Goodman's ultimate complication of the absurd comedy of multiculturalism. Here the wild mass of postmodern identities that comprise Tiki Sofer is placed in comic juxtaposition with an increasingly rarified Oxonian anglophile, Henry Markowitz. To add to the comedy, Henry reveals just as many multicultural divisions within his Yiddish, American, Anglophiliac self as does Tiki. Hence the deliciously funny rapport so quickly established between the fat, perspiring Oxford businessman and aesthete and tiny, garrulous Yemenite female taxi driver.

Tiki, unlike those who would lament the assimilation process in modern American life, revels in her multiple cultural identities. She tells the already exhausted Henry that she writes poetry in Hebrew and English, is Yemenite American, publishes the rape histories of Yemenite women on their wedding nights, has three children, has written a play, and drives her cab twelve hours a day. Her contemporary networking has helped her put together a pageant of traditional Mideastern dancing and instruments, of which she is very proud. Henry falls into the spirit of Tiki's self-narrative by concluding that she is indeed a remarkable woman: "An entrepreneurial artist living in the very thick of urban crime and decay. An artist adapted to the city, somehow managing a symbiosis" (171). Later on, after the chaos of the Markowitz family dinner table, Henry leaves—confirmed once more in his sense of the mad disjointedness of the contemporary American identity from which he has escaped.

In "The Wedding of Henry Markowitz" (1992) Goodman uses a Jewish family wedding to reveal some of the political fault lines within the contemporary American Jewish community.[15] The immersions and divisions have to do with orthodoxy, tradition, aestheticism, intellectualism, England, and America. Henry's escape from his mother's uncouth Yiddish culture, his too-American family, and the contradictions of his Jewish religious heritage has been accomplished by Edwardian retrofitting. He has become a businessman, a professional bachelor, a romantic, an Anglophile, and a collector of rare cultural artifacts. He is living the life of a nineteenth-century English aesthete, as depicted in his classic Victorian library. He has immersed himself in a more satisfying, albeit borrowed, past. Surprisingly Henry is about to get married, and his flabbergasted American family has gathered in Oxford for the high-church Anglican ceremony.

Henry's quest for beauty and spiritual development originated in his desire to escape his supposedly culturally barren, Yiddish-speaking, American Jewish background. He has surrounded himself with gourmet foods and with eighteenth-and nineteenth-century furnishings. His antique decanters, map cases, charts of the heavens, abandoned history of the Arabic-speaking peoples, calligraphy, engraved wedding invitations, brocaded armchairs, leather-bound quartos, art, rare books, and antiques suggest just how far his immersion has taken him from his old life. That life includes the "industrial academic mills" with their illusion of scholarship and mass-produced undergraduates, as well as scholars battering away at literature with the "blunt instruments" of contemporary criticism. He hates also the older scholars who "cook up Shakespeare, serve him like roast goose, stuffed with their political-sexual agendas, carve and quarter him with long knives" and for whom reading "is a boiling and a breaking, something to concoct" (27). He abhors their "deviling of art, history, social theory, politics—all mixed up and piped back in and served on a platter. These are the scholars in the journals now. They are at war with the beautiful; they are against God and metaphor" (27). In effect, they deny texture and artistry.

Henry the purist believes his brother Ed has now become one of those shapers of the "tawdry yellow thing they sell now as the Humanities" (27). Craft and light, institution and sensibility, have been cheapened and sold off into the social sciences. Ed Markowitz, who had begun as a Near Eastern historian, is nothing more than a political expert in Henry's eyes: "Another cog in the grant-getting, TV interview machine" (27). To Henry, his brother is "caught up in the American rituals. Food, kids, cars, commercials. How could one expect Edward to look up from his devouring and enter into the wedding?" (27). He has given up his Near Eastern history and "just does the political thing now" (28). He is "giving it all up to be some sort of apologist to the media for the PLO, or the Arab League. . . . He's just a pardoner selling indulgences on TV" (30–31).

For his part, Ed despairs of the hopeless Anglophile Henry, with all his "eighteenth-century *peklach*" (28). He thinks his brother is neurotically immersed in his own rerun of *Brideshead Revisited.* He does not see how Henry's aesthetic pilgrimage has culminated in Henry and Susan's joint cottage project and in the exquisite arrangements for the wedding. Ironically the least immersed member of the family, Sarah, is the one who still believes in the possibility of spiritual pilgrimage and fulfillment. She sees, as Ed does not, that Henry has retreated from the "delicate cynicism of Evelyn Waugh into the more decorated nineteenth century" (35). She understands that this self-immersion has been a courtship "more and more ornate" (35). Henry reminds her of the young Oxonians of that nineteenth-century generation who became higher and higher church until they were Catholic and their churches were Catholic. Sarah imagines "The Wedding of Henry Markowitz" as having been arrived at by his moving from "young men, to gardening, then to orchards, and finally to a cottage and a wife" (35). But then it is Sarah, the writer of fiction, who "believes in changes, secrets, and revelations" (28) and who sees these magical forces at work in Henry and Susan's beautiful wedding.

Goodman further explores the spiritual dilemmas of the Jewish American family through the ongoing pilgrimage of Ed Markowitz in "Fantasy Rose" (1992).[16] Here his immersions and spiritual impasses turn on his inability to cope with change. He does not want to lose his daughter Miriam to marriage and to face her leaving home. Nor does he want to become "father" to his aging mother's regressive "little girl" act. The coming-of-age of his oldest child and the mental and emotional decline of his aging and Percodan-addicted mother mark a major passage for Ed. Everything centers on the pink bedroom inhabited by Miriam during her childhood. Now that she has left to marry, Ed's mother, Rose Markowitz, declares that she will move in with them and inhabit the room in her old age. Whether or not to redecorate the pink room is the dilemma that reveals Ed's comic resistance to life changes. To make matters worse, he cannot find the bedrock spiritual connection he needs at the synagogue, with its buzz of inconsequential kibitzing and the rebbe's awful sermon about the divisions within the synagogue community. He will have to make do with some new pink curtains.

"The Persians" (1993)[17] focuses again on Ed Markowitz's egocentric fixation with his unpopular theory that Arab terrorists are freedom fighters who are no more immersed in violence than their Western adversaries. (We have seen this theory expounded in "Wish List," 1986.) He is flattered to be invited to a conference in Iran with an invitation written in flowery and regal language. This signals to him that his international reputation has been made. Hence he eagerly accepts an opportunity to express his theories on the Middle East on a talk show. Consistent with her earlier interest in contemporary critical theory, Goodman is clearly having fun pushing to extremes the whole postmodern Levinasian ethic of moral responsibility in the face of otherness. When the talk show degenerates into name-calling,

Ed is duly chastened and believes his performance to have been a flop. While socializing with his community at a Bat Mitzvah ceremony the following weekend, however, he realizes that everyone heard what he or she wanted to hear. The intended irony is that Ed, who understands the theory of otherness so well with regard to terrorists, cannot displace himself for a minute when it comes to the demands of others. For example, he cannot even imagine a suitable gift for a thirteen-year-old girl's coming-of-age ceremony, and he is not able to let go of narcissistic anxieties about his own performance to enjoy the reactions of family and friends.

"Mosquitoes" (1993) offers a contemporary version of Chaucer's *Canterbury Tales*.[18] These pilgrims, however, wend their way not to Canterbury, but to the contemporary Ecumenical Institute for a Jewish Catholic dialogue. Yet this experience proves one more demonstration of Ed's inability to engage in a dialogue between religious forms of ecumenical "otherness" in politically correct late-twentieth-century America. Constantly nurturing fears of an allergic response to attacks by mosquitoes, Ed imagines that he hears mosquitoes in the surrounding countryside. Worse, he is antipathetic to everyone: to Brother Matthew, the "liaison" between St. Peter's College and the Ecumenical Institute, who looks like a cross between a bear and a Buick; to Mauricio Brodsky with his yarmulke, Spanish accent, and Yiddish-kvetching lilt; to Rich Mather, the institute's director and the gathering's host, who tells the panic-stricken Ed that there will be no papers, just personal narratives about interfaith relations; and to Sister Elaine, a self-effacing, self-indulgent woman who recalls her guilty life of growing up in a dysfunctional family and then becoming a Ph.D. and a feminist.

Sister Elaine is followed by the booming masculine voice of the elderly Brother Marcus, who claims priority as the oldest pilgrim present and who recounts a lengthy narrative of his bizarre conversion from Reform Judaism to Catholicism. However, as Ed observes, Brother Marcus is soon upstaged by an even better performer, Rabbi Lehrer. This worthy medievalist historian claims to be even older, and his tale of his pious, orthodox *shtetl* origins and subsequent immigration to Toronto is dismissed by Ed as being "straight from the Judaica shop" (73).

Marthe, the German Christian baby-boomer who performs on the second day, also appalls Ed by her unearned guilt for Nazi atrocities against the Jews. When pilgrim Brodsky begins to talk, his tale is marked by complaint and anger at a God who let his people die in the ovens. Ed literally cringes when Avner Rabinovitch reveals he has lost a son to terrorism in Lebanon and has subsequently turned to discovering texts relating to his own experience—instead of studying them historically through scholarly analysis. Ed, who is now petrified because he cannot hide behind his scholarly paper, issues stern words of rebuke. He accuses them all of navel-picking, self-flagellation, and of staging mere *bubbe-mayses* and of resorting to "therapeutic back-rubbing! Interfaith tick-pulling" (79).

Goodman implies that Ed is both right and wrong. He is right in that he has seen a terrible display of ego and narcissism. He is wrong because he is quite unaware that his scholarship and personal narrative are also rife with evasion, hubris, theatrics, and more than his share of posturing. As Sister Elaine recites Isaiah 40 from memory, Ed notes that she is really an unfulfilled actress. Neither he nor any of them realize how the prophet's magnificent counsel applies to their behavior. In the final group photograph, their arms entwined like Latin lovers, those assembled give the false appearance of unity. Ed now knows that the "maddening, delicate whine, the rising voices of the mosquitoes," is not just his imagination. His personal paranoia and the general ecumenical process form the perfect metaphor for the comic discussion of irreconcilable differences and the terminal parochialism of a community seeking cross-cultural unity.

In "Sarah" (1994)[19] Goodman uses the metaphors of intertextuality and of life-as-midrashic commentary to parody the hilarious human miscommunication that ensues. Whether inside the "Creative Midrash" writing class or in real life, intertextuality is the dynamic component that orchestrates the colliding consciousness. As the students write their own interpretations, variations, and fantasies on biblical themes through the compendium of the Midrash, the resulting ironic interconnections produce a remarkable heteroglossia of voices. Thus Goodman reminds her readers that fiction, fantasy, and life are inextricably mixed. Debbie's subversive poem on Eve draws on contemporary feminist narratives. Rejecting the archetypal mother who would have her beget a patriarchal lineage, she decides instead to slip into the night garden and join the enemy, represented by the bright glow of "the eyes of my cats" (74). Brian produces an intertextual dramatic biblical piece about Jacob on the ladder talking to Thoreau and Whitman, which he claims is also inspired by *Leaves of Grass* and *Under Milkwood.* In this staged conversation, Thoreau is being promised the locomotives, as well as all of nature and numerous progeny, should he join the patriarchy. He decides, however, that he would rather sit by a warm fire than become a nation. The reader becomes aware that out of this delightful and highly ironic intertextual play Brian is also creating a new text for his own life.

In real life Sarah's mother-in-law, Rose, calls to say she is in St. Elysius Hospital, only to be corrected by Sarah, who knows that this is the name of the hospital portrayed in her favorite television show. In Rose's fantasy world, she likens herself to the displaced heroine of *Gone with the Wind*. She longs to return to the nostalgic houses of her childhood, houses that are the backdrop of the romance she has developed about her early life. She would like to write her own southern epic, but, as Sarah notes, it is hard to develop a life with memories that come from novels. Nevertheless, Rose will try desperately to involve Ed in her latest fantasy by living in his home and becoming again a child. At the same time she refuses to allow a therapist to change the script by stripping away her textual allusions and leaving her with only her identity as a Percodan addict.

Sarah observes that neither her family life nor her writing class is going well—in both, "discussion is fractured. All sniping and defensiveness, the chemistry is all wrong" (80). Returning to the biblical story of Sarah in the Midrash, she decides that she too is not much like her biblical foremother. Fertility was not her problem, but being able to develop a literary career with a husband and three small children was. She feels she has failed because it was easier to tend Ed's career than her own. Furthermore, when she offers to let Rose read the first volume of her life story, Rose comments, "Haven't you got a sequel yet?" and promptly suggests a title from *Star Trek*, "The Next Generation." For now, however, all Sarah's literary dreams are foreshortened by the delicious possibility that Rose may leave Ed's house, rewarding her with empty rooms. The reference to a room or rooms of her own in which to think and write reveals at last whose text has lain subversively in her mind during her otherwise near-total immersion in the patriarchal demands of family. However, unlike Virginia Woolf and her own antipatriarchal students, Sarah realizes that her career as a writer will probably always remain dormant and lack the dazzling poems she dreamed of writing as a child. She decides that if the Lord called her on the phone at age fifty and promised that she would write a significant book, not pulp romance, she would take down his phone number and laugh like the Sarah of old. Goodman's tale, then, proves to be a Midrash of interweaving dreaming texts and would-be texts. Metaphorical and intertextual connections create the fabric of her consciousness. For her characters real life is a Midrashic commentary.

In "One Down: A Story" (1994),[20] Goodman recounts Ed's reactions to Miriam's wedding. Although he is about to "give" away his daughter in marriage, he cannot really enter into the event. When a letter to the *Times* from Zaev Schwartz is printed, Ed is horrified to read that the man who will be the other grandfather to his future grandchild proposes a solution to the Arab-Israeli problem that is the exact opposite of Ed's own. Ed egocentrically interprets Zaev Schwartz's letter as an act of calculated disrespect to his own life's work. When his wife, Sarah, twits him with "Now, Ed did he do this just to insult you?" (33), we realize that Ed has been deeply denying his oldest daughter's marriage and its ultra-orthodox nature. It is just another mask for his resistances to one of life's passages.

Goodman deals with Rose Markowitz's reactions to the death of her second husband, Maury, in "Fannie Mae" (1995).[21] As the clock ticks down she draws into herself. When the gloomy and emotionally needy Dorothy invades her small apartment, Rose becomes angry. She calls the awkward Dorothy the angel of death because she fills the house of the dying man with her whining, accusations, and general gloominess. It is ironic that Rose, who is also an orphan and who can be just as demanding and caught up in unfinished business with her own father, fails to sympathize with the other woman. In her will she leaves Maury's money to an Israeli girls' orphanage. When Ed and Henry attempt to railroad her into investments that will fix her income and try to move her to a new house, away from her friend Esther, she puts her investments into more liquid Fannie Mae funds. Clearly she does not plan to die for a long time.

In these brilliantly ironic comedies the escape from "immersion" in the exigencies of ordinary consciousness is denied to almost every character. The failure may occur despite and because of wanderings, pilgrimages, academic endeavors, family life, liberal ideology, orthodoxy, aestheticism, subversion, or bourgeois respectability. Here repeatedly is the noise of the disjointed, postmodern collision of others, pervading as it does these hectic and humorous tales of human egocentrism. Yet Goodman's tone is never mocking, and the possible presence of *Hashem* in the midst of all these human charades is never foreclosed. Human life remains valuable, rich, comic, and dear, despite the seeming impossibility of simple human communication or of the transcendental leap beyond. Human yearning for a glimpse of the holy, for meaning, peace, dialogue, family life, beauty, law, integrity, discipline, structure, and openness characterizes all of her people, despite their hilarious parochialism. Their lives are not as spiritual because of their chaotic immersions in the postmodern America, but each one is even more obstructed by the same cultural, historical, and human conditions that have always blocked individual consciousness and formed the stuff of human comedy. All are involved in the human immersion in the "land unsown" and in the eternal convenant:

> I remember your youthful devotion, the love of your bridal days. . . . How you followed me through the wilderness, through a land unsown. . . . I will build for you an eternal covenant. ("Total Immersion," 249)

Goodman suggests that the promise still exists, and, like the Jews of old, her characters too have produced biblical laments, chronicles, confessions, parables, and even psalms to mark their eager and noisy mortal presence.

Notes

1. Allegra Goodman to Sanford Pinker, 7 November 1991, printed in *Studies in American Jewish Literature* 11, no. 2 (Fall 1992): 182–94.
2. *Total Immersion* (New York: Harper and Row, 1989), and *The Family Markowitz* (New York: Farrar, Straus and Giroux, forthcoming).
3. "Variant Text" was first published in *Commentary* 81, no. 6 (June 1986): 55–63; it also appears in the collection *Total Immersion* and in *Writing Our Way Home: Contemporary Stories by American Jewish Writers,* ed. Ted Solataroff and Nessa Rappaport (New York: Shocken, 1993). Textual page citations are from *Total Immersion.*
4. "Wish List," *Commentary* 82, no. 6 (December 1986): 48–58, and reprinted in *Total Immersion.* Citations are from *Total Immersion.*
5. "The Succession," *Commentary* 84, no. 3 (September 1987): 45–52, and reprinted in *Total Immersion.* Citations are from *Total Immersion.*
6. "Total Immersion," *Commentary* 84, no. 4 (October 1987): 45–53, and reprinted in *Total Immersion.*
7. "Oral History," *Commentary* 87, no. 2 (February 1989): 60–68, and reprinted in *Total Immersion.* Citations are from *Total Immersion.*
8. "Fait," in *Total Immersion,* 49–63.
9. "And Also Much Cattle," in *Total Immersion,* 139–67.
10. "Retrospective," in *Total Immersion,* 123–37.
11. "Further Ceremony," in *Total Immersion,* 193–212.

12. "Clare," in *Total Immersion,* 213–28.

13. "Onionskin," *New Yorker* 67 (1 April 1991): 29–35.

14. "Young People," *Commentary* 83, no. 3 (March 1987): 59–65, and reprinted in *Total Immersion.* Citations are from *Total Immersion.*

15. "The Wedding of Henry Markowitz," *New Yorker* 67 (13 January 1992): 26–36.

16. "Fantasy Rose," *New Yorker* 68 (16 November 1992): 108–19.

17. "The Persians: A Story," *Commentary* 96, no. 5 (November 1993): 41–47.

18. "Mosquitoes," *New Yorker* 69 (9 August 1993): 68–80.

19. "Sarah," *New Yorker* 69 (17 January 1994): 74–80, and in *Writing Our Way Home: Contemporary Stories by American Jewish Writers,* ed. Ted Solotaroff and Nessa Rappoport (New York: Schocken Books, 1993). Citations are from the *New Yorker.*

20. "One Down: A Story," *Commentary* 98, no. 2 (August 1994): 32–40.

21. "Fannie Mae," forthcoming in the *New Yorker.*

Writing Jewish Fiction In and Out of the Multicultural Context

Allegra Goodman

A year ago I was sitting next to Cynthia Ozick at a dinner in her honor at Stanford University. We began to talk about the term Jewish American writer, and she told me how much she resented the label. It is derogatory, she said, it is simplistic and reductive. It reduces art and ideas to ethnic commodities. The very word *ethnic,* she said, is a hateful term; it is really a slur, a term of alienation, with its root word *ethnos* connoting foreign and heathen. To label fiction as Jewish American, to think of it as ethnic, is not merely to categorize it but to attack it. Then she leaned over and asked, "What do you think?"

It is a difficult question for me: how to gauge my identity as a Jewish American writer. I fully understand Ozick's resentment at being labeled, and I share her mistrust for the trivializing and reductive capacity of labels. I certainly don't want my work stereotyped or ghettoized. When asked what I do, I say first that I am a writer; when pressed about what kind of writer, I say that I am a fiction writer, and yes, I often write about Jewish people. I do not immediately say I am a Jewish American woman fiction writer. But at the same time I understand that my most intimate and immediate audience comes from the American Jewish community, that in many ways when I write fiction I am writing not only about them but also for them. This more specialized audience overlaps but also extends my audience of general readers. The label *Jewish American* is a way of pigeonholing me, of packaging and selling my work, but it is also a symbol of an essential resource: a community of passionate readers in an increasingly difficult world for serious fiction. My parents tell me that at their synagogue in Nashville, people ask them if they are

---

A version of this essay was delivered at the 1994 Modern Language Association meeting in San Diego, California.

related to Allegra Goodman the fiction writer. My parents—proud Jewish parents that they are—immediately say, "Oh, you've read her book? You've seen her work in *The New Yorker?*"

"No, no, we don't get *The New Yorker,*" is the reply, "We read her stories in *Commentary.*"

I have come to think that a writer cannot have enough labels if they are keys to new audiences, if they are combined and subverted imaginatively. I work with as many as I can—Jewish writer, woman writer, Generation X. Each provides a different opportunity.

And yet I take Ozick's critique seriously when she speaks bitterly of the label Jewish American writer. Jewish fiction has a complex and troubling position in the United States. The Jewish writers of my generation are the inheritors of two traditions of Jewish fiction. One is the tradition of writers such as Chaim Grade, Sholom Aleichem, and I. B. Singer. They wrote in Yiddish, and their work must overcome the barrier of translation. These are writers whose aesthetic qualities and achievements are rarely isolated from their subject matter. Always they are the recorders of a lost culture and a lost language. Sholom Aleichem is always a great Jewish humorist, rather than a great writer. His texts suffer from the burden of thousands of productions of *Fiddler on the Roof* and bad art work depicting shtetl life in the Old Country. Chaim Grade's work is always the elegiac record of times past. Even Grade's prewar work bears the shadow of the Holocaust. His texts are as haunting and tragic as the photographs of Roman Vishniac, images of a fragile, vanished world. The visions of Sholom Aleichem, Grade, and even the laureate Singer become in the public imagination records of an ethnic experience that truly is foreign and strange, rendered humorously by Sholom Aleichem, elegiacally by Grade, and with a piquant semierotic spice by Singer. These writers' books are marginalized as artifacts rather than read consistently as art works.

The other tradition that comes down to us is that of Jewish American writers such as Roth and Bellow, who develop and project their self-consciousness, ambivalence, and guilt about the Jewish tradition into mainstream American fiction. If the translated Yiddish writers are marginalized as parochial, the great Jewish American writers are read as institutional. This institutional identity is in its way as limiting as that of the ethnic writer, for in the age of multiculturalism, it alienates these writers from their intimate constituency; it denies them their role as artists of the Jewish community. It is difficult to be a literary giant in the global village, to be ambassador without portfolio. Roth and Bellow have arrived and become great twentieth-century writers, and in a sense their fame makes it hard to hear them as ethnic voices. The biographical notes in *The Norton Anthology of Short Fiction* provide a fascinating index to this phenomenon. Bernard Malamud is described as being "recognized as one of the best of the writers who have portrayed Jewish life and sensibility in American fiction." But when it comes to Philip Roth, it is his "mastery of form" that the Norton editors mention, and his "gift for ribald, acid comedy." Nowhere in the entry on Roth and his work is his Jewishness or Jewish themes mentioned. Describing Isaac Bashevis Singer's work, the editors write, "Flavored with the colorful residue of folk tales, his explorations of Jewish life, past and present, are haunted allegories of the irrationality of history." But when it comes to Saul Bellow, it is impossible to tell from the biographical entry that this is a Jewish writer. In fact, the editors locate Bellow and his themes firmly in the Midwest; strangely enough he is endowed with a midwestern ethos: "He has lived in Chicago for most of his later life, teaching and writing there, and this mid-American location seems to be reflected by the spirit and subject matter of his fiction, with its discoveries of eccentrics who wrestle with the quandaries of the individual destiny in a variety of American settings." These capsule discussions of Malamud, Roth, Singer, and Bellow reveal the divide between those writers read as Jewish and those who have moved on, and perhaps up, in the world to be read as masters of form or discoverers of the quandaries of the individual. On each side of the divide Jewish writers are read, described, and introduced to students in reductive terms.

The irony is that Jewish American writers are in many ways victims of their own success. Writers like Sholom Aleichem and Singer not only record and express Jewish values, but they also have become emblems of Old World Judaism, while such ambivalent assimilationists like Bellow and Roth have in fact become assimilated into the larger mainstream tradition. So, as a working Jewish American writer, where do I stand as I look for strategies and models? I write about Jewish culture, but not merely Jewish culture. I write about religion as well. Therefore, my models are the older writers like Grade and Sholom Aleichem, who wrote of a living unself-conscious tradition. I write from the inside, taking, as they did, an idiom in which ritual and liturgy are a natural part of my fictional world, and not anthropological objects to be translated and constantly explained. From the beginning of my career I have chosen this insider's perspective. My choice was influenced not only by my reading of Jewish literature, but also by my background as a child growing up in Hawaii. I was familiar with a place that seemed exotic to others, and in my writing I chose to present the exotic as familiar.

The first story I wrote, published in my 1989 collection, *Total Immersion,* is about a Yom Kippur service that takes place on the lanai of a family in Honolulu. The whole story occurs inside the service, with dialogue, fights, speeches, and exhortations whispered between prayers and songs. Another story in the collection focuses on a strictly orthodox scholar named Cecil Birnbaum who lives in Oxford. The plot hinges on Birnbaum's horror that one of his fellow congregants has pushed a stroller to synagogue, thus violating the injunction against carrying or pushing loads on the Sabbath. I used a glossary at the end of my book to explain Hebrew and Yiddish words, but I did not interrupt stories such as these to explain or translate religious terms or rituals. I found that readers relished a feeling of total immersion. I was not trying to be obscure; I worked for clarity, but at the same time I was not apologetic about my characters and their activities. In much of my work I use ritual as both structural tool and subject. In doing so I look not only to the translated Jewish writers, but also to Chaim Potok and Cynthia Ozick, who treat not merely the ethnic but also the religious dimension of Judaism. I also find inspiration in the work of writers like Maxine Hong Kingston, another writer who lived for many years in Hawaii. Kingston developed fiction out of the interior of Chinese culture in *Woman Warrior*—an interior that she believed could speak in its own terms, without guilty nostalgia and anger or condescending bemusement.

Since *Total Immersion* I have focused primarily on characters who are far more assimilated than those of my earliest stories. There is guilt, there is ambivalence and confusion about Judaism, about Israel, about synagogues in the stories of my new collection, *The Family Markowitz.* And yet I view my characters' guilt and ambivalence with some perspective. Their guilt is not my own. I am interested in drawing on my heritage and my history, but I do not feel I must dramatize only one perspective on Judaism—or that I must take that perspective seriously all the time.

I practice this kind of writing—a fiction that is unapologetic and energetically ethnic, but like Ozick I bridle at the thought that this is all that I am about. What joy I felt, when after sending my new story about Rose Markowitz to Chip McGrath at *The New Yorker,* he called me to say it was a great piece of writing about—old age. It was not Rose Markowitz with her rent-controlled apartment in Washington Heights and her step-daughter from Israel, but old age itself that he saw as the subject. And at a deep level that was the subject of the story for me as well. Of course, it is the particulars that sustain a story, the sense of place, the idiosyncrasies of speech and character. And it is the social, political, material, biographical, literary context of a story that scholars study and discuss. But I think that few writers can hide their longing to convey the universal.

My character Sarah Markowitz suffers from this longing. She is a fifty-year-old creative-writing teacher, a would-be poet and novelist, but she has not been recognized by the world. I describe her in my story "Sarah" as she sits at her desk, thinking:

> It has been difficult for her as a poet, to be influenced by Donne, Marvell, and Herbert, but to write about giving birth, a son's bar mitzvah, Yom Kippur. . . . She has pined to have a literary career, to have her work discovered by the world. This has been her dream since her school days, when she discovered John Donne and felt suddenly and secretly clever, as if, like a safecracker, she could find the puns and hidden springs in his poetry. And when she wrote her essays in college about this image and that metaphor, what she was really wondering was how to become like Shakespeare—without seeming to imitate him, of course. When would she be called into that shining multitude of poets and playwrights, mainly Elizabethan, who rose in shimmering waves before her at Queens College? She wrote her M.A. thesis in English Literature about Emma Lazarus—not about the poem on the Statue of Liberty but about her major and forgotten works, the verse plays and poems.

Many ideas passed through my mind as I wrote that passage, among them the difficulties for women Sarah's age, would-be literary women, and the difficulties for Jewish readers and writers of every age who discover the grandeur of English and American literature and then with experience come to feel that in subtle ways they are excluded from the grand tradition. Sarah has been educated by the poets of the Protestant religious experience, Donne, Herbert, Milton, but as she writes her own poetry she finds that she will not become a literary star by writing about her Jewish experience. And it is not just that she will not be a literary lion in the eyes of the world, it is that she will not be a literary star in her own terms. She has internalized the standards and the aesthetic of Protestant England's seventeenth-century poetry. At a deep level Sarah herself believes that the language of the Protestant religious experience is profound and universal, whereas the Jewish religious experience is obscure or even earthy—somehow not as well suited to the poetic, somehow neither universal nor spiritual. As I wrote about Sarah and took her point of view, I recognized how much I share with the character, how much I sympathize with her wistful aspirations. At the same time, creating Sarah's character gave me a chance to look objectively at her ideas, to examine her from the outside, and to draw boundaries between her ideas and my own. As I wrote "Sarah," I indulged my misgivings about Jewish American fiction, about women's fiction—and then, after I finished writing the story, I felt much better. I tossed aside all of Sarah's musings and I was ready to move on.

Where should Jewish American writing move? I believe that Jewish American writers must recapture the spiritual and the religious dimension of Judaism. Ted Solotaroff goes so far as to say that only by moving into this new territory, into the post-assimilated realm of tradition, can Jewish American fiction resuscitate and sustain itself. He wrote in a 1988 *New York Times Book Review* article that "As assimilation continues to practice its diluting and dimming ways, it seems evident that the interesting Jewish bargain or edge in American fiction will be more and more in the keeping of writers . . . who are anchored in the present-day observant Jewish community and who are drawn to the intense and growing dialogue between Judaism and modernity under the impact of feminism, the sexual revolution, and the Holocaust." Solotaroff put it in darker terms in a 1991 interview with the Baltimore *Jewish Times,* prophesying of Jewish-American literature, "Only those writers steeped in Judaism will survive." I think it is a hundred years too early to tell who will survive and who will not, but I agree wholeheartedly with Solotaroff that it is time for Jewish American writers to use the Jewish religion as more than "shtick," to borrow Solotaroff's term. If literary images of Judaism are to be read seriously and not satirically or sentimentally or dismissively, they must be written that way. There must be Jewish wedding scenes other than that of *Goodbye, Columbus;* there must be alternatives to the self-deprecating rhythms of Woody Allen and the one-liners of Neil Simon. Allen and Simon seem to recognize this themselves. In *Crimes and Misdemeanors,* Allen uses the family seder, not as a raucous emblem of an overheated, distraught childhood, but as a forum for a serious discussion of good and evil. In his autobiographical trilogy, Neil Simon moves far beyond jokes as he interprets and dramatizes life in his Jewish family.

Yes, Jewish American writers have a difficult position in the multicultural context, but they are also confronting an old problem—the problem of every artist. Ultimately, I believe, all writing is ethnic writing, and all writers are ethnic writers grappling with great ambitions and a particular language and culture. Milton dared to confront the classical tradition in English. Faulkner used Shakespeare and southern dialect together. Shakespeare himself faced the formidable tradition of the Petrarchan sonnet, dismantled it, tinkered with it, mocked it, and made it new. Every writer works to develop and express ideas and emotions in the language of the particular and the mundane, to say something new and use what is old. Each strives to make a specific cultural experience an asset instead of a liability. I look at this as an old problem, and I turn to old resources—the deep Jewish tradition beneath the self-deprecating Jewish jokes, the biblical language and the poetry welling up beneath layers of satire.

Contributors

VICTORIA AARONS, Professor of English at the University of Texas, San Antonio, has written extensively on American Jewish writers, including Grace Paley (in *Jewish American Women Writers: A Bio-Bibliographical and Critical Sourcebook)* and Bernard Malamud. Her books include *Author as Character in the Works of Sholom Aleichem* (1985) and *A Measure of Memory: Storytelling and Identity in American Jewish Fiction* (1996).

GLORIA CRONIN is Professor of English at Brigham Young University. Co-editor of *The Saul Bellow Journal,* she has published *Saul Bellow: An Annotated Bibliography and Research Guide; Saul Bellow in the 1980s: A Collection of Critical Essays,* as well as an annotated bibliography of Jewish fiction writers and a book on Harriet Ne.

MIRIYAM GLAZER is Associate Professor of Literature, chair of the Literature Department, and director of the Dortort Writers Institute at the University of Judaism. A frequent contributor of essays on Jewish American women writers, she has edited *Dreaming of the Actual: Israeli Women Writers in the 1990s* (forthcoming).

ALLEGRA GOODMAN is the author of *Total Immersion,* a collection of short stories. A frequent contributor to *The New Yorker, Commentary,* and other magazines, her newest collection of stories is about the Markowitz family and will be published in 1996. She is currently completing a dissertation on Shakespeare for her Ph.D. at Stanford.

JAY L. HALIO, Professor of English at the University of Delaware, edited the *Dictionary of Literary Biography: British Novelists Since 1960.* Among his books is a recent study of Philip Roth. A Shakespearean scholar also, he has edited *Shakespeare's "Romeo and Juliet": Texts, Contexts, and Interpretations* (University of Delaware Press) and new editions of *King Lear* and *The Merchant of Venice.*

SARA HOROWITZ is director of the Jewish Studies program at the University of Delaware. She is the author of *Voicing the Void: Muteness and Memory in Holocaust Fiction* and co-editor of *Kerem,* a journal of creative explorations in Judaism. She is currently completing a book on gender, genocide, and Jewish memory.

STEVEN G. KELLMAN is Asbel Professor of Comparative Literature at the University of Texas, San Antonio. He is film critic for *The Texas Observer* and the author of *Perspectives on "Raging Bull"* and *The Plague: Fiction and Resistance.*

KAREN KLEIN has pursued a dual career as a teacher of literature and a visual artist. At Brandeis University, where she is an associate professor of English and co-director of the Humanities Interdisciplinary program, she teaches a course on lyric poetry and drawing. Her drawings and artist's books have been widely shown in six solo shows and numerous juried and invitational group shows. Her haiku have appeared in *Brussels Sprout* and *frogpond.*

SUSANNE KLINGENSTEIN teaches English at the Massachusetts Institute of Technology. She is the author of *Jews in the American Academy, 1900-1940: The Dynamics of Intellectual Assimilation.* A sequel to that volume will be forthcoming and the earlier volume will be republished.

LILLIAN KREMER is a senior faculty member in the Department of English at Kansas State University. She is the author of *Witness Through the Imagination: The Holocaust in Jewish American Literature* (1989) and essays that have appeared in *Contemporary Literature, Saul Bellow Journal, Studies in American Jewish Literature, Yiddish,* and elsewhere. She is currently completing a volume of critical essays on women's Holocaust narratives by both survivors and American-born writers.

JAMES MELLARD is Professor of English at Northern Illinois University, where he has held a number of administrative posts. His essays on modernist and contemporary fiction have appeared in *PMLA, JEGP, Modern Fiction Studies,* and the *Bucknell Review.*

His books include *The Modernist Novel in America, Using Lacan, Reading Fiction,* and *Four Modes: A Rhetoric of Modern Fiction.*

BEN SIEGEL is Professor of English at the California State Polytechnic University, Pomona. Author of *The Puritan Heritage: America's Roots in the Bible, Isaac Bashevis Singer, The Controversial Sholem Asch,* and other works, he has also edited various collections of essays, most recently (with Melvin J. Friedman) *Traditions, Voices, Dreams: The American Novel since the 1960s* (University of Delaware Press) and (with Gloria Cronin) *Conversations with Saul Bellow.*

CHARLOTTE TEMPLIN is Professor of English and chair of the Department of English at the University of Indianapolis. She is the author of numerous articles and reviews and of *Feminism and the Politics of Literary Reputation: The Example of Erica Jong.* At the modern Language Association in 1994, she organized and chaired a session on the work of Erica Jong, at which Jong was present and responded to the papers presented.

STEPHEN WHITFIELD holds the Max Richter Chair in American Civilization at Brandeis University. He is the author of seven books, most recently *The Culture of the Cold War.* He has served as visiting professor at the Hebrew University in Jerusalem, the Catholic University of Louvain, and the Sorbonne. He is a contributing editor of *Judaism* and has served as book–review editor of *American Jewish History.*

Index

Page numbers in boldface indicate an extensive discussion of an author or subject area.